Karen O'Brien

Cursing, Crisis and Customary Knowledge in Early Modern English Townships

palgrave
macmillan

Karen O'Brien
University of Sydney
Sydney, NSW, Australia

ISSN 2731-5630 ISSN 2731-5649 (electronic)
Palgrave Historical Studies in Witchcraft and Magic
ISBN 978-3-031-44044-1 ISBN 978-3-031-44045-8 (eBook)
https://doi.org/10.1007/978-3-031-44045-8

Cover illustration: Colin Waters/Alamy Stock Photo

This Palgrave Macmillan imprint is published by the registered company Springer Nature Switzerland AG
The registered company address is: Gewerbestrasse 11, 6330 Cham, Switzerland

Paper in this product is recyclable.

Palgrave Historical Studies in Witchcraft and Magic

Series Editors

The history of European witchcraft and magic continues to fascinate and challenge students and scholars. There is certainly no shortage of books on the subject. Several general surveys of the witch trials and numerous regional and micro studies have been published for an English-speaking readership. While the quality of publications on witchcraft has been high, some regions and topics have received less attention over the years. The aim of this series is to help illuminate these lesser known or little studied aspects of the history of witchcraft and magic. It will also encourage the development of a broader corpus of work in other related areas of magic and the supernatural, such as angels, devils, spirits, ghosts, folk healing and divination. To help further our understanding and interest in this wider history of beliefs and practices, the series will include research that looks beyond the usual focus on Western Europe and that also explores their relevance and influence from the medieval to the modern period.

'A valuable series.' - Magic, Ritual and Witchcraft

Contents

CHAPTER 1

The Social Context of Cursing and the Cultural Politics of Speech

> I pray that the curse of God might light on thee and all thy wares, [that] the curse of God will blow foe upon thee whereby thou might become a beggar.[1]
>
> Anne Knutsford is a very frequent curser and swearer and will ordinarily goe down on her knees and curse people grievously. Margaret Howell in a very bitter scolding and cursing manner did grivously curse Anne Knutsford and pulled her by the bosom and bid the plague of Christ take her.[2]

One cold winter's morning in 1629 Ellen Clark arose a little earlier than usual. Dressing quickly, she set out to take care of her animals. She was taken aback to find the plough stationary and her husband, John Clark, lying silently on the ground. Ellen helped John to his feet and brought him to his bed where he spent the day being wracked with fevers. She felt her world crumble around her as she watched her husband gradually slip away. Later that day when John Clark died, Ellen was grief stricken. She mourned John's loss with a heavy heart and struggled to imagine life without him. She felt helpless. How would she survive? How would she run the farm alone? Who would help her to turn up the earth? Her fears multiplied when neighbour, John Wilson, suddenly fell ill. Strange stories began to circulate in the town of Ellel. People whispered about the ghost-like figure of a woman who appeared before John Wilson, promising to

K. O'Brien, *Cursing, Crisis and Customary Knowledge in Early Modern English Townships*, Palgrave Historical Studies in Witchcraft and Magic,
https://doi.org/10.1007/978-3-031-44045-8_1

tear him apart. As days passed, the rumours grew louder, but the difficult times did not end there. Before long, the entire town was gripped by an inexplicable fever, resulting in the demise of whole families. The people of Ellel searched for an explanation. Their minds couldn't come to terms with the reality of what was happening. Seeking to understand this misfortune they looked for an answer. Why was this happening to them? they asked. What had they done to deserve such bad luck? When the memory of a bitter dispute with Jenet Wilkinson resurfaced, they questioned how they might have brought this ill fortune on themselves. It was also at that precise moment that the townsfolk were forced to acknowledge the truth. They had been cursed.[3]

The belief in cursing was widespread among early modern communities. The invocation of divine authority through pronouncing the curse stirred significant unease among the townspeople, and its utterance triggered a cascade of emotive reactions. In seventeenth-century England, the implications of cursing surpassed mere profanity, expanding into a blasphemous and, subsequently, litigious affair. The act of women ritually cursing their adversaries was perceived as an invocation of divine retribution upon the targeted individual. In a similar but different case of cursing that transpired in 1663, midwife Ann Knutsford cursed an entire community. This curse elicited an intense emotional response. They summarily denounced her for invoking God's wrath and accused her of placing a curse on them. However, on close examination it becomes obvious that the reason for Knutsford's lawsuit was not due to the fear of cursing but arose out of the disturbed nature of the relationships that pre-existed among the townsfolk, who were forced to negotiate the ideals of respectability. These were hard times. Some spouses were forced to imperil their good names when harsh conditions forced them to offer landlords sex instead of money. Money, power, reputation, and honour were at risk, and status in a social pecking order based upon reputation, good character, and credit was endlessly contested. Anne Knutsford's curse shed light on the reality of these sensitive issues.[4]

The two cases above serve as exemplars of the contexts in which cursing occurred. Though cursing varied from case to case, the elements of the cursing scenarios outlined above are characteristic of the intricate and multifaceted social background which formed the backdrop to instances of cursing. Ritual cursing was a wide-ranging affair. It was driven by the social circumstances of the time. It allowed people to express strong emotions and was regarded as a form of power that allowed individuals to assert themselves in situations where they felt powerless. Cursing played a role in shaping people's attitudes towards power and authority. It was often utilised as a form of violence and as a means of expressing anger and frustration.[5] This book delves deeply into these intricate settings, exploring the nuances of cursing, examining its social and cultural micropolitics, and accounting for its relation to the supernatural and early modern society. By exploring the intimate details of cursing and the accompanying environment, readers will gain a comprehensive understanding of cursing and its cultural significance, how it was perceived and practised in early modern society, and its connection to the supernatural realm.

Besides the interpersonal relations and the emotional responses of individuals and the perceptions of their reality, it is important to understand how townsfolk in the early modern period perceived their encounters with the supernatural world. The accounts provided by the townsfolk offer first-hand recollections of their experiences, detailing their emotional states, observations, and auditory perceptions. Overwhelmingly, they communicate that there was a strong association of cursing with crisis conditions. Although historians have pointed out the importance of the subject of vocal lawbreaking these phenomena have not fully received the attention which they deserve.[6] A thorough exploration of the traditions of customary practice is essential to properly understand the context in which cursing occurred. Engaging in cultural and linguistic analysis serves as a constructive approach to acquire a comprehensive understanding of the reality of popular beliefs. There is a theory that such 'detailed' studies of speech and conduct are warranted for several reasons: 'Firstly, they throw light on some very interesting but very obscure aspects of popular consciousness; secondly, they demonstrate the remarkable willingness of the English to settle their disputes by recourse to the courts.'[7] Some have proposed that the cases arising from disputes and tensions were 'perhaps the most dramatic consequence of the state and church providing the legal framework and ideological cosmography within which village tensions could work themselves out.'[8] Around the year 1660, during a period that aligned with the waning of witchcraft accusations, there was a discernible upswing in instances of spoken violations. By 1663, the perception of witchcraft in the Northwest region had undergone a notable shift and the phenomenon of witchcraft was increasingly perceived with reduced gravity during this period. However, regardless of the severe consequences imposed on women for their transgressions in behaviour or speech, specifically in relation to cursing, it is intriguing to note that cursing occurrences continued to intensify. Cursing was often connected with the healing methods of cunning folk, and it has been observed that materials regarding the commonplace, grassroots activities of cunning folk have been overlooked.[9] For this reason, customary knowledge in the form of magical healing forms an inherent component of this investigation.

Curses were typically pronounced by aggrieved women who wished to injure their enemies. Women who transgressed the strictly defined the laws of verbal communication and conduct were regarded as contentious. When they were taken to task and charged with the disruption of the social order it usually ended badly for them. This exploration of the prevalence of the litigation that arose from cursing and interpersonal hostility in the under-explored region of Northwest reveals several periods of acute socio-economic crisis in the seventeenth century. By incorporating the realm of customary knowledge, specifically magic and folk medicine, this finding contributes to the broader scholarship on magic and witchcraft, affirming the intricate nature of the world of healing and harming. It underscores the significance of understanding the complex circumstances surrounding these practices. Primary sources, such as pamphlets, have usefully informed several witchcraft studies, but the official correspondence of the legal system gives extensive details of the world of popular belief. The depositions of witnesses, interrogatories, town books, petitions of the townsfolk, and various manuscripts of the manorial, ecclesiastical, and secular courts positioned within a micro-historical early modern context provide the context for a textual analysis with a unique opportunity to enquire further into the backgrounds of the complainants.

This exploration of the world of cursing relates broadly to the historical exploration of the petitions of the powerless to the powerful to achieve justice. Legal appeals emerge as a significant unifying aspect within the separate domains of my historical research. By engaging in an extensive examination of documents associated with petitions and the act of petitioning, a significant body of published research has been generated, shedding light on early modern and modern societies in various cultural and geographical settings. This book expands further upon these scholarly pursuits by presenting an in-depth analysis of cursing and its intrinsic relationship with customary knowledge, within the realm of popular magic, as an integral component of the everyday existence of townspeople. It adds to the existing scholarly body of knowledge, offering valuable insights into the realities of life in early modern Northwest townships. By examining the subject from a grassroots perspective, it paints a comprehensive picture of the everyday experiences and conditions within these townships during the early modern era. It considers the supernatural world of cursing and the importance of customary knowledge in the intimate lives of townsfolk, as it is reflected in primary legal sources and contributes insights into the centrality of customary knowledge in popular practice and the impact of socio-economic crisis on early modern communities.[10]

Although cursing was traumatic for those involved, numerous historians acknowledge that examples of cursing are rare in court records.[11] In addressing the little-known world of cursing, this archive-conscious, document-driven analysis of cursing within a social context of the regional Northwest contributes an additional dimension to the eclectic historiography of magic and witchcraft. Numerous experts note that knowledge about cursing is scant. It is based purely on a general or 'symbolic' level.[12] Similarly, it has been argued that much detail about cursing is 'anecdotal and verging on the sensational.'[13] A comparative account of cursing in contemporary Ireland finds that the art of cursing is underexplored and considers the importance of the belief in magic in the community.[14] Cursing is best understood in a regional context, especially as studies of local and regional communities are important for the close and detailed view of early modern society they provide. Several historians recommend that regional and local histories must be carried out before there are further attempts to evaluate events of national importance.[15] The social and cultural milieu of local and regional communities holds intrinsic value not only in uncovering local events of significance but also in revealing the deeper social, political, economic, and ideological transformations that transpired within broader society.

Former critical investigations have unearthed a substantial correlation wherein active participation in curses emerges as a pivotal factor in the development of a distinctive societal perception. A groundbreaking inquiry into the waning influence of enchantment revealed a substantial correlation between engaging in curses and the development of a witch-like reputation.[16] A proportion of the cases of cursing examined in this book correspond with this interpretation as comprising a socio-economic function and as a 'redress for adversity.' However, this investigation highlights the profound significance of cursing in matters concerning property and the appropriation of land during enclosures, suggesting that the practice of cursing may have exhibited distinctive traits within the context of British North.

Anthropological studies have made valuable contributions to the understanding of cursing and magic. For example, an anthropological account of witchcraft, cursing, and magical beliefs finds that some individuals among French farmers in the Normandy countryside in the 1960s believed themselves adroit at removing curses.[17] In further European anthropological investigation, studies of the curse and cursing is described as 'a special kind of witchcraft.'[18] By examining the narrated details of the priests' curse amid Hungarians living in Transylvania, it is proposed that 'the kaluger's curse' was ordered by individuals to cause harm to people and to accomplish 'divine justice' as well as to resolve conflicts in the community. However, the author proposes that evidence for this anthropological observation of 'indirect and conditional inferences' is 'insufficient for a comprehensive survey.' Nevertheless, this study is important not least of all for its comparative value as it infers several commonalities with the regional Northwest of England in numerous cases of cursing. This is especially the case with the subject of conflicts in relation to 'land boundaries, family conflict, litigation and fighting among neighbours.'[19]

Several historians have made references to a significant prevalence of female participation in acts of legal transgression. Through their scholarly inquiries, these historians have highlighted a higher level of female involvement in various forms of unlawful behaviour, shedding light on the historical dynamics of gender and crime. However, there is not yet an archive-based account of cursing. Despite being somewhat dated, a regional and comparative study of Essex legal records examining the intersection of popular belief and the socio-economic sphere reveals that cunning folk (individuals associated with folk magic and healing practices) were not subjected to selective punishment based on gender. This study challenges the notion of gender-specific targeting of cunning folk in the legal system, underscoring the importance of considering socio-economic factors in understanding historical patterns of punishment.[20] More recent research proposes incorporating male experience with demonic familiars into the broader framework of witchcraft studies.[21] The dynamics of ill will that compelled the cursing cases that emanated from the community complicate the circumstances of cursing further.[22] While it is clear that women were susceptible to prosecution for magical healing and witchcraft, their male counterparts faced similar prosecutions for their involvement with witchcraft and magic.[23]

The spaces in which women historically dominated are often referred to as *female* spheres of influence but there was also a significant male presence through the practice of customary knowledge. Yet, even though women participated in symbolic crime, the offences of cursing and scolding in the regional Northwest are conspicuously ***exclusively*** female crimes. Remarkably, in the Northwest region, 100% of cursing cases were carried out by women and necessitate further investigation. Also, 75% of the cases of cursing were provoked because of the deaths of children and 40% of curses invoked starvation, plague, or death upon a recipient. Further investigation into the circumstances of these cases is required to further clarify the context of cursing during periods of socio-economic crisis.

Even though it was predominantly women that were prosecuted for cursing, there is scholarly disagreement about the gender relations involved in the incidence of scolding. There is one study that denies women's high level of involvement in the related field of scolding. It proposes that there is no special pattern of female connection above that of male in the misconduct of scolding.[24] However, conversely, scolding has been described as 'the armoury of interpersonal conflict.'[25] Although scolding has also been interpreted as 'the most distinctive offence of the early modern period' it has been insufficiently researched and is regarded as merely a branch of 'defamation' in Church court records.[26] Accordingly, the phenomenon of scolding will be incorporated as an integral component of this research.

Charting the Growth of Interpersonal Dispute Legislation

According to court authorities, women were perceived to have rejected the social order and were understood to have given rise to a situation of depraved, irreligious, and moral chaos through the enactment of the ritual curse. During the early modern period, residents of the Northwest region held great faith in the justice system, resulting in the generation of a substantial number of legal cases and disputes. Through a close reading of the socio-legal context of cursing and distribution of the causes, that is, the legal instances that were heard between the years 1600 and 1750 when the Chester Consistory Court heard a total of 7,227 causes, the material proof of discord emerges. During this turbulent period of the seventeenth century the litigation that arose out of interpersonal disharmony reveal a situation of crisis. The crisis that gave rise to cursing happened predominantly in the regional Northwest, an area that is generally under-explored outside of London. However, cursing came to be a specifically female violation of the law. Ritual cursing was reported often, and women were represented in 100% of the cursing lawsuits that were presented to secular and Church courts. Where the court chronicles a ritual cursing, there was a situation of catastrophe or dispute over property in which a female defendant was often the injured party. While the patriarchy dominated the high political world, women periodically assumed control in the lower domain through cursing. Women under pressure were aware of the power of the curse and knew how to use it to gain leverage. In a situation of crisis, the curse was an effective means of establishing a temporary new order in which women were invested with a potent vocal power and which allowed many of them to survive, and sometimes transcend, the difficult circumstances they encountered during times of disaster. In the short term, the practice of cursing extended power to women who were otherwise powerless and formed a valuable medium of expression for women who were undergoing hardship, which was a frequent motive in women's legal depositions. Situations of disaster are frequently established in the female narrative of petitions, depositions, interrogatories, responsions, sentences, and confessions. A comprehensive examination of legal jurisdictions, particularly within the consistory and secular courts, can facilitate the evaluation of the potential imposition of patriarchal standards on women perceived as troublesome by the legal system. This analysis will consequently shed light on the extent to which institutional violence was used against women in early modern English societies. The courts of the Northwest region contain accounts from women that reveal evidence of common gender-based conflicts, which are further elaborated upon later.

The following investigation addresses diverse instances of verbal lawbreaking. By referring to manuscripts that address violence against women within institutional, interpersonal, and domestic contexts, it offers an analysis of the gender dynamics presented by situations of persistent conflict and explores how such conflicts had wider implications for gender relations. The book raises questions about the social and historical context of gendered violence by investigating the socio-legal implications of gender conflict and investigates why it was that spoken crimes, such as scolding or chiding, involved a female offender. It considers the socio-legal changes that were important in laying the foundations for the systems of regulatory governance concerning women. At the heart of the study there is an investigation of the uncritical acceptance and misinterpretation of women's language as one of disreputable rumour-mongering, or frivolous conversation, or gossip. It considers cursing as a powerful force of dangerous incantation. Regardless of its arrangement, it was the passionate language of women that was censured. In place of the approach to female conversation as plain tittle-tattle, one that overlooks the subtler details of interpersonal relations and language of women in the early modern period, the records that summarise female narrative are investigated here to capture the essence of the issue that so often drove levels of interpersonal dispute involving women. Through an examination of women's petitions and depositions, this book sets out to capture the characteristics and meaning of early modern female language. It sets out the parameters of female discourse through the ritual of cursing and other censurable communication that was perceived by patriarchal authorities as scolding or chiding. It raises questions concerning its regulation and investigates why it was that the language women used was an offence against morality and makes enquiries into the circumstances that underlay the governance of the spoken violations that were carried out by women.

Closely connected to female language were the spoken rituals that were a feature of customary knowledge. Ritual healing incantation featured strongly in women's speech. These spoken rituals were closely linked to customary knowledge and formed an integral part of women's language. The intimate world of the speech of northern women is explored further below.

In early modern Northwest England, women frequently utilised the rituals of customary knowledge in their healing practices, particularly through the use of herbal remedies for treating illnesses. The petitions of female townsfolk often reveal the prevalence of this commonly shared knowledge. Eliza Cholmondeley's *Receipt Book* provides an illustrative example of the depth of knowledge women possessed in customary healing traditions. She documented some effective measures to combat smallpox and the plague in a written manuscript, which will be further examined in the subsequent sections.

In times of prolonged and intermittent crises, the governing authorities of early modern England enforced various legal restrictions on women's behaviour and speech. The secular and ecclesiastical institutions responsible for maintaining law and order produced extensive records during their operations, which shed light on their attempts to exert greater control over community affairs. The Chester Consistory Court papers, for example, are so voluminous that many records of the court remain to be 'unsorted and unlisted.'[27] The manuscripts of the Chester Consistory Court record the particular circumstances of moral crimes between the years of 1525 and 1755 and serve as a crucial source for this study.

The present publication prompts inquiries into the reasons behind the belief that women's speech had the potential to disrupt the social order and undermine the authority of governing institutions. It examines what it was that the legal authorities were afraid of. To properly understand the growth in interpersonal dispute legislation, this research investigates the social, legal, and economic complexities that underscored female speech contravention beginning with the reasons for the growth of interpersonal dispute legislation in early modern Northwest England. The link between cursing and female speech lawbreaking is examined by analysing court records that implicate women, to provide a comprehensive explanation for why cursing was viewed as a significant aspect of female speech infringement. The records of cursing cases in both secular and ecclesiastical courts frequently contain such details. This investigation examines all aspects of the factors that led to cases of ritual banning and cursing, with a focus on understanding why women were exclusively involved in all cursing cases.

Legal, religious, and patriarchal social groups, despite having competing ideologies, were united in their efforts to exert legal demands on women's conduct and speech. Through a combination of legal restraints, they collaborated in their aim to shape or abolish what was once a powerful female voice in public and private affairs, while prohibiting aspects of female conduct that did not conform to religious expectations.[28] These coercive forces combined over time to compel what was seen as 'contentious' women to comply with the rigorous standards of conduct that was expected, especially by non-conformist groups.[29] It was through such deliberate attempts as these to govern female conduct and space that the regulation and governance of female opinion and conduct was carried out. As early modern English interpersonal connections were reflected by word-of-mouth and the dynamics of personal relationships expressed through spoken language, speech was charged with special meaning and power and fear about the influential nature of verbal communication was manifested frequently in the discord that arose within the society. As the performance of traditional healing practices involved vocal incantations and remedies, women were perceived as overtly dangerous by both the local populace and law enforcement officials. To gain complete comprehension of why disputes so often manifested in the realm of symbolic and linguistic expression, it is crucial to consider the wider societal backdrop. Because of reliance on the oral tradition, the battle for control and authority frequently occurred within the domain of speech, which held the greatest potential for exerting dominance and influence. The mid-seventeenth century, marked by the English Civil War, represented a significant turning point in traditional customs. During this period, numerous towns in England underwent rapid expansion and witnessed alterations in social organisation. Social and economic instability frequently culminated in disputes within the community. These conflicts were often presented as legal cases before the courts.

While there has been extensive research on Church court records regarding sexual behaviour, archival sources related to other aspects of social history have been relatively neglected and archival sources remain underexplored.[30] Research confirms that there was an overtly Protestant concern about the unholy nature of magical procedures. There was a process of change in orthodox religions, which competed with the 'lower' expressions of religious phenomena when English society was alienated from its shared past. This change was owing to the transition from an oral to literate culture and there was a battle for control over traditional belief that commenced shortly after the Reformation. The result was that by the twentieth century, popular belief became relegated to the realm of proposed 'superstition.' It has been argued that the struggle to control popular belief occurred for the most part during the seventeenth century.[31] Catholic, Anglican, and Protestant clergy disapproved of magical intervention. They were critical of individuals whose practices might be associated with magical traditions and, however innocuous their customary rituals such as 'blessings' or 'casting water' may have been, they still became subject to unforgiving regulation and vocal infringement incurred harsh penalties. In Nantwich in 1627, when Margaret Knowsley presented a petition to the Justices asking for the remission of the third penalty in her sentence for slandering the minister, Mr. Jerrome. She was to have 'three manners of punishments on three several Saturdays.'[32] This meant that she was first to be whipped, second to make acknowledgment of her crime in 'as many places as the Justices of Nantwich shall think fit', and third to be 'carted' and 'bound' to 'her good behaviour.'[33] Despite her plea, she was forced to endure all three penalties. She was whipped, proclaimed at the cross, and carted before all Nantwich.[34] In 1688, Elizabeth Hayes of Etchells, was convicted for stealing 12 shillings from her employer, John Ryle. She was placed in safe custody, where she was to be punished by 'putting fetters and gyves upon her and by moderate whipping of her and that you allow no more for her maintenance than what she shall earn for her labor, in case of sickness.'[35] Community tension in Nantwich was especially pronounced in 1663.

The complexities of societal transformation have received comparable scrutiny within early colonial communities. Scholars have noted that the occurrence of witchcraft in early modern North America cannot be simplistically attributed to irrational dread or superstition. Rather, it serves as a reflection of the intricate dynamics of a shifting world, wherein conventional sources of authority were being confronted and contested. It has been suggested that colonialism played a decisive role in shaping the social and political context that gave rise to the pursuit of witchcraft.[36] As Anglicanism was the official religion of the British Empire, the Anglican Church sought to establish itself in the colonies by sending missionaries and building churches but faced opposition from other religious groups who saw it as a threat to their own beliefs and practices. It met with significant challenges in the colonies due to the prevalence of other religious groups, such as Puritans and Quakers.[37] Religious tensions between Puritanism and Anglicanism contributed to the prevalence of witchcraft accusations and in the context of cursing, warrant closer examination. It has been noted that the religious context of early modern North America was complex and contentious and religious beliefs and practices intersected with other social and cultural factors. Puritans, who were in the majority in many colonies, often accused Anglicans of being overly tolerant in their religious beliefs and practices and saw them as potential allies of the devil. As a result, accusations of witchcraft often became intertwined with accusations of religious heresy, and those accused of witchcraft were often Anglicans or other religious minorities.[38] Protestantism, in the company of other religious groups, was a leading participant in a battle that took place to control women's speech and conduct. As a result of competing religions and theology in early modern England, Calvinism came to dominate other ideological competitors within the scope of Protestantism.[39] Calvin's doctrine of predestination, which took a hold on so many religious Christian minds in the second half of the sixteenth century, emerged at a crucially important time because it was rapidly accommodating itself to the capitalist objectives of the emerging bourgeoisie. Scholars have put forward the idea that the seventeenth century saw extreme variability in America, especially in Massachusetts where the advancement of government began to threaten the Puritan supremacy and where voting rights of religious groups were later replaced with landowners.[40] However, a consideration of speech as a cultural system in early modern New England investigates the influence of the Puritan worldview on its inhabitants and indicates that Puritan attitudes to gender were complicated. For example, *Governing the Tongue: The Politics of Speech in Early New England* is an exploration of numerous pamphlet materials and verbal testimonies in a series of episodes ranging from 1620 to 1690. It offers an insight into Puritan rules of 'right speaking' and the appropriate ways of modest expression through the strict government of natural language.[41] It is argued that nonconformists in the sixteenth and seventeenth centuries 'made the relationships between words and flesh words and deeds central tenets of their faith' and confirms that verbal exchange for New Englanders was very important to the extent that speech and conduct were the same entity.[42] The Puritan doctrine, which achieved so much in the arena of competing ideologies, was of paramount importance to the ideological modelling of male and female relationships. Based upon a model of inherent inequality, the model of master and slave that was dominant in the economic sphere was reproduced and institutionalised by the Church on the social level. Such standards were similarly influential in Northwest England. Building upon Calvinist ideology, Puritan clergy members extended their reach through the Quarter Sessions courts and a discourse that marginalised women while elevating their own authority to divine status, thus seeking to dominate, disempower, and subjugate women in early seventeenth-century Northwest England. The standard works of the church fathers and the leaders of the Reformation influenced ministers of this faith.[43] Copies of this literature were found in the wills and inventories of Puritan ministers. In the figures derived from civil and ecclesiastical court papers, visitation records of the diocese and archbishopric of York, quarter session documents, probate records, published sermons and Puritan devotional literature, a total of 160 clergymen were working in the area at one time.[44] In areas such as the western part of Lancashire, where Catholicism retained its strongest hold, it was 'relatively isolated from the main trading network of the county. Educated to a doctoral standard, English

Puritan ministers succeeded in their attempts to shift the ideological ground in Calvin's direction.[45] Puritan ministers of the Northwest were in the vanguard of Calvin's 'Godly reform,' and by the 1630s were in a dominant position among the local clergy.[46]

Significantly, in the context of the cultural politics of speech, Calvinism was dependent on the power of preaching and included language which reproduced and dictated Puritan ideals of inequality and Calvinists believed that such models were ordained by God. Close control of language was paramount in the quest to convert non-believers and so was preaching the 'word.' Accordingly, close linguistic control of speech was crucial to the success in promulgating the doctrine. Exemplars of acceptable and unacceptable language and conduct were formulated according to strict Calvinistic principles. The implementation of religious doctrine played a significant role in the prosecution of women for verbal transgressions in early modern Northwest England.

Godly Discipline and Female Repression

The waning importance of religiously-inspired elite ritual magic within the upper echelons of English society can be attributed to the prevailing influence of a Protestant cultural milieu.[47] Calvin's concept of Godly law came to be widespread in early modern Northwest England between the years 1580 and 1642.[48] In certain townships, such as Nantwich, for example, an infrastructure was by this time in place, where commercial routes could be used more frequently and the consequence of having an existing structure was instrumental in intensifying existing commercial relationships and with it nonconformist ideals. The growth of chapel houses is an indication of the growing influence of stricter government. The town of Nantwich saw a growth in the numbers of non-conformist meeting houses. Evidence from the Cheshire Record Office demonstrates that there was a strong growth of nonconformist belief in Nantwich. Between the years of 1689 and 1699 there was a growth in the number of chapel houses erected, so demonstrating the growing influence of the ministry in this town. There are no figures available for the period from 1660 to 1670. There were 21 chapel houses erected between the years 1689 and 1699.[49] This high proportion of chapel houses established in a short time is indicative of the growth and influence of nonconformism in Nantwich. There was a total of 43 chapel houses erected between 1689 and 1853. Just under half of the total number were established by 1699.

The success of Calvinist indoctrination can be attributed to a few clerical figures who preached dramatic sermons designed to perturb an audience with powerful invective against sensuality and in favour of 'Godly' discipline. Preaching in the 1630s, ministers such as Edward Fleetwood, John Angier, Richard Mather, and Christopher Hudson held a derisive view of the female body and the most natural human impulses of sensual pleasure were attributed to women.[50] Desire of any kind was perceived as self-indulgent and explicit sexual engagement, drinking beer, drunkenness, and swearing were reviled.[51] Hard work, self-denial, and observing the Sabbath, however, were qualities that were much revered. Metaphors of female submission were employed to ensure religious conformity. The ministers referred to themselves as 'the chief workers, the master builders' whilst all others were 'God's labourers.'[52] Religious exercises in the home were the responsibility of the male, although women, in the absence of men, were occasionally called upon to do the preaching. Cheshire minister, Samuel Torshell believed that 'women may and must privately and familiarly exhort others where men are not present.'[53] By 'others' he referenced those further down the social scale such as servants, children, and those of low social standing. Through an ideology that was socially unjust and strictly anti-female, women of the righteous household were obliged to repeat a belief that was based on the master and slave dichotomy. Typical of such a creed and writing during the 1630s, the attitude of minister, Nicholas Byfield, reflects Puritan ambivalence and confusion about women. Byfield explicitly encouraged women to exert cautious wifely pressure upon her husband when he wrote: 'she may admonish and advise her husband with certain cautions.'[54]

Silencing Women: Censoring Female Speech and Conduct

The religious requirements imposed on women in the holy household were instrumental in the process of censoring female speech and conduct where 'Women were best to preserve themselves quiet, undisturbed and impassionate.'[55] Women speaking publicly on any matter contravened the uppermost authority where it was 'against God's ordinance and against church order and modesty for women to publicly preach.'[56] Such attitudes as these presaged severely for women those women in the broader community who were perceived as contentious. The characteristics of ordinary women, and the radical sectarian groups such as the Quakers were depicted in sharp contrast to the Puritan ideal:

> The common people and especially the female sex, [are] apt to be seduced, strong in their affections and loving too much independency, [but] weak and easy in their understanding, [and] not able to examine grounds and reasons not to answer you.[57]

Some mothers had definite views about the rituals of 'churching.' Several Puritan women found the ceremony obnoxious because it implied that childbirth was 'an impure rather than heroic act.'[58] Cressy, however, argues that churching represented a woman's new-found status in society. He argues that childbirth put women centre-stage as opposed to at the rear of the church, proposing that 'the ceremony celebrated her survival, and offered the comforts of religion.' Opposition to the ritual of churching was rare. But the fact that such incidents took place at all is evidence that women, even Puritan women, did indeed challenge the status quo.[59] The legitimacy of certain rituals associated with childbirth was fiercely contested. The Anglican Church inherited some Catholic childbirth rituals. Protestants continued with the practice of churching, but stressed it was a gesture of thanksgiving for a safe birth rather than a rite of purification. The Catholic Church allowed midwives to administer baptismal rites to children.[60] Protestants disagreed, accusing those involved of a transgression of Calvin's law, and citing Calvin's opinion that 'Christ did not command women, or men of any sort to baptise.'[61] An essay about the constructions of early modern motherhood explores the ideologies which attempted to shape motherhood.[62] This assessment of the deterioration of the status of women corresponds with a general decline in the status of women.[63] Such analyses find support in theories of a looming seventeenth-century crisis in gender relations presented in the essay entitled 'The Taming of the Scold' which traces the punitive measures imposed on women for verbal misdemeanours. It proposes that punishments against women increased between the years 1560 and 1660.[64] It has been noted that there were ideological pressures placed on women through the 'new professions,' but instead of concentrating on the ways in which women were forced out of their traditional roles, the unique role of motherhood in early modern England is emphasised. It has been noted that the role of women as mothers has been neglected by modern historians. An investigation of midwives, their relationships with the women they worked for, and the social circumstances of childbirth can, by contrast, tell us more about the dynamics of female-to-female relationships in early modern England and may allow an insight into the hidden world of women's business.[65] The context of midwife Anne Knutsford, is discussed further below.

In Cheshire, as everywhere in the early modern period, bringing forth children was a risky business. Women came close to death and were aware of the dangers they took in experiencing confinements.[66] The circumstances of a woman's delivery were a social equaliser. These circumstances applied to all women regardless of their social standing.[67] Crawford argues that the biological experiences of maternity, parturition, and lactation were socially constructed. In the seventeenth century they were defined as 'natural to women.'[68] She refers to medical treatises, sermons, domestic advice books, and Justice handbooks which aimed to understand the biology of reproduction; in so doing they, therefore, give an important account of the ideology of motherhood.[69] In many respects these views are sound. It has been noted that preaching ministers taught how 'the ideal good woman was the good mother'.[70] The Bible was the authority on the subject. A woman was believed to be 'saved' by childbirth. Contraception or abortion was seen as murder. The pain of childbirth was regarded as a punishment for Eve's sin. To ease the pain, Protestantism offered prayer, while Catholicism allowed 'supernatural' aid to women through relics such as the 'girdle of a saint.'[71] Supernatural aid was not well regarded. Protestant ministers, as with earlier Catholic priests, affirmed that women should be subject to male authority. This point is endorsed by most historians of early modern women's history who largely agree, that a husband's position 'was strengthened after the Reformation.'[72] It is less clear whether they agree with the argument that the veneration of women's reproductive ability was lost after the Reformation, through the 'ridicule of the cult of the virgin Mary' and the Catholic doctrine of 'divine Motherhood.'[73] Certainly, sexual desire, other than that which was directed at motherhood and marriage, was termed 'unnatural'.[74] Similarly, male authority was enhanced after the Reformation when the notion of 'bastardy' was intensified. The status of women was controlled by an ideology which approved only of motherhood within marriage.[75]

There is a further aspect to this denigration of womanhood. The Justices of the Peace, who punished female verbal violation, were also responsible for creating the category of bastardy. The punishments for transgressing the law were severe. Whipping or incarceration in the house of correction was imposed to control reproduction outside of wedlock. Families attempted to control female sexuality. The daughters of peers and gentlefolk had to be virgins to marry. At the other end of the spectrum, dowry-less states and greater sexual license were connected. This may have been how working women came to be known by Puritan ministers, as noted above, as headstrong, yet 'apt to be seduced.'[76]

The prosecution of prenuptial pregnancies varied in seventeenth-century England. Presentments in partly industrialised Wiltshire ranged from 60 to 75%. 'In more sparsely populated uplands country, only 7% of cases were presented'.[77] There was an increase in the numbers of women brought to court for verbal violence, witchcraft, and cursing. Evidence shows how these crimes disguised issues that were related to land, money, or property. In the analysis of the Cheshire and Lancashire Quarter Sessions and Church court records, it was found that in 95% of the cases related to witchcraft, cursing, or scolding, there was a concurrent dispute concerning property, land, or monetary matters.

There is a theory that 'by definition only women were adulterous' and that 'double standards' operated in religious and parliamentary law.[78] The 'law' certainly made it 'impossible' for a woman to legitimately have more than one lover, but this could depend upon where the offence was tried. Ecclesiastical courts may have differed from parliamentary law, perhaps imposing a lesser sentence. The Puritan parliament in 1650 introduced the death penalty for transgressing wives, who were rarely put to death but were 'strongly criticised.' All children born in wedlock were deemed 'legitimate' unless a husband could prove otherwise.[79] The system whereby the onus was upon a husband to prove the 'legitimacy' of his child may have been true of some regions but not all. Evidence from Lancashire and Cheshire, which relates details of women giving evidence against their husbands for adultery, complicates the issue. Chester Consistory Court also investigated cases of rape and adultery. Adulterous men were certainly punished, and in one instance, in 1610, a woman allegedly paid to obtain the sexual favour of a man. While such evidence exists, we cannot be certain that the Church law always operated double standards. Wealth, property and inheritance laws certainly operated in favour of husbands who, by default of an adulterous wife, were at risk of producing illegitimate children or 'bastard heirs.'[80] It has been noted that Puritan divines sought to make men as culpable as women but without success. In some areas, they triumphed in persuading some men to conform to the Godly model.[81] Historians of Puritanism in Northwest England have been constrained by the limited availability of evidence within the legal system because the government before 1630 did not systematically attack Puritanism. While this may be true of Puritanism in general, there is no lack of information about women in the ecclesiastical and secular records. Charges of cursing, witchcraft, and attendant forms of spoken violence that were brought against women gave females a high profile in the legal institutions of early modern Northwest England. The quarter sessions courts were regularly governed by Puritan Justices of the Peace. Throughout the Northwest, but especially in the town of Nantwich, there is evidence of women who presented challenging attitudes to the authorities and their role in community affairs. Those who brought cases of cursing to court demonstrated in their depositions an outlook of desperate, bereft, and sometimes unreasonable townsfolk. Such hostility to such verbal outbursts might suggest a reason for an increase in the prosecutions of cursing and magical healing throughout the decade of 1630 to 1640. The enthusiasm with which the judiciary reacted to such accusations in this decade, arose out of their efforts to rid the regional Northwest not only of self-determining women but also what they believed were surviving remnants of 'papish ritual' in the practice of cunning women. The legal emphasis in 1660 to 1670, however, suggests a shift away from charges of customary magical healing and sorcery, in favour of a stronger focus on cursing as a possible manifestation of female social protest. Consequently, the language used by women, as evident from accusations of cursing and scolding, as well as overt displays of female sexual tendencies, underwent intense scrutiny and became increasingly subjected to regulation.

Between 1630 and 1640, there was a surge in legal disputes brought before the Chester Consistory Court and quarter sessions courts, primarily targeting cunning women and charging them with engaging in sorcery or related practices, which encompassed a broader range of traditional activities. The populace, who held superstitious beliefs and whose customs might have been deemed by Puritan Justices as having ties to Catholicism, regardless of how benign their actual rituals, such as 'blessings' or 'casting water,' were, were frequently subjected to strict legal enforcement. However, the litigation against cunning women was often initiated by ordinary people, who, with no explanation to hand for the disastrous occurrences that overtook them, accused cunning people of resorting to the darker side of magic. As with the crimes associated with speech, the harmless 'charms' of the cunning women were depicted as 'inchauntements,' or, even worse, as 'sorcery.' The accusations, however, were rarely inspired by ideology alone; as with cases of cursing, the accusers repeatedly referred to the deaths of children, sickness, the loss of goods, and fear of starvation among the reversals of fortune so provoking their allegations against cunning folk. Such evidence very clearly expresses the desperate situation in which these petitioners existed. The ensuing pages enquire into the social and economic forces that shaped and regulated women's attitudes and investigates how these ideologies affected legal decisions and violent crime. Specifically, it examines the underlying animosity that fuelled accusations against women in greater depth.

Why Northwest England Matters: The Importance of Context in Understanding Female Speech Infringement Laws

The region of the Northwest has been chosen for this study for three specific reasons. First, female spoken crime of the cursing kind is customarily associated with this region. Indeed, it was a distinctive feature of *only* the Northwest region and owing to this exclusivity warrants particular investigation.[82] Second, aside from research into poverty in Lancashire, the Northwest region is, in the main, underexplored.[83] Third, Northwest England is valuable for its historical, cultural, or geographical significance, its unique features and characteristics, and as a potential point of comparison or contrast with other regions. The incidence of cursing spoken crime along with other kinds of verbal infraction is noticeable in a range of sources that are important to this inquiry such as the courts of Northwest England, Lancashire and Cheshire quarter sessions, the Liverpool Town Books, the various manorial courts of Cheshire, and other subsidiary regulating bodies of the Northwest of England. In addition to the records of various influential legal institutions, official documents can also aid in gaining a deeper comprehension of the socio-legal milieu surrounding what the court considered as verbal offences.

The records of the Chester Consistory Court which takes both Cheshire and Lancashire into its diocese establishes that there were three distinct intensifications in the prosecutions of women's' spoken infringement. Female verbal lawbreaking increased in the decades preceding the

Civil War, and in the decade following the collapse of the Commonwealth. In each of the decades 1610 to 1620, 1630 to 1640, and 1660 to 1670, there was an increase in the number of cases. However, between the years from 1660 to 1670—the decade of the Restoration—the number of cases increased sharply. The high incidence of female spoken crime during the decade from 1660 to 1670 was related to an especially traumatic period and one of extreme social hardship. This adversity is expressed in the manuscripts of the court cases. The depositions of the people of Nantwich, a Cheshire town, conveyed their hardships and distress in the records of both ecclesiastical and secular courts. Their depositions provided detailed descriptions of the challenges they encountered. For example, the people of Nantwich communicated the details of the adversities they faced in their depositions. Several cases confirm a dynamic of ill-will that had gathered momentum over previous decades, and which erupted in legal chaos in the year 1663. During this time a wave of litigation arose from one incident of cursing and continued until the end of the decade. It was also during this decade, and in the particular year of 1663, that a record number of 126 cases was heard by the Chester Consistory Court. As documents drawn from this court feature prominently in this enquiry, the Consistory Court itself deserves a brief explanation.

The ecclesiastical courts or church courts were also traditionally referred to as the 'Bawdy Courts.' The role of the Chester Consistory Court was to control public morality. It was, in addition, often consulted to settle matters of property ownership between individuals. The Church Court had its hierarchy of more than 250 courts, which had come down from the Middle Ages, as with the rest of the institutional backbone of the State, little modified by the Tudor monarchy. It has been argued that although they came under attack from Protestant reformers, they 'emerged unscathed.'[84] The church court concerned itself with tithes, probates, the dividing of lands under laws of inheritance, and alimony, as well as the fining of individuals for debts and defamations. Church courts had jurisdiction over the goods and livings of midwives, doctors and ministers. Most importantly, the charges of cursing came within the Church courts' responsibility for moral welfare in the Northwest, and cases involving cursing were typically heard there.

Societal Dynamics in the Northwest: Examining Government, Politics, and Conflict

Society in the Northwest was structured according to wealth and ownership of land. The landed nobility was at the highest point in the hierarchy and the poor at the lowest. A seating plan of a church in Acton illustrates the social hierarchy exactly as it was in Cheshire in 1635. The chief landowners, peers, and gentlefolk had the best seats, closest to the chancel. The yeomanry and husbandry had the remaining seats with all other churchgoers standing at the back of the church.[85] The bequest of heirlooms revealed by examinations of wills and inventories, and the spending of funds on better houses are indicative of the rise in the position of the yeoman during the early seventeenth century.[86] The situation that existed in Cheshire is much in keeping with the rest of England where the yeomanry possessed a greater proportion of land than they did in the late medieval period because the rising prices of produce meant greater profits. This is only partly true of Cheshire where the land was pastoral. It appears that the profits of industry played a greater part in the increase of wealth in this region.[87] It is generally accepted that the English gentry benefited greatly by the dissolution of the monasteries and that by the Civil War, they owned twice as much property. This was not the case with the Northwest, which was distinct from the rest of England in this regard since substantial amounts of the monastic property remained in the hands of the crown, or were controlled by the ancient hospitals of places such as Nantwich, or were consumed in the administrative costs of the huge diocese of Chester.[88]

Government and Politics

The Northwest region was disciplined in the same way as other English regions were, by a three-way structure of civil, military, and ecclesiastical control. The Justices of the Peace, who held quarter sessions at four annual meetings and moved intermittently between them, supervised the civil courts. Both counties were Palatinates that controlled assize courts and civil courts. In Cheshire, quarter sessions were held at Chester, Nantwich, Knutsford, Middlewich, and Northwich. The county was large and very difficult to oversee.[89] Military supervision was carried out by the Lord-Lieutenant, (the Earl of Derby) and his deputies. The sheriff had a formal role, and was an important figure in legal administration, but was not involved in parliamentary elections.[90] There was a routine connection with the Privy Council in London and the local governors through judges of the assizes who visited twice yearly. After 1578, the Justices of the Peace, sheriff, and assize judges met twice a year in Lancashire (Lancaster) in contrast with Cheshire (Chester) where Justices attended sessions infrequently. Justices did, however, meet regularly at monthly intervals in their hundreds.[91]

The Significance of Depositions, Petitions, and Letters in Historical Research

There are obvious advantages and disadvantages to using documents generated by lawsuits as a source for historical research. One disadvantage is that of legibility. These old manuscripts are filthy and in varying states of decay. Most accounts are often written in a mixture of Latin and English with varying degrees of paleographic complication. Some suits contain only partial evidence, whilst others are abundantly rich and informative in subject matter. Compiling case studies from primary source materials is a difficult process. It is not always easy to find a range of documents that will relate to a particular case. Where possible, documents relating to one incident are accumulated to offer an extended case study. In a case where there is limited information, the background story relating to the cursing is put forward. Noticeably, overall the sources give no hint concerning the final judgment of the court. However, on the positive side, the great advantage to using such a source lies in its originality and the quality of the narrative that is expressed in the deposition. It was the case that, in the past, scholars had acclaimed the richness of the original documents but lamented the disorganisation of the material.[92] Some scholars question the completeness of archival sources while others question the reliability of the 'female voice' in the sources.[93] There have been some changes with the introduction of digital materials, and some primary manuscripts being made digitally available and placed online, however, the sources consulted for this study are mostly archived.

During the early modern period in London, it has been noted that women dominated oral mores, and that the Church courts offered women 'a rare official institutional weapon.'[94] The manuscript documents produced by the Church courts are renowned for their richness. This may be especially true of court depositions which contain original narratives and female opinion. In their depositions, the witnesses and litigants in the courts put forward many fine points concerning the contested events of the matter. Of the London courts, it has been observed that men's adultery was seldom exposed. However, it has been noted that women 'publicised their husband's behaviour through the words of insult.'[95] Without a doubt, such litigation as this often placed women at the heart of community affairs.[96] Unfortunately, the same cannot be said of the court of Chancery, where the surviving records of equity proceedings, although voluminous, are incomplete.[97] Nevertheless, the court of Chancery is useful in reflecting on the visible developments in English institutions and society. Studies of the records of the Chancery court, claim that 'the surges and ebbs in the level of business were characteristic of the central courts as a whole.'[98] One particular impressive study identifies a growth in commercial and artisanal litigants and researchers have detected a 'pronounced rise in suitors from the metropolis.'[99] The increase was found to be linked with concomitant economic and demographic trends, a fall in debt cases, a rise in estate cases, and shifts in the mix of suits associated with changes in statutory law. Chancery court research has identified 'a falling off of litigation business in the Chancery and an avoidance of the central courts by the provinces.'[100] It has been suggested that 'the problem cries out for answers, and it is now evident that the answers do not lie at the centre.' [101] Considering the finding that further research is required in other local courts beyond those of London to regional towns, it is, for this reason, crucial that this investigation takes as its focus the largely under-researched region of Northwest England.

For this study, a wide range of national, regional, and local sources were consulted. However, the bulk of the manuscripts used in this research were sourced from the comprehensive, abundant, and informative records of the Chester Consistory Court. Cases were presented in this court from 1525 to 1860 and the instances consulted for this study comprise some 3,000 documents. However, for practical manageability purposes, a focus is placed on documents concerning the period from 1590 to 1675. Additional sources from numerous shire record offices, such as the quarter sessions records from Lancashire and Cheshire are also consulted as they are helpful in providing an understanding of interpersonal dispute. While some manuscripts, consist of a few lines giving brief details of the crime, some cases record a more extensive account of events. The scope of the cases exhibited considerable variation, with certain instances spanning up to 60 pages of depositions, meticulously unravelling the intricate minutiae of a specific incident. In the majority of situations, the Chester Consistory Court records documented essential information such as the names of the individuals involved, and specific details pertaining to the crime, as well as the ages and occupations of the individuals implicated in the proceedings. In certain cases, the sentence which an offender received was also recorded, in some instances it was not. For the most part, in the instances heard by the Consistory Court, there are recorded extensive elements in the 'depositions', 'interrogatories', 'responsions', 'sentence' and, in some cases there might also be a Schedule of Confession. Schedules of Confession are advantageous in providing evidence about the kinds of punishment that was imposed on women for verbal communication violation. Similarly, details of verbal communication infringement are present in the records of quarter sessions. The Quarter sessions documents consulted in this study are informative about the responses of Puritan Justices of the Peace, as well as about the social and economic circumstances of verbal crime. In addition, hearth tax records, state papers, and parish records are useful in providing the details relevant to perceived female criminal discourse.

While the investigation of prohibited female speech continues to hold significance, the primary focus of this inquiry revolves around comprehending the multifaceted conflicts that arose within early modern townships. Specifically, it aims to explore how women utilised cursing as a strategic tool to confront their adversaries and assert their agency in the face of challenging circumstances. The following chapters analyse the extent of social and legal control that institutions exerted over women during periods of crisis and investigates the distribution of 'causes' during some of the peaks of prosecutions and legal cases heard by the Chester Consistory Court between the years 1541 and 1755, when a total of 7,227 causes were brought before the court. The Consistory Court records indicate that there was a steady increase in court business with three distinct high points in the distribution of prosecutions. From 1541 to 1600 court business rose steadily, but after this period there were three peaks in what was an otherwise even rhythm of prosecutions. These high junctures in suits occurred during the periods of 1610 to 1620, 1630 to 1640, and 1660 to 1670. In the first increase that occurred in the decade 1610 to 1620, the numbers of cases increased sharply from 766 in 1600, to 1,168 cases in 1610. After a decrease between 1620 and 1630 to 722 causes, a second remarkable increase occurred in 1630 to 1640, when the Consistory Court instances peaked at 1,284. The rise was then followed by a sharp decrease. The obvious fall in causes is accounted for by the upheaval of the Civil War, when from 1642 to 1650 there were only 119 causes, and no court matters heard during the interregnum between 1650 and 1660.[102] When the Consistory Court resumed business in 1660, however, there was a third rise with 841 causes being heard between 1660 and 1670.[103] The highest annual increase within the second peak decade of 1660 to 1670, took place in 1663, when 126 causes were heard by the court in a single year.[104]

Some Consistory Court papers give intimate and precise details about the attitudes of the litigants and witnesses who were involved in spoken crime.[105] These sources, however, are problematic as there is a gap owing to the Civil War when the functions of the court stopped. Fortunately, during the Civil War period, the quarter sessions courts continued, and where a gap in the evidence occurs, the documents from Lancashire and Cheshire quarter sessions are consulted, and these make evidence available from testimonies. These documents, as with the Consistory Court papers, confirm that prosecutions intensified during the period from 1630 to 1640. These causes are rich in a narrative of the social disharmony which is so revealing about the issues relating to the charges of verbal infringement. Townsfolk often sought assistance through petitioning and petitions were brought by many troubled members of the community. These petitions are informative about the social dimensions that framed cases of cursing and are revealing about the context of speaking 'inchauntements' as well as sorcery. In addition to being illuminating about the perspectives of sorcery and cursing, some documents from the Quarter Sessions courts, unlike the Chester Consistory Court, are to some degree revealing about the attitudes of the Lancashire Justices of the Peace, many of whom were Puritan. Certainly, Puritan Justices of the Peace formulated the parameters of acceptable and unacceptable language and behaviour according to strict Calvinistic standards and such doctrines were a significant contributing factor in the prosecution of women for verbal transgression in early modern Northwest England.

This exploration of crisis and cursing does not include *all* the evidence relating to charges of defamation; it centres on manuscript evidence that is concerned with the crime of cursing as it appears in the secular and ecclesiastical courts. It explores court documents which relate distinctively to *female* spoken violation. The evidence discloses that cursing was, overall, regarded more tolerantly by church court authorities than it was by the Justices of the Lancashire and Cheshire quarter sessions. The Chester Consistory Court often dealt with accusations of cursing in a more evenhanded way than did the quarter sessions courts of Lancashire and Cheshire.[106] The Puritan Justices of Lancashire Quarter Sessions, were severe in the prosecution of female spoken transgression. They took a particularly harsh approach to those women who were involved with ritual cursing.[107] Even though the Justices took a stern view of female cursing activity, their reaction in the early seventeenth century was more moderate in comparison to the judiciaries of continental Europe.[108]

The following study confirms that townsfolk were certainly accustomed to the enactment of ritual cursing.[109] Throughout the sixteenth century in the Northwest, the testimonies and depositions of female litigants indicate that cursing was common practice and there was a steady pattern of prosecutions of women for scolding and cursing. Numerous testimonies produced by the courts substantiate the view of cursing as a cultural continuity of popular belief. Overall, they refute an interpretation of a spontaneous witch hunt.[110] Cursing and scolding were commonplace features of everyday life. During intermittent periods of community pressure, scolding and cursing accusations increased. Quarter sessions documents clearly characterise a transition from the degree of tolerance that was often extended to the acceptable face of popular magic of cunning women, that is, popular medicine for healing purposes, to one of stern disapproval of what was perceived as the dark arts of sorcery. The increases in prosecutions which occurred during the decades 1610 to 1620, 1630 to 1640, and 1660 to 1670 and the evidence from the records which sheds light on these three intervals will form the basis of the enquiry which is set out in the subsequent chapters.

In a rare insight into the thoughts, feelings, and experiences of those involved in legal disputes, depositions provide a unique glimpse into the events, offering an intimate portrayal of the thoughts, emotions, and experiences of those embroiled in legal conflicts. Indeed, it has been proposed that the deposition offers a 'limited area of transparency on the otherwise opaque surface of regular, uneventful social life. Through it we are enabled to observe the crucial principles of the social structure in their operation.'[111] Although the Chester Consistory Court records offer limited evidence regarding the social and economic aspects of perceived criminal activities attributed to women, the narratives found in women's letters, depositions, petitions, and supplementary documents provide a more nuanced understanding of the specific types of verbal offences committed. These records offer a comprehensive depiction of community conflicts, allowing for a more comprehensive portrayal of the overall situation. The records reveal how legal institutions regarded certain types of female language and behaviour and verify the alleged reasons behind why women's activities were so often perceived unfavourably.

Undoubtedly, the involvement of the courts added an additional layer of urgency to the situation of those who were already experiencing distress. An examination of the causes relating to cursing from the Chester Consistory Court between 1590 and 1700 reveals a steady increase in cases of cursing. Some incidents relate to one particular series and continue until as late as 1675. However, one peak, that of 1660 to 1670, discloses that there was an unusually high proportion of cases that related to cursing that occurred in one distinct area. Although the case numbers are a small proportion of the overall total of 7,227 causes heard by the Consistory Court between the years 1541 and 1755, while there were many incidents involving cursing, *formal* cursing charges were rare elsewhere in England during this period. Therefore, *any* information at all about cursing is worthy of close attention and especially those with a long history centred in one area. The decade from 1630 to 1640 was particularly socially unstable. While much of the business of the Consistory Court, related to moral crime, a large proportion of its business involved defamation causes. However, consideration of the Quarter Sessions depositions implies that during this period the records reveal that those who practised the healing arts were pursued most vociferously, notably because their customary practices were perceived as sorcery

As with the other areas of England, women were well represented in cases involving defamation. Women were involved in 90% of Consistory Court cases and 100% of cursing situations were carried out by women. Just under 75% of the cases of cursing were provoked because of the deaths of children. In addition, 40 of curses besought starvation, plague, or death upon the injured party. However, since cursing was then a *singularly* female socio-legal violation, it is a worthy objective to investigate the personal history of this paradigm of the regional Northwest that might set it apart from such areas as Devon, London, Somerset, and Wiltshire. Although the increase in numbers of cases relating to spoken crime undertaken by women increased in proportion to the general rate of increase in Consistory Court business, investigation of the entries involving cursing in the period from 1660 to 1670, contain more details about women's encounters and aspects about midwifery, childbirth, women's work, and attitudes to women. These elements shed light on a range of broader social questions relevant to women's history, especially the debate about the possible erosion of their position in society. As indicated above, socio-legal, and religious attitudes towards women are well represented in court proceedings and these provide some important insights into gender relationships as well as the association between women and the law. Such evidence provides a portrait of the social and economic dimensions of speech crime committed by women during the decade from 1660 and 1670 and conveys the micro-political circumstances relating to one woman, a midwife, of one township of Nantwich in the regional North-west, who was accused of cursing for the duration of one turbulent period of 1663.

The court proceedings of the Consistory Church Court offer a detailed perspective on how the language and conduct of women were governed in early modern England. These court records are particularly informative about the kinds of verbal communication that were judged by the ruling authorities to be offensive against morality. The language that the Court thought contentious was female language that was often associated with identifiable regions of the cultural and bodily low.[112] The societal taboos that were progressively introduced demonstrate clear-cut associations with expressions of female sexuality. Those who disturbed the peace of the community were reprehended. Such censoriousness was primarily concerned with the opinions and the language that expressed such opinions that were voiced by women.[113] For example, healing charms, curses, magic and spells of popular culture were held by the Court to be objectionable. Female language of containing these characteristics offended religious groups where female expression of the supernatural world was perceived as word-magic and it a transgression against church order and modesty.[114] In theoretical terms, such perceived degradation of female bearing is usefully explained by Bakhtin's theory of the 'grotesque' body of the carnival, and of popular culture in general, which is one of ambivalence where orifice, protuberance, apertures, the genitalia, particularly the phallus and bowels, are exaggerated and sexual intercourse, defecation and over-indulgence are accentuated.[115] However, most significant in this analysis is the continuous flow of female *speech*. The grotesque body exists in perfect opposition to the manners and culture of polite society and this perception was applied more rigorously to women. The association of grotesque imagery with the social domain, is also circumscribed geographically, spatially and bodily. In early modern Northwest England, certain spatial areas were ruled as being 'out of bounds' to women. Such spaces included the alehouse and the marketplace which were in conjunction with women's speech and perceived to have been related to the bodily 'low' region. Certain gamblingactivities such as laying a bet were supposed to be unsuitable for well-thought-of women. Gambling, cursing, scolding, witchcraft, and ill-wishing were related to the symbolic 'low' and were deemed to be out of bounds for women. The kinds of feminine behaviour that were associated with these locations existed in perfect opposition to the standards that were imposed by 'polite' society. Significantly for this study, between the years 1630 and 1670 the traditional verbal rituals of popular culture such as pronouncing charms and magical healing became more closely associated with the rituals of Catholicism and consequently women's speech and conduct became subject to more rigorous control by Puritan Justices of the Peace.

The regulation of female behaviour in Northwest England and the underlying crisis that led to the deterioration of gender relations provoke inquiries. These include questioning the motivations of legal authorities, exploring the concerns behind the restrictions imposed on female social space and language, identifying the implicit ideological driving force behind the imposition of behavioural restraints on women's social speech, examining why female bodies were a matter of concern, and uncovering the circumstances revealed by an analysis of gender interactions and crisis hotspots. The upcoming chapters aim to explore the meaning of the multiple competing ideologies that lay behind the suppression of female social space, language, and conduct. These chapters will address the complexities of the regulating ideological forces that emanated from religion and its convergence with popular beliefs under certain circumstances.

Numerous court depositions pertaining to female illicit discourse indicate that women expressed distress about their circumstances. Through their narratives, it becomes evident that religion in Northwest England played a significant role in intensifying an enduring and impassioned struggle for religious nonconformist control over the female realm. The narratives of women consistently reveal the presence of hardship. These accounts disclose distressing details about experiences such as abandonment during pregnancy and lack of support from their partners. There is often expressed fear regarding the absence of paternal assistance and apprehension about illness. The prevailing conditions of impoverishment are frequently described, along with the pervasive fear of starvation. The cases frequently expressed various forms of crisis that revealed the underlying conditions leading women to seek retribution and engage in verbal aggression towards fellow townspeople. These circumstances also compelled women to resort to cursing as a means of expressing their frustrations and grievances.

In raising questions about gender and taking into consideration the question of why female discourse and social space was a prime target for restraint; it is crucial to consider the construction of gender in the early modern period. It has been noted that time is gendered and is influenced significantly by the social order.[116] Moreover, there exists a contention that gender cannot be perceived solely as an ideological construct that has been forcibly imposed upon a biological basis and that the physical body is not devoid of any social or cultural influences. The body is not merely a natural fact but is a 'volatile entity.'[117] Any historical investigation of the female body requires an examination which questions the construction of gender. It would be a mistake to assume that because the female body is arguably gendered in the present that it has always been so in the past. The performative world of early modern theatre demonstrates the centrality of gendered knowledge in the mentality of early modern society.[118] Similarly, theoretical approaches to gender have established the ways in which the power of heterosexual hegemony shapes bodies, sex, and gender.[119] A gender theoretical framework offers a structure for examining cursing, crisis, and customary knowledge. Understanding the process by which the female body became gendered is essential for comprehending the extensive discursive production of female behaviour in early modern England. This understanding naturally applies to the association of female activity within the realm of magical healing which was not well regarded by Justices of the Quarter Sessions courts. Considering this line of reasoning, the impact of popular belief and socio-legal restraints on the perception and proposed governance of female discourse and conduct in early modern England is discussed in more detail below.

The Policing of Women's Language and Behaviour: Increased Control and Restrictions

When conducting research on the wider context of magical practices related to health and healing, it is crucial to have a clear understanding of the role and status of women. Traditionally, women's part in sorcery and witchcraft is often misunderstood as that of victim.[120] Often women appear in witchcraft history identified as a 'victim' of male dominance.[121] This situation is even true of deliberately 'feminist' accounts which have the result of undermining the possibility of female agency in spite of being consciously 'feminist' exposés.[122] In such accounts, sensationalised pamphlet information is considered from the perspective of the 'victim' of patriarchal dominance. Numerous investigations that attempt to re-establish women's centrality and importance to the witchcraft phenomenon question why it was that women were perceived and prosecuted as witches in early modern Europe.[123] It has been noted that the psychological dimensions of witchcraft in early modern Germany are important to the symbolic domain and that women involved in witchcraft were 'fantasy targets' for their enemies. It has also been noted that studies of witchcraft belong to psychology as much as to history along with the 'sociological characteristics of women as a group.'[124] Such an interpretation positions a psychological emphasis upon women through a study of the 'dilemmas of the psychic identity of womanhood,' which proposes that the psychic conflict attendant upon oedipal relations and motherhood that provided witchcraft with a psychic drama allowed a '*fantasy* of witchcraft to unfold.'[125] In explanation of the phenomenon, it is argued that the ambivalent effects of sexual regulation can be dated back to the period before the eighteenth century where gender is an issue, and where 'psyche and body are at stake.' These are necessarily cultural or psychological areas.[126] Since sexualities and gender issues remain largely unexplored in early modern history, *Oedipus and the Devil* was among the first study to chart new ground.[127] It explores the ideas of Weber and Elias arguing that the early modern period saw a 'renewed interest' in magic and the irrational. While this may have been so in early modern Germany, English sources demonstrate that interest in magic and witchcraft was not 'renewed' but was rather a 'continuity' of popular culture. The evidence supports the view that in England it was owing to the systems for the regulation of witchcraft that were renewed or changed.[128] Such a psychoanalytical approach is based upon the *inquisitorial* proceedings against witchcraft in continental Europe. There have been doubts expressed about adapting a 'model of psycho-analytical enquiry to an entire society.' These doubts are well founded, for it is not possible. An examination of English secondary sources and pamphlet materials that extend representations of witchcraft, recommends that the behaviour of both male and female witches was portrayed similarly and not according to gender but rather by their perceived association with the diabolical.[129] However, the sensational nature of pamphlet materials involved no popular narrative and cursing involved an invocation of Godly authority as opposed to the diabolical. Moreover, while relevant English archival sources and regional investigations remain relatively unexplored, any broad-based generalisations about women and witchcraft in early modern England are inconclusive until the regional variations of female experience are evaluated in closer detail.

From a literary perspective, the depiction of witches has taken on diverse forms in literature, art, and popular culture, evolving over time. However, the image of the witch has consistently served as a source of both anxiety and fascination within Western culture. This is obvious in the ways that witches have been represented that have reflected wider social and cultural concerns. During the early modern period, witchcraft was often associated with political subversion and the threat of social disorder, while in the nineteenth century, the figure of the witch was used as a symbol of female empowerment.[130] The potential of a cultural-linguistic approach and socio-economic framework have been noted for achieving an understanding of the diverse ways in which magic practices are understood, presenting new perspectives on the relationship between these practices and broader social, economic, and political factors.[131] It is likely that, from local studies and research upon parish and village, a complex and divergent account of local and regional issues will emerge to contribute to the national picture.[132] Recent research of early modern Scottish magic and witchcraft and the role of gender and the influence of popular culture is considered in relation to the beliefs that shaped Scottish society. The social, political, and cultural contexts that shaped these beliefs and practices, including the impact of the Reformation and documents show that magic and witchcraft were not products of superstition or religious fanaticism, but were also integral to early modern Scottish culture and society. Scottish witchcraft was driven by a combination of factors, including the influence of Calvinism, the tensions between different social and political groups, and the impact of the wider European witchcraft.[133]

According to English legal records it has been suggested that the cunning folk were not specifically selected for punishment according to gender.[134] From 1630 to 1640 in the Northwest of England, the strict regulation of women's language and behaviour led to the categorisation of traditional knowledge and practices of magical healing as sorcery. As a result, the frequency of prosecution for offences related to sorcery and enchantments increased significantly. Since it was not solely the legal elite that principally *initiated* the accusations, the questions relating to gender are complicated by the fact that it was ordinary members of the community that drove the accusations. Individuals who were the most marginalised and vulnerable in their communities were most susceptible to being accused, particularly women, poor people, and the elderly.[135] The complexities surrounding magical healing arise from the interplay of negative emotions within the community. To gain a deeper understanding of the events, it is crucial to examine these circumstances closely.[136] It is evident that women were at risk of being prosecuted for various spoken transgressions beyond those related to witchcraft, although their male counterparts on occasion faced prosecutions for witchcraft and magical healing.[137]

A gender-based analysis offers a useful approach for the identification and evaluation of the criteria and circumstances that authorised the legal control of other certain types of female behaviour. The presence of female power in early modern England was multifaceted and complex, necessitating a diverse range of questioning approaches when exploring women's activities during that period. Over recent years, much has been achieved in recovering female experience from the margins of early modern history.[138] Studies on women in early modern England consistently debunk the notion of female passivity and actively dismantle the myth of their lack of involvement in the community. Although women were primarily accused of symbolic crimes such as cursing, scolding, and witchcraft, they were also involved in actual criminal activities such as murder and robbery. However, it is important to stress that while women participated in symbolic crime, verbal offences such as cursing and scolding remained *singularly* female crimes. The spaces most often associated with women, commonly referred to as 'female' domains, often featured a male presence as well. This is particularly evident in the realm of magical healing. However, despite the presence of men, women were more frequently accused of engaging in mystical verbal offences compared to their male counterparts.

Traditional cursing was certainly perceived as legal misconduct. Women who were accused of cursing were believed to have disrupted the social harmony of their communities. To prevent them from expressing their grievances through the act of cursing, legal constraints were imposed on their speech. By cursing they contradicted the norms of polite society and transgressed a religiously imposed rule. Due to the intricacies of the verbal realm of cursing and malediction, it is essential to examine how such language functioned within the social context to fully grasp the circumstances surrounding cursing in the Northwest. Additionally, it is crucial to investigate the reasons behind the legal limitations placed on cursing. Despite facing severe criticism from the broader community, women who cursed others continued to engage in this practice, as cursing remained an intrinsic vocal expression within popular culture. Several theoretical propositions seek to explain cursing. It has been argued that there is much value in applying a cultural-linguistic analysis to the expression of belief in popular culture.[139] Cultural verbal interdictions become greatly intensified and complicated because the language in the social setting is highly charged. It has been noted that a curse might produce a 'whole family of words in exact parallel.'[140] This supposition echoes Malinowski's view that language is to a greater extent more potent in non-literate societies and proposes that 'the word has power of its own; it is a means of bringing things about' and that 'language in its primitive function is to be regarded as a mode of action rather than as a countersign of thought.'[141] It has been stated that the semantic history of 'curse' is unknown but its meaning in old English was 'to damn.'[142] 'Flyting' was a similar verbal enunciation which was a convention of a ritual insult which means 'to contend or strive.' Flyting had a similar negative verbal association which meant 'to chide, wrangle or scold.'[143] It has been noted that insults are 'deliberately provocative' and designed to 'egg' people into action. Of such language in the early English North, the following assessment of the term applies:

> Although the language is often gross, even grotesque and astonishingly scatological, there is a certain element of play. Skill in barbed insult, dexterity in the wounding phrase, is very much part of the heroic language of the North, where the complexity of wordplay reaches astonishing proportions in skaldic verse, which was delivered *ex tempore*. It is the verbal equivalent of virtuoso sword-play.[144]

In a similar manner, in a restrained linguistic regime an affront or a curse might act as a 'safety-valve' in society. Such language found its place in popular culture and its function allowed for the alleviation of unresolved tensions.[145] This may well have been true of the early modern Northwest during a time of social and economic change and when the speech of popular culture underwent a transformation and where new 'polite' modes of conduct and terms of reference were introduced by ruling groups. Explicit verbal dexterity in the community, and especially as expressed by women, was often at odds with the restraint of the more austere etiquette of the genteel classes of Northwest England. It is crucial to examine how repressive measures were employed to restrict female rhetoric, particularly language that conflicted with societal norms of politeness. Conducting a thorough exploration of the economic and social context of early modern townships is crucial for gaining a more accurate understanding of the significance of cursing. The examination of factors such as social hierarchy, gender roles, and economic conditions in later chapters will provide insights into the motivations that were behind the use of the curse.

Notes

1. Cheshire Record Office (hereafter CRO) EDC5/48 Grappenhall, 1633.
2. CRO EDC5/1663/4/16. Deposition of Margaret Birkerton. Anne Knutsford cites Margaret Howell for cursing her and pulling her by the bosom.
3. Lancashire Record Office, (hereafter LRO) QSB1/64/21–23, 1629.
4. CRO EDC5/1663/4/16.
5. J. Sharpe, *Instruments of Darkness: Witchcraft in Early Modern England* (Philadelphia: University of Pennsylvania Press, 1996), p. 98.
6. J. Sharpe, *Crime in Early Modern England 1550–1750* (London, New York, 1984).
7. Ibid. p. 87.
8. Ibid.
9. O. Davies, 'Cunning-Folk in the Medical Market Place during the Nineteenth Century', *Medical History* 43 (1999): 55–73.
10. See, for example K. O'Brien *Petitioning for Land: The Petitions of First Peoples of Modern British Colonies*, Bloomsbury (2019). This book confirms how First Nations challenged British colonial authority from the earliest days of colonisation through the act of petitioning. In an analysis of First Nations petitions, it investigates First Nations rights and the range of legal encounters that initiated the many petitions of the first peoples of modern British colonies. Similarly, see K. O'Brien, The Larrakia Petitions for a Treaty and Land Rights. *UK Parliaments Petition*

Committee, (October 2019). See also the use of charms and blessings in diverse healing and ritual customs in *White Magic and the Cunning Folk: Charms and Blessings in Northwest England*, The Bluecoat Press, Liverpool, (2001). For cursing in local and social context see K. O'Brien, 'Petitioning, Sexual Impropriety and the Dynamics of Ill Will in Daily Urban Life.' *Urban History* 43, no. 2 (2016): 177–199 and for intimate relationships see 'Companions of Heart and Hearth: Hardship and the Changing Structure of the Family in Early Modern English Townships.' *Journal of Family History* 39, no. 3 (2014): 183–203, and 'Intimate Worlds: Kinship Relations and Emotional Investment Among Nantwich Women 1603–1685.' *Journal of Family History* 41, no. 2 (2016): 131–143.
11. J. Sharpe, *Crime in Early Modern England 1550–1750* (London and New York, 1984), p. 87.
12. W. de Blécourt, and O. Davies, *Witchcraft Continued Popular Magic in Modern Europe* (London: Manchester University Press, 2004), p. 191.
13. W. de Blécourt, R. Hutton, and J. S. La Fontaine, *Witchcraft and Magic in Europe the Twentieth Century* (London: Athlone Press, 1999), p. 191.
14. T. Waters, 'Irish Cursing and the Art of Magic, 1750–2018.' *Past & Present* 247, no. 1 (2020): 113–149.
15. D. Rollison, *The Local Origins of Modern Society: Gloucestershire, 1500–1800* (London and New York, 1992), p. 45. Suggests that English history may well be rewritten from the local and regional level, bottom up. K. Wrightson, *English Society, Poverty and Piety in an English Village, Terling 1525–1600* (London, 1986).
16. K. Thomas, *Religion and the Decline of Magic Studies in Popular Beliefs in Sixteenth- and Seventeenth-century England* (London, 1971), pp. 599–637.
17. J. Favret-Saada, *Deadly Words: Witchcraft in the Bocage* (Cambridge, Cambridgeshire: Cambridge University Press, 1980).
18. É. Pócs, 'Curse, Maleficium, Divination: Witchcraft on the Borderline of Religion and Magic' in Willem de Blécourt, Ronald Hutton, and J. S. La Fontaine (Eds.) *Witchcraft and Magic in Europe the Twentieth Century* (London: Athlone Press, 1999), pp. 174–176.

19. Ibid. p. 176.
20. A. Macfarlane, *Witchcraft in Tudor and Stuart England: A Regional and Comparative Study* (London, 1970), p. 160.
21. C. R. Millar, 'Diabolical Men: Reintegrating Male Witches into English Witchcraft.' *The Seventeenth Century* 36, no. 5 (2021): 693–713.
22. See, for example, K. O'Brien, 'Sexual Impropriety, Petitioning and the Dynamics of Ill Will in Daily Urban Life' 43, no. 2 (May 2016), pp. 177–199.
23. Macfarlane, op. cit., pp. 255–309. Macfarlane analyses the gender distribution of those accused of witchcraft in early modern Essex. He argues that though the proportion of women accused of witchcraft was high overall, men were accused at a lower rate than women and that it is difficult to establish a gender bias.
24. For further discussion of historiography of scolding see K. O'Brien, 'Sexual Impropriety, Petitioning, and the Dynamics of Ill Will', pp. 4–6.
25. Ibid. pp. 4–6.
26. Ibid. pp. 4–6. See discussion of scolding. 'The greatest threat to community order came not from thieving, rape or murder but from 'scolds.' It was a crime which was usually dealt with by the church court or local manorial court.
27. CRO Catalogue of Consistory Court Papers. Cheshire Record Office, hereafter referred to as CRO.
28. D. Underdown, 'The Taming of the Scold: The Enforcement of Patriarchal Authority in Early Modern England', in A. Fletcher and J. Stevenson (Eds.), *Order and Disorder in Early Modern England* (Cambridge, 1985).
29. The term 'nonconformist' in this book is contemporaneous with early modern terminology as it appears in the manuscripts.
30. O. Davies, *Popular Magic: Cunning Folk in English History* (London, England: Hambledon Continuum, 2007), p. 15.
31. Thomas, Religion and the Decline of Magic.
32. Ibid. p. 83.
33. Ibid. p. 81.
34. See S. Hindle,'The Shaming of Margaret Knowsley: Gossip, Gender and the Experience of Authority in Early Modern England', in *Continuity and Change,* Volume 9 (Cambridge, 1994), pp. 391–419. It has been noted that 'the world of private

women's speech was independent of a male patriarchy and was a powerful tool which posed considerable political problems on the streets of early modern England'.

35. F. A. Bailey, *op. cit., p.* 89.
36. M. Gaskill, *The Ruin of All Witches: Life and Death in the New World* (Oxford University Press, 2020).
37. Ibid. pp. 26–27.
38. Ibid. pp. 53–54.
39. For the influence of the Reformation upon England see C. Haigh, *English Reformations: Religion. Politics and Society Under the Tudors* (Oxford, 1993) and D. Loades, *Revolution in Religion: The English Reformation 1530–1570* (Cardiff, 1992) and E. Cameron, *The European Reformation* (Oxford, 1991). For the slightly later period see D. MacCulloch, *The Later Reformation in England. 1547–1603* (New York, 1990). Rosemary O'Day addresses the historical controversy associated with the Reformation in *The Debate on the English Reformation* (London, 1986). For the influence of the Reformation within a broader geographical context in Europe in general, see C. Lindberg, *The European Reformations* (Oxford, 1996). Patricia Crawford in *Women and Religion in England 1500–1640. 1500–1720* (London, 1993), provides an informative and much-needed analysis of the religious effects of the Reformation upon English women, particularly during the changes that occurred.
40. Mendez, 'Feeling with Demons' pp. 11–12.
41. J. Kamensky, *Governing the Tongue: The Politics of Speech in Early New England* (New York: Oxford University Press, 1997), pp. 5–16.
42. Ibid.
43. R. C. Richardson, *Puritanism in Northwest England, A Regional Study of the Diocese of Chester to 1642* (Manchester, 1972).
44. Ibid. Puritan ministers consulted the following literature: Calvin's *Commentary on Psalms*, and *Institutes of Religion*. Foxe's *Book of Martyrs*, Thomas Cartwright's *Second Reply to Archbishop Whitgift* and *The Geneva Bible*.
45. Ibid.
46. Ibid.
47. F. Young, *Magic as a Political Crime in Medieval and Early Modern England: A History of Sorcery and Treason*. International

Library of Historical Studies (London, New York: I.B. Tauris, 2018), p. 23.
48. Ibid. p. 57.
49. Ibid.
50. Richardson, Puritanism in Northwest England.
51. Ibid. Richardson argues that there was 'largely unmolested growth of Puritanism in the diocese of Chester.' He also states that between the period '1580–1642 at least 160 clergymen in the diocese of Chester can be labelled Puritans.' p. 23.
52. Ibid.
53. Ibid.
54. Ibid.
55. Ibid. p. 107.
56. Ibid.
57. Thomas Edwards, *Salvation Certain* (London, 1642). Cited by Richardson, *op. cit.,* p. 108. Thomas Edwards was also the author of *Gangraena,* which is a tract denouncing sectarian preachers for their activities.
58. See, also, David Cressy's alternative view of ritual Churching, 'Purification, Thanksgiving and the Churching of Women in Post Reformation England', *Past and Present*. Numbers 138–141, (1996), pp. 106–114. Churching recognised her endurance of the pains and the perils of childbearing and focused on the woman rather than her baby. See for example, p. 145.
59. Ibid.
60. P. Crawford, 'The Construction and Experience of Maternity' in Valerie Fildes, (Ed.), *Women as Mothers in Pre-Industrial England: Essays in Memory of Dorothy McLaren* (London and New York, 1995), p. 11. See also, M. Brazier and S. Fox, 'The Regulation of Midwives in England, c.1500–1902.' *Medical Law International* 20, no. 4 (December 2020): 308–338.
61. Ibid.
62. Ibid.
63. A. Clark, *Working Life of Women in the Seventeenth Century* (London, 1992). (First edition, 1919). Clark consulted archaeological collections, private diaries, biographies, books of midwifery, Churchwarden's accounts, court leet records, rolls of parliament, Quarter Sessions, wage assessments for twenty-five cities in England, letters, and workhouse accounts.

64. D. Underdown, 'The Taming of the Scold: The Enforcement of Patriarchal Authority in Early Modern England' in A. Fletcher and J. Stevenson (Eds.), *Order and Disorder in Early Modern England* (Cambridge, 1985).
65. The latter part of this book provides an analysis of the social circumstances of childbirth in Nantwich in the seventeenth century.
66. Regarding the dangers of pregnancy in early modern Europe, see chapter five, of O. Hufton, *The Prospect Before Her: A History of Women in Western Europe, Volume One, 1500–1800* (London, 1995). See also J. Gelis, *History of Childbirth: Fertility, Pregnancy and Birth in Early Modern Europe* translation by R. Morris (Cambridge, 1991). For an informative guide to childbirth in England, see V. Fildes (Ed.), *Women as Mothers in Pre-industrial England: Essays in Memory of Dorothy McLaren* (London, 1990), and an earlier work by A. Eccles, *Obstetrics and Gynaecology in Tudor and Stuart England* (London, 1982). For an enlightening account of the privileged position pregnant women enjoyed in Germany see U. Rublack, 'Pregnancy, Childbirth and the Female Body in Early Modern Germany,' in *Past and Present*, Number 150 (February 1996), pp. 84–110. See also L. Gowing, 'Secret Births and Infanticide in Seventeenth Century England', *Past and Present* (August, 1997).
67. R. C. Richardson, *op. cit.,* p. 111.
68. P. Crawford, op. cit., p. 6.
69. P. Crawford, op. cit., p. 6. The treatises referred to are L. Lemnius, *The Secret Miracles of Nature* London, 1658, p. 23. N. Fontanus, *The Woman's Doctour* (London, 1652), refers to 'women's desire for men's seed.'
70. Timothy, Ch. II, Verse, V.
71. P. Crawford, op. cit., p. 8.
72. P. Crawford, op. cit., p. 9.
73. A. Clark, op. cit., p. 239.
74. P. Crawford, op. cit., p. 9.
75. On the issue of the loss of female authority after the Reformation, see O. Hufton, *op. cit.,* pp. 173–216, and P. Crawford, *Women and Religion in England* 1500–1720 (London, 1993), P. Collinson, 'The Role of Women in the English Reformation Illustrated by the Life and Friendships of Anne Locke' in *Godly People:*

Essays on English Protestantism and Puritanism (London, 1983), and C. Levin, 'Women in the Book of Martyrs as Models of Behaviour in Tudor England', *International Journal of Women's Studies*, 4 (1981).

76. R. C. Richardson, *Puritanism in Northwest England: A Regional Study of the Diocese of Chester to 1642* (Manchester, 1972), p. 108. Tract of Thomas Edwards the author of Gangraena.
77. P. Crawford, op. cit., p. 9.
78. Ibid. p. 10.
79. CRO EDC5/1630/45 and CRO EDC5/73/1638.
80. P. Crawford, *op. cit.*, p. 10. This was the situation in Nantwich, 1663 when a midwife's words cast doubt upon the parentage of James Cliffe, the heir to the Cliffe estate. See CRO EDC5/1663/16.
81. In those areas with a strong Puritan element, men were also required to conform to the standard of fidelity. See, for example, CRO EDC5/1630/45 where Anne Hough brought a legal action against her husband Thomas Hough of Runcorn.
82. K. Thomas, *Religion and the Decline of Magic: Studies in Popular Beliefs in Sixteenth- and Seventeenth-century England* (London, 1971), p. 606.
83. For some recent research into poor relief in Lancashire, see J. Healey, *The First Century of Welfare—Poverty and Poor Relief in Lancashire, 1620–1730* (Boydell and Brewer, 2014). For a broader exploration of law and the relationship between law and religion in the communities of England see also J. Bogiato, A. Green, M. Lobban, *Law, Lawyers and Litigants in Early Modern England*, Essays in Memory of Christopher W. Brooks (Cambridge, 2019).
84. C. Hill, *Society and Puritanism in Pre-Revolutionary* England (Middlesex, 1964), p. 289.
85. C. B. Phillips and J. H. Smith p. 19. The seating plan they refer to is examined by J. Livesey, 'Acton Church Seating Arrangements,' Transactions of Historic Society of Lancashire and Cheshire, LXIV. See, also a seating plan of St. Mary's church in Nantwich, 1633. A copy of the uniformity of the church of Nantwich, 1633, P120/4525/253.

86. G. J. Piccope (Ed.), *Lancashire and Cheshire Wills and Inventories from the Ecclesiastical Court at Chester*, Chetham Society, old series, LI and LV, 1860 and 1861 (London, 1985).
87. C. B. Phillips and J. H. Smith, op. cit., p. 21.
88. J. Addy, op. cit., p. 12. and C. B. Phillips and J. H. Smith, op. cit., p. 70.
89. The Victoria County History of Cheshire, Volume III (London, 1980), p. 3.
90. C. B. Phillips and J. H. Smith, op cit. p. 55.
91. Ibid.
92. See, for example, J. Milhous and R. D. Hume, 'Eighteenth Century Equity lawsuits in the Court of Exchequer as a Source for Historical Research' *Historical Research* (The Bulletin of the Institute of Historical Research), Volume 70, Number 172, (June 1997).
93. The view that the female voice is diluted in the records is also shared by R. Cust. See, for example his article 'Honour and Politics in early Stuart England: The Case of Beaumont versus Hastings' in *Past and Present*, Number 14, (November, 1995), pp. 57–94. This view is contrary to the findings presented by L. Gowing, 'Language, Power, and the Law: Women's Slander Litigation in Early Modern London', in J. Kermode and G. Walker, (Eds.), *Women, Crime and the Courts in Early Modern England* (London, 1994), p. 43.
94. L. Gowing, 'Language, Power, and the Law: Women's Slander Litigation in Early Modern London' in J. Kermode and G. Walker, (Eds.), *Women, Crime and the Courts in Early Modern England,* (London, 1994), p. 43.
95. Ibid. 43.
96. Ibid. 43.
97. H. Horwitz, 'Record-Keepers in the Court of Chancery and Their Record of Accomplishment in the Seventeenth and Eighteenth Centuries', *Historical Research*, Volume 70, Number 171 (February 1997). Horwitz gives an account of record-keeping and explores the surviving records of chancery equity proceedings contained in the Public Record Office. He questions the completeness of this source but is emphatic about the vastness.
98. Ibid. 43.

99. H. Horwitz and P. Polden, 'Continuity or Change in the Court of Chancery in the Seventeenth and Eighteenth Centuries', *Journal of British Studies* 35, no. 1 (January 1997): 24–57.
100. Ibid. 57.
101. Ibid.
102. See K. O'Brien, 'Sexual Impropriety, Petitioning and the Dynamics of Ill Will in Daily Urban Life.' *Urban History* 43, no. 2 (2016): 177–199. p. 5. There were also 44 citations to individuals to appear during this period which I have not included in the overall figure. This cursing case forms the basis for an extended case study.
103. Ibid.
104. Ibid.
105. Ibid.
106. See CRO EDC5/1662/63, Nantwich, Anne Wright contestes [sic] Mary Briscoe, April 1663. The manuscript contains the libel, depositions, interrogations, confessions, and sentence.
107. Lancashire Justices of the Peace, Roger Nowell, Edmund Assheton [sic] and William Leigh, were also Puritan ministers. They prosecuted cursing severely.
108. Studies of continental witchcraft demonstrate an inquisitorial dimension to witchcraft. Such inquisitions did not occur in Northwest England.
109. P. Rushton, 'Women, Witchcraft and Slander in Early Modern England: Cases from the Church Courts of Durham, 1560–1675', *Northern History* Volume XVII–XVIII (Manchester, 1986). Rushton highlights the 'ordinariness' of the social circumstances of female speech crime in Northumberland and Durham where cases arose in the domestic setting, in the home or on the street.
110. For information about witch hunts more broadly in earlier research see, for example, N. Cohn, *Europe's Inner Demons* (London, 1976), B. Levack, *The Witchhunt in Early Modern Europe* (London, 1987), E. W. Monter, Witchcraft *in France and Switzerland; the Borderlands During the Reformation* (Ithaca, 1976), and H. C. E. Midelfort, *Witch-Hunting in South Western Germany, 1562–1684* (Stanford, 1972). See also, A. Mendez, *Hell is Empty: Demonology, Witch Hunts, and Reformation in Early*

Modern England in Sixteenth and Seventeenth Centuries (University of Valencia Press, 2020). This more recent study explores the ideas, representations, and treatises that were published by members of the cultural elite such as religious ministers, theologians, and doctors in England between the sixteenth and seventeenth centuries and how the authors sought to explain the relationships between the human, the divine, and the unholy throughout the Protestant Reformation.

111. A. Macfarlane and S. Harrison, *The Justice and the Mare's Ale* (London, 1987), p. 24.
112. For more details on the origins of 'foul language,' see M. Bakhtin, *Rabelais and His World*, translated by Helene Iswolsky (Bloomington, 1984), and P. Stallybrass and A. White, *The Politics and Poetics of Transgression* (London, 1986).
113. Underdown, 'The Taming of the Scold: The Enforcement of Patriarchal Authority in Early Modern England' p. 128. Underdown broadly argues that an increase in verbal crime was recorded in most southern counties, particularly towns which had a high economic profile with high immigration and passing tradesfolk between the years 1560 and 1640.
114. G. Hughes, *Swearing: A Social History of Foul Language, Oaths and Profanity in English* (Oxford, 1991), p. 14.
115. M. Bakhtin, *Rabelais and His World.*
116. M. Wiesner-Hanks, *Gendered Temporalities in the Early Modern World* (Amsterdam: Amsterdam University Press, 2018).
117. E. Grosz, *Volatile Bodies. Towards a Corporeal Feminism* (Bloomington, 1994). See also J. M. Bennett, *History Matters: Patriarchy and the Challenge of Feminism* (Philadelphia: University of Pennsylvania Press, 2006). Demonstrates an achievement of a more feminist future relies on a rich, plausible, and well-informed knowledge of the past. Patriarchal gender roles were similarly imposed on Indigenous Australian society with damaging consequences. See, for example, A. McClintock, *Imperial Leather: Race, Gender and Sexuality in the Colonial Contest* (Routledge, 1995), A. Moreton-Robinson, *Talkin' Up to the White Woman: Aboriginal Women and Feminism* (St Lucia: University of Queensland Press, 2000), pp. 179–186.
118. S. D. Amussen and D. Underdown, *Gender, Culture and Politics in England, 1560–1640 Turning the World Upside down* (London:

Bloomsbury Academic, an imprint of Bloomsbury Publishing Plc, 2017).

119. J. Butler, *Bodies That Matter: On the Discursive Limits of Sex* (London: Routledge, 2014).
120. These studies approach witchcraft as a 'persecution' N. Cohn, *Europe's Inner Demons* (London, 1975). B. Levack, *The Witch-hunt in Early Modern Europe* (London, 1987), E. W. Monter, *Witchcraft in France and Switzerland; the Borderlands During the Reformation* (Ithaca, 1976), H. C. E. Midelfort, *Witch-Hunting in Southwestern Germany, 1562–1684* (Stanford, 1972), and L. C. Ewan, *Witch Hunting and Witch Trials* (London, 1929/1971). Some studies which take alternative approaches to witchcraft include Bengt Ankerloo and Gustav Henningsen (Eds.), *Early Modern European Witchcraft* (Oxford, 1990), G. Scarre, *Witchcraft and Magic in Sixteenth- and Seventeenth-century Europe* (London, 1987), C. Ginzburg, *The Night Battles: Witchcraft and Agrarian Cults in the Sixteenth and Seventeenth Centuries* (Baltimore, 1983).
121. This is regrettably true of Mariane Hester's study *Lewd Women and Wicked Witches: A Study of the Dynamics of Male Domination* (London and New York, 1992).
122. Ibid.
123. L. Roper, *Oedipus and the Devil: Witchcraft, Sexuality and Religion in Early Modern Europe* (London and New York, 1994).
124. Ibid. p. 4.
125. Ibid.
126. Ibid. p. 3. Roper's work emphasises how approaches influenced by Weber have dominated the way subjectivity is conceptualised for the early modern period. She argues the following 'Michel Foucault's emphasis on the power of language and the importance of discourse in the constitution of the individual subject enables exploration of the construction of sexual desire through language.'
127. See also, E. Donoghue, *Passions between Women: British Lesbian Culture 1668–1801* (London, 1993), explores women as a 'distinct sexual and social group'. There is evidence in women's Wills and Inventories that women openly lived together in early modern Nantwich. See, K. O'Brien, 'Companions of Heart and Hearth: Hardship and the Changing Structure of the Family in

Early Modern English Townships.' *Journal of Family History* 39, no. 3: 183–203. See also, L. Gowing, *Domestic Dangers: Women, Words, and Sex in Early Modern London* (New York: Oxford, 1996).

128. See, for instance, A. Macfarlane, *Witchcraft in Tudor and Stuart England: A Regional and Comparative Study* (London, 1970). K. Thomas, *Religion and the Decline of Magic: Studies in Popular Beliefs in Sixteenth- and Seventeenth-Century England* (London, 1971). Both historians contend that witchcraft was a continuity of popular belief with an identity that is entirely separate from Continental witchcraft.
129. C. R. Millar, 'Diabolical Men: Reintegrating Male Witches into English Witchcraft.' *The Seventeenth Century* 36, no. 5 (2021): 693–713.
130. D. Purkiss, *The Witch in the Western Imagination* (London: Routledge, 2012).
131. E. Bever, 'Popular Witch Beliefs and Magical Practices: New Directions for Research.' *International Journal of Humanities and Social Science Research* 5, no. 1 (2017): 1–10.
132. See, for example, J. Healey, *The First Century of Welfare—Poverty and Poor Relief in Lancashire, 1620–1730* (Boydell and Brewer, 2014). For a broader exploration of law and the relationship between law and religion in the communities of England see also J. Bogiato, A. Green, and M. Lobban, *Law, Lawyers and Litigants in Early Modern England* Essays in Memory of Christopher W. Brooks (Cambridge, 2019). For earlier proponents of local and regional archival history see Keith Wrightson, *English Society, 1580–1680* (London, 1982) and K. Wrightson, and D. Levine, *Poverty and Piety in an English Village, Terling 1525–1700* (New York, 1979), and David Rollison, *The Local Origins of Modern Society: Gloucestershire, 1500–1800* (London and New York, 1992).
133. J. Goodare, L. Martin, and J. Miller. *Witchcraft and Belief in Early Modern Scotland* (London: Palgrave Macmillan UK, 2007).
134. Macfarlane, op. cit., pp. 255–309. An analysis of gender distribution of those accused of witchcraft in early modern Essex proposes that the proportion of women accused of witchcraft was high overall, men were accused at a lower rate than women and that it is difficult to establish a gender bias. See also, C. R.

Millar, 'Diabolical Men: Reintegrating Male Witches into English Witchcraft.' *The Seventeenth Century* 36, no. 5 (2021): 693–713, p. 706, who stresses the importance of viewing the male equivalent of female involvement in magical belief.

135. J. Sharpe, *Instruments of Darkness: Witchcraft in England 1550–1750* (London: Penguin Books, 1997).
136. See, for example, K. O'Brien, 'Sexual Impropriety, Petitioning and the Dynamics of Ill Will in Daily Urban Life' 43, no. 2 (May 2016): 177–199.
137. See J. Sharpe, Instruments of Darkness: Witchcraft in England 1550–1750, (London: Penguin Books, 1997). A. Macfarlane, Witchcraft in Tudor and Stuart England: A Regional and Comparative Study (London, 1970), p. 160.
138. See also A. L. Erickson, *Women and Property in Early Modern England* (London, 1993), Laura Gowing, *Women, Sex and Honour: The London Church Courts, 1572–1640* (London, 1993), L. Gowing, 'Gender and the Language of Insult in Early Modern London', *History Workshop*, No. 35 (Spring, 1993), pp. 1–21. L. Gowing, *Domestic Dangers: Women, Words, and Sex in Early Modern London,* (Oxford: New York, 1996). L. Gowing, *Common Bodies: Women, Touch, and Power in Seventeenth-Century England* Haven: Yale University Press, 2003. S. Amussen, *An Ordered Society: Gender and Class in Early Modern England* (Oxford, 1988), G. Walker, *Crime, Gender, and Social Order in Early Modern England*, Cambridge Studies in Early Modern British History (Cambridge, 2003).
139. E. Bever, 'Popular Witch Beliefs and Magical Practices,' in *The Oxford Handbook of Witchcraft in Early Modern Europe and Colonial America* (Oxford University Press, 2013).
140. Ibid.
141. Ibid.
142. Ibid.
143. Ibid.
144. Ibid.
145. Hughes, in Swearing argues that cursing is also a type of social safety-valve among Indigenous Australians.

CHAPTER 2

Cursing in Early Modern Townships

Cursing certainly evoked powerful feelings. The emotional intensity within which English cursing took place was similar to that of witchcraft.[1] The investigation of emotions within the domain of magic represents a nascent and burgeoning area of historical scholarship, and this study makes a constructive contribution to the advancement of this field.[2] The context surrounding the occurrence of cursing is characterised by a potent emotional charge, primarily attributed to the invocation of divine wrath through the curse. In contrast, witchcraft typically called upon diabolical forces and held distinct associations with diabolical power. The fact that the curse invoked Godly authority caused townsfolk great disquiet. In subsequent pages, a comprehensive exploration is presented to develop a nuanced understanding of the emotional impact generated by the act of cursing. This investigation aims to shed light on the multifaceted emotional responses that arise in relation to cursing. It will assess the impact of cursing as well as evaluate the degree to which male-dominated ideologies have sought to regulate female language and space. While the complexity of magical belief is well known,[3] some scholars advocate for an exploration of how gender-based or socio-economic pressures have contributed to the complexity of magical traditions.[4] Taking this observation into account, this book focuses on the socio-economic context to gain a deeper understanding of the origins and connection of curses with

K. O'Brien, *Cursing, Crisis and Customary Knowledge in Early Modern English Townships*, Palgrave Historical Studies in Witchcraft and Magic, https://doi.org/10.1007/978-3-031-44045-8_2

social adversity. As previously discussed, cursing was primarily committed by women, prompting gender-related inquiries as to why it was exclusively women who faced charges for this crime in early modern Northwest England. The broader gender, social and economic contexts of cursing raise important questions and they are addressed further below. Such inquiries prompt an exploration of why only women were charged with this offence and what specifically symbolises cursing as a distinctly female illegality. Furthermore, it calls for an examination of the circumstances that shape the broader gender dynamics, social structures, and economic contexts surrounding the act of cursing. In the contemporary sense, cursing might simply mean to swear or to use offensive language. In seventeenth-century England, however, the meaning of the curse went beyond a simple act of swearing to encompass a blasphemous and subsequently litigious situation as women who ritually cursed their antagonists were seen to invoke God's wrath upon an individual. The curse was regarded as a heinous offence against God. Within the early modern legal and religious context, to curse an individual was a crime which was punishable with extremely harsh penalties. Despite the risks involved, women in the townships of early modern England resorted to ritual cursing as a powerful and effective means of attacking their enemies, particularly in times of hardship. They were not afraid to place a curse upon those who opposed them, knowing full well the potential consequences. Ritual cursing was a complex phenomenon that was influenced by a variety of circumstances and factors. The curse was typically administered by women who were undergoing severe adversity. The specific background of the disputes that led women to curse is significant, and the circumstances in which it occurred reveals a world filled with anxiety and hardship.

While patriarchal norms may have limited women's agency in the realm of high politics, women were able to exert influence and organise at the grassroots level through the use of verbal power. The demonstration of female agency is best understood within the broader social and economic context of early modern communities and the everyday lives of women. It is at this community level that the true extent of women's agency becomes apparent. While cursing could take place in various contexts, it was predominantly in situations of great distress or adversity that women resorted to cursing. Women turned to cursing as a last resort to assert themselves and gain a sense of power in situations where they were otherwise helpless. The circumstances that led to the curse included a wide range of issues such as determining the father of a child, dealing with illnesses, experiencing material loss, losing one's home, facing poverty, or dealing with the sudden death of family members. Cursing provided women with a potent means to fight back against their adversaries and gain some measure of power in dire circumstances. For women facing desperate situations, the ritual of cursing could offer a quick path to freedom from their struggles. In some cases, a well-executed curse prevented further attack from adversaries. Examination of the correlations between cursing, economic hardships, and other forms of prohibited female speech within the depositions and petitions from the period reveals the underlying, hidden anxieties of the popular community. By exploring the meaning of curses within the community, this investigation sheds light on the wider social and economic ramifications of female discourse-related crimes. It unravels the deeper implications of such actions and their impact on the social fabric and economic dynamics of the community. It is at this juncture that historians propose that further investigation of female participation is warranted, especially in the most developed commercial areas of the country.[5] The discussion below encompasses numerous female narratives of hardship and desperation in a close examination of interpersonal dispute litigation and spoken transgression in the townships of the Northwest of England.

When women engaged in cursing, they became the subject of critical scrutiny and faced social and legal constraints that limited their ability to openly express their distress. To adequately address this issue, it is imperative to inquire into the intricate connection between social hardships and verbal transgressions, while concurrently undertaking a thorough investigation of spoken violations. A multifaceted approach will provide a comprehensive understanding of the interplay between adverse societal conditions and the use of verbal infractions. Such an approach serves to elucidate the degree to which cursing might embody female agency within the community's everyday affairs and offers an understanding of how instances of speech misconduct might have facilitated female empowerment. In the context of the correlation between socio-economic downtimes, and women cursing, and who were experiencing various forms of social deprivation, these interrogations are explored further below.

Although transgressions of cursing and further associated verbal misdemeanours provoked an increased governance of female language, cursing was deeply associated with underlying socio-economic changes and these changes underscore the high rate of presentments that occurred in Northwest England throughout the seventeenth century. To further explore the socio-economic factors behind cursing, it is important to consider the increase in legal cases involving interpersonal disputes as well as the use of female speech that was considered transgressive, such as cursing, scolding, and chiding. These forms of language were often associated with criminal behaviour and were frequently used by female offenders. The records indicate that in crisis hotspots of deprivation there was a high incidence of such female verbal contravention. Broadly, between 1600 and 1750 the Chester Consistory Court heard a total of 7,227 causes. During a turbulent period from 1630 to 1640 there was a period of loss and high child mortality in the region. Hardship was a frequent motif of the petitions and depositions that were presented by women. There was a steady increase in court business with three distinct high points in the distribution of prosecutions during the three decades of 1610 to 1620, 1630 to 1640, and 1660 to 1670. The production of female dialogue in social situations and narratives was linked to female healing and the practice of popular medicine. In an exploration of the narratives of desperation and hardship, it becomes clear that the fear of impoverishment and starvation was a frequent motive that drove women to resort to cursing.

Challenging Patriarchy: Women's Verbal Transgressions and Acts of Agency

The over-emphasis on the absence of female influence in the high political domain means that there is a tendency to overlook the extent of female agency in the early modern community. Scholars have put forward the idea that it was owing to patriarchal norms and constraints that the 'incorporative dimensions of state formation' did not afford novel degrees of agency to women and 'that it would be difficult to argue that women could have been involved in state development.'[6] While there may have been a lack of female agency in the high political domain, the same is not true of the low political context. In terms of the levels of agency presented by women who were successful in achieving their aims, cursing and other forms of female language that were perceived as female spoken affront enabled female agency at the community level. Recent research confirms that female involvement in testimony offered an opportunity to demonstrate the level of standing within their community.[7] The accounts given by women in court depositions and successful petitions provide additional evidence to support this idea and are worth exploring further. Scholars propose that women often influenced proceedings purely by participating in Church court proceedings.[8] The power that women exerted over the spoken word and the cursing power that was exerted by women in the community is an important example of the ways in which women sought to subvert patriarchal norms in early modern communities.[9] While cursing did not necessarily offer agency in the legal context, it was a quite different story in the local community. It was within the social framework of the early modern township that the power of the curse offered desperate women significant leverage.

Cursing and Customary Knowledge in Social and Historical Context

The practice of ritual cursing certainly has a long history. Its enactment was most prevalent among women in the north of England. The earliest evidence of a curse in England is comparable northern European cursing which can be traced to the Celtic period, 50 years BC. Tablets bearing magical inscriptions have been found in several parts of the country.[10] Evidence of formulaic cursing at this time was also found in northern England where curses were inscribed upon stone tablets. One particular curse, which was discovered at Covetina's Well near Hadrian's Wall, was written on a tablet of lead and the curse invoked the wrath of the local goddess upon a person whose identity is unknown.[11] Experts are unable to say whether the goddess referred to in the curse was familiar in popular culture, or whether popular reverence of the goddess was a feature of German common culture and brought to Britain by German troops.[12] The ritual of cursing was carried out regularly in Anglo-Saxon England and the curse was also a commonplace expression that took place throughout the Middle Ages and continued throughout the medieval period.[13] The practice of ritual cursing increased sharply in the Northwest region during the seventeenth century.

Cursing was an elaborate form of ritual magic that was exerted to produce a political outcome. It was a practice that held authority in the community through the fear of the malediction. Some curses were written, and these bore magical signs and were written on stones and buried. One cursing stone that encompassed a curse was found at Lincoln's Inn and it bore an inscription that said: 'that nothing may prosper nor go forward that Ralph Scrope taketh in hand.'[14] It has been noted that such curses as these were a substitute for political action, and that curses took many forms. For example, there was the curse of the beggar; the priest's curse; the curse of individuals against enclosing landlords; the widow's curse against those taking her property. However, the most potent of all curses was the curse of the impoverished. The belief that the poor possessed unparalleled maledictory prowess was strong in popular culture. It has been acknowledged that the refusal of charity to the unfortunate was often followed by a much-feared curse. Religious ideas provided cursing with a powerful impact. Although the community felt that it was wrong to pronounce a curse, they never undermined its power or destructive potential.[15]

Undoubtedly, the curse wielded significant power as a weapon. There is certainly evidence to support the claim that 'it exploited the universally held belief in the possibility of divine vengeance upon human evil-doers and it could strike terror into the hearts of the credulous and guilty.'[16] Similarly, there is confirmation that cursing from a scattered number of regions is suggestive of an undisclosed socio-economic impetus for cursing.[17] During the Middle Ages the Church had the power to pronounce curses. Priests used curses to control the behaviour of parishioners.[18] Such maledictions were pronounced against lawbreakers who stole or who were violent. Similar curses were issued against those who sinned against the Church. In townships, Churchwardens and constables were alerted to members of the community who would swear, bann, or curse. During the visitations of church officers, inquiries were made about whether any members of the community had offended by cursing. Churchwardens reported cursers, swearers, scolders, and chiders. Their reports were often the first step on the road to presentment before the Church courts. At this point any offenders who ritually cursed were often excommunicated from the Church.

The Art of Verbal Healing: Rituals and Practices

Notwithstanding subsequent attempts to condemn the practice of ritual cursing, there is substantial evidence that attests to the existence of a robust customary tradition of verbal ritual which exerted a significant influence on the widespread utilisation of magic within the early Anglo-Saxon society. Spoken rituals were embraced by the earliest herbalists of early England and they were present in the language of Old English, which, by the tenth century, expressed scientific thought. Bede's book on times and tides, was translated by Aelfric, who was then a leading astronomer and mathematician, while Byrhtferth, a monk affiliated with the Ramsey monastery, wrote an astronomical calendar.[19] Customary knowledge of herbal healing is present in these manuscripts. The Old English herbal and medical books, prescriptions, and recipes record a great understanding of science, folklore, and healing. Some spoken rituals and charms were written down and presented in manuscripts of the tenth and eleventh century. These are described by experts as 'the very oldest surviving pieces of Germanic literature.'[20] Spoken charms reach back to the time before migration of peoples from Europe arrived in Britain. The manuscripts are full of charms to cure backache, charms to protect from witchcraft, charms against cattle rustling, and spoken remedies to guard against the dangers of childbirth.[21] One charm explicitly refers to pre-Christian rites and mentions Erce, who was the earth mother goddess of fertility.[22]

Bald's Leechboo*k*, a substantial medical manuscript of this period was compiled in Winchester in the ninth or tenth century ('leechbook' being the Old English term for medicine book). The manuscript is divided into three sections with 88 prescriptions to cure every part of the body from head to toe. Bald's Leechbook addresses internal problems, their symptoms and diagnosis. It emphasises the curative properties of charms and magical remedies.[23] Bald's remedies put an end to such everyday problems as backache, loss of virility, shingles, hair-loss, headache, and dog bites. On occasion, magical skills were called on to cure an attack on a person by evil spirits. In 1846, Oswald Cockayne transcribed such prescriptions in his work entitled *Leechdoms, Wortcunning and Starcraft of Early England*. Historians have noted that the affirmation of charms were believed to protect early Anglo-Saxons from thieves. These charms of protection were similarly recited by individuals who feared that their animals would be stolen. One recorded example of a charm used to ward off cattle theft is as follows:

> May nothing I own be stolen or concealed, any more than Herod might steal or conceal our Lord. I thought of Saint Helena and I thought of Christ hanging on the cross thus I desire to find these cattle, not let them be carried off; to hear word of them, not let them be injured; to look after them, not let them be led away. Garmund, God's servant, find those cattle and fetch those cattle and capture those cattle and guard those cattle and bring those cattle home! May he never own land where he may lead the,

> nor ground to which he may carry them off, nor byre where he may hold them! And if perchance he does, may it never profit him! Within three nights may I know his strength, his might and power to protect.

Aside from the healing spells found in Bald's Leechbook, herbal medicine was also a significant aspect of early Anglo-Saxon medicine. The remedy below is Bald's prescription for the bite of a mad dog. The potion drew out poison, soothed inflammation and healed the wound. The directions for the treatment were written down as follows:

> Mix agrimony and plantain with honey and the white of an egg; treat the wound with that. For a wound from a dog: boil burdock and groundsel in butter; anoint with that. Again: bruise betony; apply it to the bite. Again: beat plaintain; apply it. Again: seethe two or three onions; roast them on ashes; mix with fat and honey, apply it. Again: burn a pig's jaw to ashes; sprinkle on. Again: take plantain root; pound it with fat; apply it to the wound so it casts out the poison.[24]

In early Anglo-Saxon England, it was believed that both excessive sexual activity and sexual inactivity could lead to negative health consequences. To maintain a balance, remedies were prescribed to address these extremes. Bald, a renowned Anglo-Saxon medical practitioner, offered several such treatments. One of his remedies, is aimed at countering the harmful effects of sexual promiscuity or under-activity. In the seventeenth century, the remedies for extreme sexual behaviour and fertility issues continued, and cunning women offered solutions to those seeking to conceive. Bald's remedy below is considered to address both excessive sexual desire and virility problems:

> If a man be over-virile, boil water agrimony in Welsh ale; he is to drink it at night fasting. If a man be insufficiently virile, boil the same herb in milk; then you will excite it. Again: boil in ewe's milk: water agrimony, alexanders, the herb called Fornet's palm, so it will be as he most desires.[25]

Some early English herbal remedies were accompanied by the summoning of curative magical powers. The ritual application of herbs, and, in some cases, of smoking the afflicted part of the body, could bring about a cure. In the following example, Bald recommended placing burning animal hair down the patient's trousers to smoke out the problem:

> For the dorsal muscle, seethe green rue in oil and in wax; anoint the dorsal muscle with it. Again: take goat hair; let it smoke under the breeches against the dorsal muscle. If a heel-sinew be broken, take Fornet's palm, seethe it in water, foment the limb with it, and wash the limb with it; and make a salve of butter; anoint the fomentation.[26]

There is an historical continuity with disquiet about powerful women who expressed ill will against others. Just as charms were an effective cure, so loose talk, or gossip, especially if executed by women, created alarm. It was believed that women who spoke dangerous words could bring much harm to a person. To thwart the effects of spoken ill will, Bald suggested the following prescription 'against a woman's chatter': 'Eat a radish at night while fasting; that day the chatter cannot harm you.'[27]

Most of the herbs in Bald's medicine would have grown commonly in the hills and fields from place to place. As with the early Anglo-Saxon healing formulas, the herbal remedies usually included charms to recite, and often, they contained elements of magic. In one remedy used to repel evil, Bald alluded to 'elves, goblins and those women with which the devil copulates.' 'Those women with which the devil copulates' we might take to mean witches. His remedy and directions to thwart the evil effects of witchcraft were written down as follows:

> Take the female hop-plant, wormwood, betony, lupin, vervain, henbane, dittander, viper's bugloss, bilberry plants, cropleek, garlic, madder grains, corn cockle, fennel. Put those plants in a vat; place under an altar; sing nine masses over it; boil in butter and in sheep's grease; add much holy salt; strain through a cloth; throw the herbs into running water. If any evil temptation come to a man, or elf or goblin, anoint his face with this salve, and put it on his eyes and where his body is sore, and cense him and frequently sign him with the cross; his condition will soon be better.[28]

Bald's therapy above, for the condition that he describes as 'temptation,' is an illustration of why the cunning folk came to be known as 'Blessers.' The directions for protecting one from evil are very reminiscent of the 'blessing' ceremony that takes place in church with some minor variations. Incense is used, the sign of the cross made frequently, and, instead of holy water, holy salt is applied.

Without a doubt, articulating 'charms' were clearly a part of healing in Bald's time. Strongly featured in the early Anglo-Saxon use of charms of words and the selection of charms from Bald's Leechbook are remedies to cure various kinds of illness and charms to repel goblins, elves, witches, and thieves. The rituals were directly inherited from the religious ritual of 'blessing.' The cunning people, Bald, and in the seventeenth century, perhaps, Culpeper, with their remedies and charms, clearly enjoyed a distinct place in the history of early English healing. Such practices may well have continued undisturbed but for the authorities of the social order that perceived the vocal expression of curative charms as sorcery or curses and the customary practice of ritual herbal medicine and blessing came to be perceived negatively. The regulation of healing practices in the early modern period was implemented by the Justices who enforced strict controls. Conflict arose between women who practised ritual cunning and their antagonists owing to the magical language they used together with customary healing methods that took place during the seventeenth century. The many components of the practice of customary knowledge are discussed in more detail below.

Traditional Wisdom and Healing Practices

The application of traditional knowledge and its associated practices has historically played a crucial role in promoting the overall well-being of the community.[29] Indeed, gaining a deeper understanding of the social and political contexts in which cunning folk operated is essential for an accurate comprehension of them as practitioners of customary knowledge in community life. Regional differences in the use of magic and medicine, as well as popular politics, likely contributed to variations in their practices and reputations. Further research is necessary to fully grasp the nuanced ways in which cunning folk mediated in community affairs, as well as how they lived and operated within their respective communities. By shedding light on these aspects, scholars can gain a more comprehensive view of the complex and multifaceted world of cunning folk and their place in early modern society.[30] However, in times of danger the local community perceived their customary healing activities inconsistently. During times of cyclical illness and during periods of acute distress cunning women were careful not to offend the community as they might find themselves subject to community-driven belligerence. Regardless, cunning women were popular. Where possible, their healing provision was provided to all comers. Often, they did not work for financial reward but instead offered remedial treatment to people in exchange for a meal or would accept some other gesture of appreciation. Equally, however, townsfolk were worried about the power cunning women possessed as they were perceived as potentially dangerous. There is a long tradition of resorting to the skills of both cunning men and women to obtain cures for themselves and domestic medicine was a common feature of everyday life. It has been noted that a further exploration of actual practices of magical healing need to be explored to acquire a better understanding of the efficacy of magical practices.[31] Their procedures and details of their expertise are well recorded in petitions and depositions and documents drawn from these sources form the basis for this investigation. The Warden of Manchester and astrologer, John Dee in the 1580s was famous for possessing powers of magical healing. In 1640, Thomas Broadbent who was also well versed in the art of health-giving was affectionately known as Old Daddy and was a servant of the Stanley family.[32] However, an important feature of early local medicine was the emphasis that was placed on 'cunning.' A broad scope of healing was undertaken by those who were knowledgeable in this work and their endeavours were recorded in their manuscripts. Macer's Herbal, discussed further below, offers significant knowledge about medical cures and is known to have contributed to medicinal knowledge and healing.[33] Macer's Herbal has been dated somewhere between thethirteenth andfifteenth century and several abridged translations of Macer's Herbal in middle English were printed in 1543 and consulted throughout the early modern period.

Apothecaries were essential to the health of the community and domestic medicine was common in most households of the broader population. Gentlewomen possessed significant medicinal knowledge, for example, the knowledge of Cheshire gentlewoman, Eliza Cholmondeley in 1677, which is discussed more extensively in Chapter 5. She recorded her familiarity with domestic medicine in a household remedy book entitled 'Eliza Cholmondeley's Book of Receipts.'[34] Botanists, such as Frederick Hornby of Liverpool, imparted knowledge about the appearance and the history of the known healing powers of herbs that would have been commonly familiar to the popular community, and the exquisite hand-coloured engravings of William Kilburn identify the appearance of healing herbs as well as disclose where, in the local environment, poorer townsfolk might have found them. Curtis, between the years of 1777 and 1787, assembled an astonishing accumulation of drawings of herbs with a clarification of the medicinal value of each herb.[35] In this work, Curtis refers to the use of herbs, and, by using the system of an early botanist known as Linnaeus to index his findings, he catalogued a great many herbal remedies. Among these remedies were some that were put to everyday use by the townspeople. These remedies are explored below as they shed further light on female discourse and knowledge and the contribution of women to the practice of customary healing in the community.

Although many women possessed customary knowledge, as well as practising time-honoured treatment broadly, few women were formally recognised as apothecaries. King James I gave apothecaries their own guild in 1618, and the Company of Apothecaries and the later Apothecaries Act of 1815 continued the formal regulation of the practice of herbal medicine. Women, nevertheless, applied treatment within the home. Customary healing took place extensively in the homes of many of the wealthier families of seventeenth-century Northwest England. While the broader populations of the Northwest regularly made use of herbaceous plants mutually as food and for medical treatment, the early modern healing repertoire was influenced by apothecaries and learned experts such as Bald, Macer, and Culpeper. The use of popular herbal remedies was constant throughout the fifteenth century and the eighteenth century. A selection of popular herbs is illustrated in William Kilburn's hand-coloured engravings and showcased in William Curtis' 'Flora Londensis.' As its name suggests, the herbs, plants, and flowers mentioned in this collection were commonly found in the surrounding countryside of London. Many of the plants and herbs that were used in traditional recipes grew universally around England. Curtis affirms that most herbs were commonly available throughout England.

The herbs and plants that were used for curative purposes in early modern Northwest England were most used throughout society by therapists and layfolk alike. For the hungry and impoverished it was crucial to their continued existence to have customary knowledge of where to find edible plants and herbs. Some herbs were ordinarily located by roadsides or at the entrances to towns and villages. In certain circumstances healing herbs and plants were cultivated in gardens. The quality of the ground they grew in obviously determined their geographical location and naturally some plants and herbs were more available than others. Foxglove, for example, grew in dry and gravelly soil. According to Curtis, foxglove was to be 'found common enough over most parts of England.'[36] There were herbs, such as 'common wild thyme' that preferred to grow in a slightly richer soil. Indeed the quality of the soil might even determine where people settled. Some herbalists recommended settling in those areas where herbs such as 'common wild thyme' grew, as it was believed that the ground was particularly fertile and therefore most advantageous to social settlement. For example, Curtis quoted the following lines from an old customary maxim:

> Mark where the dry champaign swells into cheerful hills, where marjoram and thyme, the love of bees, perfume the air. There, bid thy roofs, high on the basking steep Ascend: There light thy fires.[37]

While many herbs were used for their curative ability, herbs that grew wild around England were consumed by townsfolk for their nutritious value and they were widely sourced. Some plants and herbs were used in stews and soups, while other were eaten as salad leaves. Burdock, for example, was very nutritious and was often used in salads. Its secondary healing benefit was found in its application on the skin to relieve nettle sting. Among those edible herbs widely consumed were a variety of grasses which were combined with salad leaves which also grew wild.

Wild rocket was a popular herb. It grew wild in many places throughout England, and it was also cultivated in gardens for medicinal purposes. The seeds were popularly known to contain aphrodisiac qualities. Its power of healing was not the only reason that it was so well liked; it was also eaten as a salad leaf, as it is today. According to Curtis, wild rocket was to be found specifically near Hyde Park. It also grew 'on all the old walls and castles throughout England.'[38] One of the most popular of these leaves was known as 'corn salad.'[39] As its name suggests, corn salad was a salad herb, and was usually combined with other leaves and eaten. 'Wild marjoram,' was popular as a herb and was well known for its aromatic and pungent aroma. It was infused and drunk as a tea and assisted with fragilities of the stomach.[40] Wild marjoram was also added to beer as it was customarily known to enhance its power of intoxication. One of many popular eating herbs was one known as the 'common wood pea.' This plant grew abundantly in woods and in towns all over England. It was consumed by the desperate poor to stave off the pangs of hunger. Of this herb to repel hunger pangs, Curtis quoted a minister, Mr. Lightfoot of Uxbridge, who observed its use in Scotland. His account appears below:

> Common in lowlands and highlands of Scotland and Hebrides wood pea is called in the Erse language Cor-meille. The highlanders dig up the roots

> and dry them in their pockets, and chew them like tobacco or liquorice root, to relish their liquor and to repel hunger and thirst. In Breadalbane and Rosshire they sometimes steep them in water, and make an agreeable fermented liquore with them, which they esteem to be good for disorders of the thorax. It has a sweetish taste somewhat like liquorice roots. Fond as the highlanders were of this root, they frequently used to change it with me for some pig-tail tobacco, their favourite indulgence.[41]

A herb known as 'common arens' had an aromatic flavour like that of cloves. It was often infused in beer to stop it from spoiling. It was customarily chewed to sweeten the breath.[42] A popular and common herb used for cooking was known as 'sauce alone.' This herb possesses the pungent aroma of garlic. As its name suggests, it was a well-known and powerful flavouring agent, which, when added to meals, provided them with much tastiness.[43] The pot herb 'common mallow' was widely consumed in places around the world. It was as popular in England as it was in Egypt and China.[44]

In testing times edible plants offered great relief to the impoverished. The herb known as 'field scabious,' for example, was to be easily found in cornfields and meadows. It was recommended to cure 'coughs and asthmas, malignant fevers, epilepsy, scurvy, itch, scabies,' and was used to cure a disease known as 'tetters.'[45] 'Centory' was a herb that was applied widely in domestic medicine. It was used regularly by the broader population, the cunning folk, and just about everybody else concerned with healing. It was known in most places by early herbalists as 'gall of the earth.' This herb, however, was usually only to be found growing wild and was difficult to cultivate. It was used in the main to remedy stomach disorders. Its curative powers extended to alleviate the symptoms of such other illnesses as 'jaundice, green sickness, worms, agues, gout and scurvy.'[46] There was wide-ranging customary knowledge of the herb known as 'vervain.' This herb was a domestic plant and was useful in cases of scrofula, or the King's Evil, as it was commonly known. The remedy was devised by a herbalist, Morley, who advised his patients to include in a vervain amulet such additional herbs as 'mercury, antimony, hemlock and jalep.' It was recommended that the amulet be worn on the body 'which consists in hanging the root which is to be of a larger or smaller size according to the age of the patients, be tied with a yard of white fattin ribband round the neck, there to be worn until they recover.' Speaking of the gratitude that his patients expressed Morley stated:

> Many, many guineas have been offered me, but I never take any money. Sometimes indeed, genteel people have sent me some small acknowledgments of tea, wine and venison. Generous ones, small pieces of plate or other little presents. Even neighbouring farmers, a goose or turkey by way of thanks.[47]

A popular herbal remedy to ward off illness is 'common St John's wort'. According to conventional legend this herb was harvested on with great ritual on St John's Day in France and Germany and was regarded by many people with great admiration. Curtis, however, derided the use of herbs as charms. He wrote disparagingly about popular superstition and of popular belief he wrote 'they hang it near window as a certain charm against storms, thunder and evil spirits.'[48] Similarly, the herb, which was believed to have possessed magical powers, was popularly known as the devil's bit, or 'meadow scabious.' Of this herb Curtis wrote:

> Fabulous antiquity (the Monkes and Fryers as I suppose being the first inventors of the fable) said, that the Devil envying the good that this herb might do mankind, bit away part of the root and thereof came the name Devil's bit.[49]

A herb known as 'good King Henry' was recognised for its emollient qualities. The leaves were commonly applied for 'healing slight wounds, cleaning old ulcers, and other corresponding purposes.'[50] The popular healing herb known as 'clowns all heal' was recognised by Gerard as a vulnerary. Clowns all heal was also known by the names of 'clown's wound-wort' or simply 'all-heal'. Curtis named a case in point of a 'labouring man' whose 'deep gash in the leg' was healed by applying this herb.[51] Similarly, 'sharp-pointed dock' was used externally for healing wounds, and was applied to the skin 'in ointments, cataplasms and fomentations.'[52] 'Common ladies-smock' was found to be effective for 'various spasmic complaints.' Among the diseases it cured, were those such as 'asthma, spasms of the abdominal and other muscles, St Vitus dance and epilepsy.' The measure Curtis prescribed to alleviate the symptoms was 'a scruple to half a dram morning and evening.'[53]

Among the poor, internal complaints were many. To alleviate internal symptoms the herb 'comfrey' was highly functional. Comfrey was highly praised for its medicinal properties and it was taken 'internally' for 'spittings of blood, purgings, fluxes, and ulcers of the bladder.' In addition, it was applied externally, 'in poultices to fresh wounds, fractured bones, bad ulcers, bruises and gouty swellings.'[54] An important healing herb that was widespread and used extensively by the popular community was known as 'agrimony.' A drink was made by infusing the leaves with other ingredients which were known to purify the blood. According to Curtis, this herb was widely made use of and was to be located in Europe, Virginia, and Japan. It was regarded primarily as a medicinal plant and a mild corroborant. It was employed by most people and was known to work well against 'habitual diarrheas and many indispositions.'[55]

Some popular remedies that had been used for centuries were later rejected by several eighteenth-century botanists and herbalists. A particular botanical specimen which had been used traditionally to cure stomach disorders, and 'obstructions of the liver and biliary ducts and in epilepsies and palsies,' was the herb known as 'woodruff.' This herb, Curtis claimed, was rejected by 'modern medicine.'[56] However, despite the derision of popular practice many fragrant flowers, plants, and herbs were used to treat diseases besides those delineated above. The herbs and the remedies presented here are some of the most popular of these herbal remedies. Many of these were also sourced in Europe as well as the regional Northwest and are discussed further below.

The Use of Herbal Medicine in the Sixteenth and Seventeenth Centuries

In the sixteenth and seventeenth centuries there was a 'retrieval of classical drugs.'[57] *On Materia Medica* was responsible for a resurgence of Hellenism in medicine.[58] Some have argued that the subject of 'botany did not exist in the sixteenth century' and that the classification of plants and nomenclature did not appear until the seventeenth century.[59] Experts suggest that there was a medical revolution during the seventeenth century. Some have proposed that it is important to explore the social circumstances in the transmission process of medical ideas to have a complete understanding of the development of medicine.[60] An investigation of 11 case studies between 1630 and 1730 examines what is defined as a classical Renaissance and a history of ideas, and which takes as its focus an 'intellectual rather than social history.'[61] Experts propose that Dioscorides' *On Materia Medica* was the foundation upon which most knowledge of herbal medicine was based. Cheshire herbalist, John Gerald in his *Herball*, took his knowledge from this source. It is not certain whether Nicholas Culpeper, the famous astrologer-apothecary, who left behind a vast collection of herbal remedies in his book *Culpeper's Complete Herbal*, and whose work was broadly influential was influenced to the same extent. Culpeper, in 1653, worked at grassroots level, freely advising poor people at his practice in Red Lion Street, Spitalfields.[62]

There is a theory that a text such as *On Materia Medica* was unavailable to Western Europe in the Middle Ages and that it became accessible when translated into Latin in 1450 by Theodore Gaza. Galen's *On the Powers of Simple Remedies,* did not surpass in importance the work of Dioscorides which had been around since AD 50–70.[63] It is Dioscorides' work which experts believe is responsible for the revival of medical botany. However, not all experts agree that classical sources dominated the subject of medical knowledge. Some, in their research, have found that the earliest physicians existed in the valley of the Nile since c.2700 BC and have argued that 'doctors and medical thinking existed thousands of years before the first Greek physician appeared on the scene.'[64]

The world vision of many Europeans was 'totally transformed by the Portuguese and Spanish.'[65] Exotic plants such as cinnamon, nutmeg, and cloves were new medicines which appeared through the influence of the work of scholars such as Nicolas Monardes (c. 1493–1588) in *Dos Libros*. Monardes analysed the properties and uses of plants from the new world and cited the ways in which American Indians utilised plants for healing. His work was translated into Italian, English, French, German and Latin.[66] There was an interest in Aztec culture through a manuscript which contained drawings of hundreds of medicinal plants used in Aztec medicine. The manuscript was translated into Latin and used in Spain. Similarly, India also provided new cures for healing. Garcia D'Orta published, in 1563, a book which was the culmination of a lifetime's work in Goa. This book, it is believed, was also influential in shaping European medicine. The information it included on eastern drugs, life and society, the etymology of plants, their preparation and therapeutic use was derived by D'Orta from Arabic and classical sources.[67] In early modern Europe, objects such as amulets and charms were an essential part of magical practice, and that the use of these objects played a significant role in the lives of those who believed in magic. Magical objects were produced and traded, highlighting the role of markets and fairs in the distribution of magical goods. A detailed analysis of objects and artifacts offers a nuanced view of the practices and beliefs.[68]

Medicines described as 'exotic' were too expensive for poor people. Medical reformers, on moral grounds, opposed their use. One such disputant, Timothy Bright, (1551–1615), wrote a pamphlet entitled *A Treatise Wherein is Declared the Sufficience of English Medicines for the Cure of All Diseases Cured by Medicines* (1580). In this work, Bright condemned physicians for dealing with such expensive drugs.[69] He insisted that God had provided the ways in which the sick could cure themselves using plants growing nearby. Although the work was aimed at the wealthy, neither the poor, nor the public in general, required a treatise to inform them about the efficacy of the curative powers of herbs as they were aware of the healing potential of nature, which they depended on for their survival. When their illness went beyond the power of their own knowledge, they sometimes relied on others who were better informed than they were, believing that their skill and customary knowledge had been passed down in particular families from generation to generation. Such were the cunning folk, who, in times of health crisis, were called on to treat some of their wealthier neighbours on the principles of healing. Sometimes situations such as these arose during times of endemic illness. Historians argue that treatises, such as Bright's, stressed that 'local remedies' written in the vernacular, challenged the hegemony of Galenic learned medicine written in Latin.[70] Whilst Galenic and learned traditions may well have been recorded in Latin, there are some manuscripts, such as Macer's Herbal, for example, that confirm a familiarity with the healing strategies of classical Greek medicine. Macer's Herbal similarly demonstrates an appreciation of some of the Latin, German and French healing traditions. Mostly, the knowledge expressed in the manuscripts—especially Macer's Herbal—demonstrates a clear understanding of local herbal medicine. Moreover, in conformity with the work of Culpeper, the manuscripts provide evidence of a knowledge of the environment in which the herbs grew, as well as the illnesses that they remedied, and demonstrate significant customary knowledge, which was so often expressed in the depositions of cunning women who, in the seventeenth century, were charged with sorcery.

Macer's Herbal

Macer's Herbal broadly influenced customary knowledge and the use of domestic medicine through written instructions for the preparation and application of treatment for a wide range of illnesses. It is a meticulous exposition of 'the virtues' of 42 herbs and a summary of many diseases and how to cure them. This herbal comprises a catalogue of decoctions, ointments, applications, 'plaisters,' a variety of beverages, tinctures, and herbal solutions, and usefully suggests alternative cures for the many ailments of the day. A herb was known to cure more than one illness and the 'virtues' of a herb might number more than.20

Macer's Herbal can be dated variously to the fifteenth or sixteenth century. This investigation refers to the handwritten Middle English archived manuscript.[71] The healing repertoire pertained to plants, herbs, and flowers gathered to provide medical prescriptions for over a hundred maladies that ranged from 'toothache' to 'swollen bollockes.' Macer's prescriptions cured most illnesses and mishaps, from the prevention of conception to the cure for snake bite. Some of his formulas include those 'for the head-ache'[72] and those 'for the ache of feet.'[73] For conjunctivitis, he devised a herbal remedy 'for clene eyen.'[74] For the short-sighted there was a remedy to improve vision.[75] There was also a prescription 'for the venym of snakes.'[76] For those suffering from urinary tract infection, or cystitis, Macer suggested a remedy 'for the ache of the bladder.'[77] In those cases where one suffered the ravages of excessive sexual libido, there is a handy remedy 'for lecherie,'[78] and, for the sexually adventurous, there is another 'for the ache of the thyes.'[79] Macer's remedy for 'lechery' involves the use of a herb known to him as 'coutherenweed.' He suggests that it be 'layed oonly under the pillow at thine head and it shall steer thee hugely to lechery, also drink the same herbe and it shall quench thee of lechery and it helpeth against the gout.'[80] Macer also recommends ways to assist conception in animals. The following prescription was devised by him to bring about the right conditions for animals to bring forth young. For example, the manuscript states: 'Throut well a barren beasts cunte with nettle leaves or with the juice of it and the beast shall conceave.'[81] For nursing mothers, Macer recommended 'hemlock green' to be useful for drying up a mother's milk. For, according to Macer, 'if a mayde anoint her tetes with hemlock, the hemlock drieth the mylke.'[82] The selection of remedies presented in this book draws attention to Macer's general application of herbal medicine. However, in addition to simple remedies, the use of charms surfaces regularly. Often, the application of medicine for a remedy was ritualised alongside a spoken charm.

Healing Women's Medical Conditions: Macer's Popular Herbs and Plants

Women's medical problems were well documented in herbal casebooks. For example, the common problems that were associated with the female menstrual cycle, were known as 'the flux of the womb.'[83] Many herbs were found to be useful in bringing about a balance in described as 'women's floures.' A troublesome menstrual cycle, or 'the bloody menstrun,' as it was known, was relieved by several herbal remedies. One such course of action was to combine the herbs 'wermeede' and 'moderweede.' A great number of women's remedies were sought and were treated with herbs, which when 'stamped together so, shalt purge women's floures sovereignly.'[84] Among the remedies were those that treated pregnant women. The remedies which featured most strongly in Macer's Herbal were those designed to assist the complaints of women in childbirth. A prevalent recurring condition involved stillborn infants, and various methods were employed to manage the delivery of stillborn children, as well as medicinal strategies to facilitate the removal of the placenta. For example, the herbe known as 'ache' assisted both with 'women's floures, and the dead children to be born.'[85] Similarly, to remove the afterbirth, the following procedure was put forward: 'if thou put honey with wermeede and make a subfumigation, it shall dry up the skin for the child that leyeth in his mother's womb, and make the fluid for to come out fast.'[86]

There were numerous illnesses mentioned such as 'tennerseenen', 'the podagre', 'embolers of the spleen', the 'boachers', and 'sickness of the toon.' Some of the most troublesome and recurrent of complaints were 'the cowshe', 'the chinke', and 'boaches' or 'boachers'. 'Boaches' was a condition which resulted in unpleasant skin eruptions during a fever, as sometimes did 'boylinges' (boils). 'Jaundice' appeared often in the manuscript and so did cures for 'rotten woundes.' Another common health problem was that of water retention. Accordingly, cures 'to make for to pysse' appeared regularly in the casebook, and snakes were common. Various herbal repellents to cure snake bite and thwart the effects of several venoms appeared throughout.

The 'falling cuel,' was an affliction which particularly affected young children. This illness was treated regularly. Complaints such as 'worms', the 'sighing', 'paulsey', and 'dropsy' were also common. A variety of remedies for such common symptoms as 'toothache', 'ache of the ear' and 'headache' appeared regularly. One such remedy to cure earache was achieved using the herb known as 'rowe' and the instruction to 'Chafe the juice of rowe in the pill of a pomegranet and hold it into the ear and that shall heal the ache of it.'[87] For a headache, the herb 'nettle' was prescribed. The direction was to 'anoint well with the oil that nettle is sodden in and make it sweet, take the juice of nettle seed and anoint the head and it shall heal and repress the aching of the head.'[88]

Macer's Herbal was intended for use as a medicinal handbook and the day-to-day practice of treating illness. However, an army of practitioners used whatever skills they possessed. Apothecaries healed a great many people with their cures. They were well acquainted with women's common complaints. During the seventeenth century, customary healing knowledge and the herbal practices of the popular community, especially those involving ceremonially spoken charms came to be prohibited by the ruling authorities.

One such organisation which ruled over the practice of common knowledge in medicine was the Consistory Court and as it had control over public morality it was also involved with sexual matters. In this regard the world of speech was rigorously controlled. The speaking of charms, scolding, cursing, witchcraft, ill-wishing, and defamation were similarly scrutinised. Such varieties of speech as these were often associated with crimes of a sexual nature such as adultery and cuckoldry and was the domain of the Church court also known as the 'bawdy' court. The Church court employed Churchwardens to guard the sexual and religious morality of the community and while the Church courts were usually involved with moral offences against the community, they also had control over incidents which disrupted the peace, such as spoken infringement. Churchwardens kept a close eye on local affairs and listened carefully to any rumour and gossip which was circulating in the community. On their report individuals were cited to appear in the court. A 1624 Act of Parliament was passed which tightened the laws against cursing and swearing. This Act meant that women were exceptionally predisposed to these charges. Later a similar ordinance was issued against offenders under the Commonwealth.[89] Nevertheless, the law was defied. Religious groups, for example, employed the expression of the curse. Puritan ministers who were aware of the power of the imprecation, themselves adopted this female practice. They cursed those who did not sit through their sermons. Similarly, during the Civil War, Royalist clergy, the Ranters, and Quakers invoked the wrath of God upon the Anglican Church.[90]

Although the Church used the power of cursing to its advantage, the efficacy of the curse was derived, not from theological sources, but from common belief. Cursing was powerful not because it had ritual connections with the Church, but because people believed it could work. It was owing to such beliefs that the curser was endowed with potency. A powerful weapon against adversaries, the reputation for being a successful curser, could, and often did result in a formal charge of witchcraft. Unlike other forms of power, such as high-ranking social status or financial power, the power of the curse could be wielded by any member of society including those of the popular domain. According to Thomas, the curse was at its most destructive when uttered by the least successful member of the community.[91] Owing to its power, the impotent resorted to the power of the imagination. Crucially, the social meaning of the curse was important, and it was noted to be as 'effective a means of destruction as it was of healing.'[92]

It is clear from the Church court records that the reputation for successful cursing among the general population could easily lead to a formal charge of witchcraft. As Thomas explains, people in the early modern period perceived the link clearly: 'Cursers are murderers, for if it please God to suffer their curse to take effect, the party cursed is murdered by the Devil.'[93]

Cursing and Banning

The earliest varieties of cursing were unconnected to any region and cursing cases were sparse.[94] Legal records beyond the English context, in France, reveal that there was a preoccupation with herbal treatment.[95] However, there is evidence to suggest that the incidence of cursing was more common in the north than it was in the south of the British Isles.[96] Further, the examination of cursing, in early modern Cheshire and Lancashire certainly establishes that there were high levels of ill-concealed uncertainty, disquiet, and dread among the townsfolk. Testimonies confirm that cursing had a clearly defined function and that it operated to influence and change difficult circumstances. The female motivation for cursing is discernible in the broad spectrum of spoken affronts, and legal records shed light on the ways women dominated the 'symbolic' vocal world of cursing, swearing, and scolding. Evidence from the Consistory Church Court records confirms the well-known proposition that those who had the power to heal also had the power to harm. This view also finds support in the documents associated with ritual healing and spoken charms. The manuscripts confirm that some women executed the kinds of crimes that are most often associated with men.[97] In the regional Northwest, cursing cases disclose that there is a well-established social and historical evolution of cases that escalate from a situation of conflict to one of cursing that remains unexplained.

As indicated above, cursing was greatly favoured by the powerless to procure power over the powerful. While charges that related to spoken affront such as sexual slander and defamation, were commonly directed at women, cursing was regarded by contemporaries as most culpable. However, as a system of revenge for those women who sought retaliatory power, cursing worked efficiently. Cursing achieved even better results when the persons cursed were anguished with guilt or with anxiety, or when the recipient of a curse believed themselves to have transgressed the well-defined laws of morality.

While it has been noted that 'barratry' is the male equivalent of female ill-speaking, and 'barratry' is noted as a possible male equivalent of scolding, mysteriously, there are no records that might connect scolding offences with a male offender. Neither are there any which describe an action that might be interpreted as 'barratry.'[98] The records of the Oxfordshire archives, yielded several cases of scolding but the records are also silent in this respect.[99] However, some sources demonstrate that the spouse, lover, or partner-in-crime of those *women* who commit verbally related crimes were occasionally punished. However, men who ***associated*** with women who were accused of verbal crime or drunkenness, prostitution, and physical violence were subjected to regulation. However, in no record is there a reference implicating men as chief perpetrators of scolding.[100]

The cucking stool was sourced for the punishment of scolds. It has been noted that this kind of punishment occurred infrequently.[101] However, this view is not borne out by evidence from Lancashire and Cheshire where the cucking stool was used regularly to punish verbal crime. Records from 1542 onwards confirm that it was a common instrument of punishment in Lancashire. This view is borne out by local folklorists and antiquarians.[102] James Hall found that the same was true of Cheshire.[103] It has been suggested that the associated crimes of chiding, brawling, and verbal abuse were ascribed to female behaviour, yet scolding was an exclusively female crime. It is claimed that women were verbally aggressive because they did not have access to litigation.[104] However, the situation in the Chester Consistory Court was similar to other regions, as women often resorted to authorised legal action and were capable of manipulating it to their advantage. Through a meticulous examination of the Wiltshire Church court records spanning from 1570 to 1640, a comprehensive study on marriage and sexual relationships has emerged. Notably, the records highlight the significance of scolding, warranting further in-depth analysis.[105] It proposes 'delving deeper into the actual circumstances of scolds and scolding in order to get closer to the reality of the lives both of women and of men in the past.'[106] Experts of the London circumstances propose that scolding was 'the armoury of interpersonal conflict.'[107] However, little analytical emphasis has been placed upon the incidence of ritual cursing. As this study will demonstrate in subsequent chapters, women of the Northwest regularly fought, and won, legal cases in Church courts and often appearing as witnesses they initiated the presentation of petitions to Justices of Quarter Sessions. The records leave little doubt that in the regional Northwest, scolding, as with cursing, was an acutely female crime.

The presence of women in figurative crime is well documented and though it has been noted that women were 'predisposed' to verbal wrongdoing there is little explanation of how or why it came about that those women 'came to be labeled' as scolds.[108] The argument that women tended to avoid physical violence is not borne out by evidence from the Northwest as manuscript evidence from this region suggests that female participation in this area of crime was also high. Women frequently violated the law and were involved in crimes like stealing and receiving stolen goods, violent violations, and assault. The evidence on this issue can be swiftly summarised. First, evidence from Susan Amussen's *Punishment, Discipline and Power: The Social Meanings of Violence in Early Modern England* indicates that violence within the household was a regular event in early modern England.[109] Second, as the studies of Thompson, Gowing, and Erickson have indicated, women had access to legal channels, and studies confirm that litigation taken against women, by women was also commonplace.[110] Suit and countersuit were executed regularly in the Chester Consistory Court, often in a subsequent maze of litigation that followed. Women were unquestionably aware of the procedures of the legal system in the Church and secular courts. They initiated lawsuits against each other, against relatives, neighbours and, in some instances, against husbands. Women of high and low standing in the community were tested in legal battles which, in some cases, went on for three years, sometimes longer, in a tangle of suit and countersuit. Some women took successful legal action against their husbands for violent affray. In the Northwest it was not remarkable for a woman to bring a husband to court for domestic violence. Some women fought, and won, legal battles against their husbands for rape. It was not considered to be outlandish for women to fight. In some cases, men terrorised the women they were married to, and, as the evidence below will demonstrate, women sometimes resorted to physical violence to resolve issues.[111] Similarly, some women resorted to the court for legal redress and cases such as these are also explored further below.

According to the records of the Chester Consistory Court, the Manorial Court records of Cheshire, and in the Liverpool Town Books, scolding was a feature of everyday life and prevalent, and the evidence from these sources is explored in Chapter 3. Cursing, however, was a completely different matter. Cases of cursing sustained a high profile in the Church court at Chester and cursing was reported with greater frequency than it was in other parts of the country. Indeed, as noted above, historians confirm that cursing, unlike scolding, may have been a phenomenon that was especially common in the Northwest regions of England. The numbers of people involved in any single incident of verbal misconduct varied from a handful to as many as 100 people.[112] The following focuses on cases involving a significant number of people and their reported incidents of cursing in the Northwest region between 1590 and 1670. While this research is based on an analysis of all reported cases of cursing in the Northwest between 1590 and 1670, it concentrates more precisely on those cases which involved relatively large numbers of people. The documented large-scale occurrences of cursing in the Chester Consistory Court offer valuable insights into the popular consciousness of the time. Since spoken crime was predominantly associated with women, these records provide a lens through which to examine the female sphere and the society in which these offences arose. Whether women were scolding, chiding or cursing, it is clear from the evidence that women figured most prominently in this sphere. The upcoming pages provide an in-depth examination of the context and prevalence of female-spoken crime with a particular focus on the connection between such offences and financial survival, and offer insight into the broader societal factors that contributed to the emergence of such offences.

Notes

1. C. R. Millar, *Witchcraft, the Devil, and Emotions in Early Modern England* (Taylor and Francis, 2017), pp. 182–185.
2. See, for example review by W. de Blécourt; *Emotions in the History of Witchcraft*, by Laura Kounine and Michael Ostling, (Eds.), *Witchcraft, the Devil, and Emotions in Early Modern England*, by Charlotte-Rose Millar and 'Imagining the Witch. Emotions, Gender, and Selfhood in Early Modern Germany' by Laura Kounine, *Church History and Religious Culture* 100, no. 1 (2020): 85–93.
3. J. Barry, *Witchcraft and Demonology in South-West England, 1640–1789*. 1st ed. 2012 (London: Palgrave Macmillan UK, 2012). https://doi.org/10.1057/9780230361386.
4. J. Sainsbury, 'Barry, Jonathan. Witchcraft and Demonology in South-West England, 1640–1789.' *CHOICE: Current Reviews for Academic Libraries*. American Library Association CHOICE, 2012.
5. See, for example, L. Gowing, *Domestic Dangers, Women, Words and Sex in Early Modern England* (Oxford, 1996); L. Gowing, 'Language, Power, and the Law: Women's Slander Litigation in Early Modern London' in J. Kermode and G. Walker, (Eds.), *Women, Crime and the Courts in Early Modern England* (London 1994), p. 43; A. Shepard, Worthless Witnesses? Marginal Voices and Women's Legal Agency in Early Modern England, *Journal of British Studies,* 58 (October 2019), 717–734. See also, K. O'Brien, 'Sexual Impropriety, Petitioning and the Dynamics of Ill Will in Daily Urban Life.' *Urban History* 43, no. 2 (2016): 177–199.
6. A. Shepard, 717.
7. A. Shepard, 717.
8. A. Shepard, 734.
9. For an account of the social and gender complexity of the circumstances in which women subverted norms see K. O'Brien, 'Sexual Impropriety, Petitioning and the Dynamics of Ill Will in Daily Urban Life.'
10. K. Thomas, *Religion and the Decline of Magic: Studies in Popular Beliefs in Sixteenth- and Seventeenth-century England* (London, 1971). p. 607.

11. H. E. Davidson, *The Lost Beliefs of Northern Europe* (London, 1993), p. 131.
12. Ibid. p. 131.
13. K. Thomas, op. cit. pp. 599–637. Thomas argues that the connection with cursing contributed very strongly to the reputation of an individual as a witch.
14. K. Thomas, op cit. p. 607.
15. Ibid.
16. Ibid. 609.
17. Ibid. 608. Thomas highlights the importance of cursing to issues relating to property and ownership of land particularly during enclosures of land.
18. Ibid. p. 600.
19. K. Crossley-Holland, *The Anglo-Saxon World: An Anthology* (Oxford, 1984), p. 268. See also, A. L. Meaney, 'Variant Versions of Old English Medical Remedies and the Compilation of Bald's Leechbook,' *Anglo-Saxon England* 13 (1984): pp. 235–68. J. F. Payne, *English Medicine in Anglo-Saxon Times* (Oxford: Clarendon Press, 1904).
20. K. Crossley-Holland, op. cit. p. 269.
21. Ibid.
22. Ibid.
23. Ibid.
24. K. Crossley-Holland, op. cit. p. 273.
25. Ibid.
26. K. Crossley-Holland, op. cit. p. 276.
27. Ibid. p. 276.
28. K. Crossley-Holland, p. 277.
29. See, for example, K. Thomas, *Religion and the Decline of Magic: Studies in Popular Beliefs in Sixteenth and Seventeenth Century England* (London, 1971) and A. Macfarlane, *Witchcraft in Tudor and Stuart England; A Regional and Comparative Study* (London, 1970). See also M. Chamberlain, *Old Wives Tales: Their History, Remedies and Spells* (London, 1981). Chamberlain's study identifies women who continued to nurse patients back to health and were consulted despite the church's long history of stopping women from healing. W. de Blécourt, Witch Doctors, Soothsayers and Priests. On Cunning Folk in European Historiography and Tradition, Social History, Vol. 19, No.

3 (October 1994), pp. 285–303. De Blécourt's article stresses the need for further research into the activities of the cunning folk. T. D. Walker, '*Doctors, Folk Medicine and the Inquisition: The Repression of Magical Healing in Portugal during the Enlightenment', The Medieval and Early Modern Iberian World, No. 23,* (Boston, 2005). Walker's portrait of folk medicine draws on a broad range of materials to offer a nuanced picture of the environment and work of practitioners. See also E. Bever, *Realities of Witchcraft and Popular Magic in Early Modern Europe* (New York, 2008). See also R. Porter, (Ed.), *Patients and Practitioners: Lay Perceptions of Medicine in Pre-industrial Society* (Cambridge, New York, 1985). See E. Wilby, *Cunning-Folk and Familiar Spirits: Shamanistic Visionary Traditions in Early Modern British Witchcraft and Magic* (Brighton, 2005). O. Davies, *Cunning-Folk: Popular Magic in English History* (London, 2003). For an interesting investigation of magic and the material culture of early modern healing, see the doctoral thesis of A. Thwaite, 'Magic and the Material Culture of Healing in Early Modern England.' https://doi.org/10.17863/CAM.63593. Accessed 26 April 2022.

30. M. Gibson, and O. Davies. *Cunning-Folk: Popular Magic in English History* (New York: Hambledon and London; Dist. by Palgrave, New York, 2003), pp. xv, 246 *Albion*, 2004.
31. E. Bever, 'Popular Witch Beliefs and Magical Practices: New Directions for Research.' *International Journal of Humanities and Social Science Research* 5, no. 1 (2017): 1–10.
32. See, for example, the recipes for healing of the Stanleys of Alderley, CRO DDX/361. Some of these recipes were probably passed on by 'Old Daddy.'
33. Macer's Herbal, Cheshire Record Office, D/4398.
34. CRO D/4367/1AQ2 BES Eliza Cholmondeley, 1677, Receipt Book. For more information about 'Receipt Books' see E. Leong, https://recipes.hypotheses.org/about a project which is a collaborative international research community that brings together and showcases interdisciplinary research on healing recipes across a broad temporal and geographic area.

    See A. Rankin and E. Leong, (Eds.), *Secrets and Knowledge in Medicine and Science, 1500–1800* (London: Routledge, 2011). See also, E. Leong, *Recipes and Everyday Knowledge: Medicine,*

Science, and the Household in Early Modern England (London: University of Chicago Press, 2018).

35. W. Curtis, *Flora Londensis, 1777–1787* Plates and descriptions of plants that grow wild in the environs of London, (Illustrations engraved by William Kilburn, Sansom and Sowerby from drawings by Kilburn, Sowerby, Pts. 1–5, roy. fo. London (1777–1799) pl. 434, hand-coloured, Hugh Frederick Hornby Library, Liverpool.
36. Ibid. p. 48.
37. Ibid. p. 47.
38. Ibid. p. 38.
39. Ibid. p. 4.
40. Ibid. p. 39.
41. Ibid. p. 53.
42. Ibid. p. 36.
43. Ibid. p. 48.
44. Ibid. p. 56.
45. Ibid. p. 13.
46. Ibid. p. 22.
47. Ibid. p. 41.
48. Ibid. p. 57.
49. Ibid. p. 10.
50. Ibid. p. 17.
51. Ibid. p. 35.
52. Ibid. p. 21.
53. Ibid. p. 40.
54. Ibid. p. 18.
55. Ibid. p. 32.
56. Ibid. p. 15.
57. L. Conrad, M. Neve, V. Nutton, R. Porter, and A. Wear, Members of the Academic Unit, The Wellcome Institute for the History of Medicine, London, *The Western Medical Tradition, 800 BC to AD 1800* (Cambridge, 1995), p. 300.
58. Ibid.
59. Ibid.
60. J. Barry, 'The Medical Revolution of the Seventeenth Century.' *The English Historical Review* 108, no. 427 (April 1993): 466.
61. R. French and A. Wear (CambridgeThe Medical Revolution of the Seventeenth Century, C.U.P., 1989).

62. N. Culpeper, The *Complete Herbal* (London, 1953).
63. L. Conrad et al., *The Academic Unit*, p. 300.
64. J. Thorwald, *Science and Secrets of Early Medicine* (London, 1962), p. 5.
65. L. Conrad et al., The Academic Unit, p. 306.
66. L. Conrad et al., The Academic Unit, p. 307.
67. L. Conrad et al., The Academic Unit, p. 309.
68. O. Davies and T. Easton, 'Cunning-Folk and the Production of Magical Artifacts', R. Hutton, (Ed.), 'Cunning-Folk and the Production of Magical Artefacts,' in *Physical Evidence for Ritual Acts, Sorcery and Witchcraft in Christian Britain* (United Kingdom: Palgrave Macmillan UK, 2015).
69. L. Conrad et al., The Academic Unit, p. 310.
70. L. Conrad et al., The Academic Unit, p. 309.
71. CRO D/4398/1, Macer's Herbal p. 68.
72. Ibid. p. 91.
73. Ibid. p. 66.
74. Ibid. p. 96.
75. Ibid. p. 137.
76. Ibid. p. 120.
77. Ibid. p. 120.
78. Ibid. p. 114.
79. Ibid. p. 130.
80. CRO D/4398/1, Macer's Herbal, p. 56.
81. Ibid. p. 45.
82. Ibid. p. 114.
83. Ibid. p. 26.
84. Ibid. p. 56.
85. Ibid. p. 74.
86. Ibid. p. 57.
87. Ibid. p. 67.
88. Ibid. p. 58.
89. Ibid.
90. Ibid.
91. Ibid.
92. Ibid. p. 609.
93. Ibid. p. 610.
94. K. Thomas *Religion and the Decline of Magic*, pp. 599–680.
95. E. L. R. Ladurie, *Jasmine's Witch* (France, 1983), p. 7.

96. Ibid.
97. See, G. Walker, *Crime, Gender and Social Order in Early Modern England*. Cambridge Studies in Early Modern British History, (Cambridge: Cambridge University Press, 2003), G. Walker, 'Framing Premodern Desires Between Sexuality, Sin and Crime: an introduction,' in S. Lidman et al. (Eds.) *Framing Premodern Desires. Sexual Ideas, Attitudes and Practises in Europe* (Amsterdam: University of Amsterdam Press, 2018). See also an older study of women and the courts, entitled 'Women, Theft and the World of Stolen Goods.' in J. Kermode and G. Walker, (Eds.), *Women, Crime and the Courts in Early Modern England* (London, 1994). Walker provides an analysis of 'real' crime in Cheshire illustrating the range of female crime.
98. M. Ingram, 'Scolding Women Cucked and Washed' in J. Kermode and G. Walker, (Eds.), *Women, Crime and the Courts in Early Modern England'* (London, 1994).
99. An analysis of the Oxfordshire Church Court Depositions from 1542 to 1660 revealed no cases of cursing. There were no incidents of 'barratry,' although scolding involving women was frequently punished.
100. Evidence from the Liverpool Town Book reveals that Tugar Bolde of Liverpool, in 1597 was fined six shillings and eight pence for his association with a scold, p. 660, f224r.
101. M. Ingram, 'Scolding Women Cucked and Washed.'
102. J. Harland and T. Wilkinson, *Customs, Lancashire Legends, Traditions* (1883).
103. See J. Hall, *A History of the Town and Parish of Nantwich* (Manchester, 1883).
104. M. Ingram, p. 51. 'Scolding Women Cucked and Washed.' 'Women tended to eschew physical violence and did not ordinarily have access to effective substitutes such as manipulation of the legal system; and such verbal aggression, when perpetrated by women, had come to be labelled as a specific category of female offence.'
105. M. Ingram, *Church Courts, Sex and Marriage in England*, 1570–1640 (Cambridge, 1987).
106. M. Ingram, 'Scolding Women Cucked or Washed,' in J. Kermode and G. Walker (Eds.), *Women, Crime and the Courts in Early Modern England,* (London, 1994).

107. L. Gowing, *Domestic Dangers: Women, Words and Sex in Early Modern England* (Oxford, 1996), p. 264.
108. M. Ingram, 'Scolding Women Cucked or Washed.'
109. S. Amussen, 'Punishment, Discipline and Power: The Social Meanings of Violence in Early Modern England,' *Journal of British Studies* 34, no. 1 (January 1995): 13. See also, J. Warner and A. Lunny, 'Marital Violence in a Martial Town: Husbands and Wives in Early Modern Portsmouth, 1653–1781,' *Journal of Family History* 28 (2003): 261.
110. See J. A. Thompson's analysis of defamation in Devon, from the records of the Diocese of Exeter in her PhD book entitled '"Her Good Name and Credit": The Reputation of Women in Seventeenth-Century Devon,' (University of Cincinnatti, 1984), p. 124. Her analysis shows that between the years 1634–1688 the lowest percentage of cases in which both plaintiff and defendant were female was 13%, and this was during the year 1675–1676. The highest percentage occurred during the years 1661–1663, and this was 57%. See also L. Gowing, *Domestic Dangers: Women, Words and Sex in Early Modern England* (Oxford, 1996).
111. See, for example, CRO DDX96/5, 'The Misdemeanours of Elizabeth Brynne of Tarvin.'
112. See the case of Anne Knutsford, midwife of Nantwich discussed extensively in this book, that in 1663, involved ten separate litigations. One incident alone involved 100 people.

CHAPTER 3

Spoken Transgression and the Courts

> What thou forsworne man, thou villaine, I hope to see hellish divelles to steale awaie thy soule when thou art deade. May god looke upon Robert Jure and poore his plague upon him for he hath molested me and troubled me this manie yeares.[1]

Desperate for a way to defend themselves women under attack called on the power of God to bring down a terrible plague on their enemies. The curse usually took the form of a pronouncement summoning Godly supernatural powers. It was usually accompanied by an invocation of the wrath of God and a visitation of demons. It sometimes besought a common dread of illness by procuring the hand of God to induce a fatal plague on an individual. The curse mentioned above exemplifies a typical form of imprecation that a woman might employ against an adversary. This particular type of curse was employed as a means to deter aggressive intrusion. However, upon closer examination, it becomes evident that behind the curse lies a history of preceding violent actions. The motivation behind the curse was driven by the necessity to bring an end to the violence inflicted by Robert Jure. By voicing her disapproval of the harassment she had endured from him, the woman aimed to deter future acts of aggression. Thus, the curse served a dual purpose, functioning both as a defensive shield and an offensive weapon.

K. O'Brien, *Cursing, Crisis and Customary Knowledge in Early Modern English Townships*, Palgrave Historical Studies in Witchcraft and Magic,
https://doi.org/10.1007/978-3-031-44045-8_3

Curses were usually brought to the attention of the Church court through the conversations of women or communicated by an informant of the Church Warden. Their depositions provide a valuable female perspective on the practice of cursing, shedding light on the social contexts in which it occurred and the degree of violent incursion into female spaces. The narratives pertaining to women accused of engaging in cursing offer valuable insights into the intimate relationships of individuals residing in early modern townships. Women were often perceived as the 'mouths' of community affairs. As such, their conversations were closely monitored by Churchwardens, who were the 'ears' of governance in the community and the Church court. This is the legal route that hearsay followed before it eventually came to the attention of the Church court functionaries. Churchwardens were sometimes cursed by the women they reported.[2] Although cursing was iniquitous, the approach to women's speech was an ambivalent one. On the one hand, female conversation might be regarded as mere idle talk, while on the other, beyond certain bounds, the female word of mouth was rigorously censured.[3]

Women's transgressions in speech were frequently reported to local authorities, who considered them as violations of the law. The increase in cases of spoken crime during this period reflected a growing social concern with controlling women's behaviour and speech. According to York Consistory Court records, speech crime increased four times in the seventeenth century.[4] In Lancashire and Cheshire discursive crime doubled.[5] It has been argued that the rise in litigation was a sign of the failure of the mechanisms of informal social control.[6] The examination of female discourse is instrumental in aiding our understanding of the social context surrounding the significant increase in such discourse. It also supports the argument of patriarchal control being enforced in this context. There is evidence of female vocal crime from its prosecution by secular and ecclesiastical ruling bodies, such as the Chester Consistory Court Papers and Lancashire and Cheshire Quarter Sessions, highlighting the social and economic circumstances underlying the ritual of the curse. Two peak decades are examined in subsequent chapters to achieve a closer understanding of the broad range of issues that were involved in female speech crime during what was a peak decade in Consistory Court business between the years of 1630 and 1640 and during the third rise in court business which occurred between the years of 1660 and 1670.

The abundant evidence provided by female discursive regulation targeted the perceived transgressions of cursing and scolding which were often associated with sexual behaviour and matters pertaining to the bodily low. Such violations were frequently labelled using derogatory terms such as 'whore.' The records of the Chester Consistory Court reveal a notable decrease in societal tolerance towards such activities as drinking, gambling, fornication, and adultery. An ongoing regulation of female language between 1610 and 1670 was accompanied by restrictions on the social space of women. The regulation of female social space meant that some professional areas were prohibited to women, and social territories, such as the alehouse and places of gambling, were out of bounds for women.[7] Similarly, in the world of high politics and during the Reformation, magical practice was directly associated with treason. Catholic belief and the popular beliefs that were expressed in magic were considered to be dangerous to the rule of government.[8]

The regulation of female speech was progressive with periodical sharp increases in presentments. The court records in the sixteenth century disclose a consistent pattern of prosecution, which spiked suddenly at specific times during the seventeenth century. Female speech was closely monitored, and harsh punitive measures were imposed on women who were found to be at odds with others in the neighbourhood. There was a significant increase in the prosecutions of women who expressed their opinions too vehemently and the courts concluded that women who paraded a hot-blooded temper or presented fervid speech had disrupted the peace. It was perceived as unsociable and contrary to Christian charity and led to those women being charged with disrupting the peace.

Punishing Female Speech and Conduct

The legal infrastructure had existed since the thirteenth century to deal with social problems.[9] The pervasive violence prevalent in the larger society is exemplified by the legally sanctioned punitive measures implemented to control and manipulate female speech and behaviour. The functions of the court and the 'complexities of applying the law in specific situations' are well known.[10] Assize courts and Quarter Sessions give the names of those who were accused, their occupation, residence, the names of the people involved, and some details of the punishment they received. In addition, residents of the Northwest who were disturbed by 'troublesome' females resorted to the Consistory Court.

Throughout the sixteenth century, members of the community customarily reported to Manorial courts or Portmoot courts. In Cheshire, certain kinds of verbal misconduct were reported to, and controlled by, the Baronial and Manorial courts. Other ruling bodies such as the Court Leets and Baron, the Manor Court Rolls of Audley Fee, in Nantwich, and the Countess of Warwick Fee, in Nantwich, demonstrate a predisposition to regulate female spoken crime and to keep it restrained. In Lancashire, the regulation of female spoken crime was consistently recorded in Prescot Court Leet and the Liverpool Town Books. In general, regulatory procedures were imposed on women who expressed their opinion too loudly or in a way which was at odds with an existing situation. Constant government of the female voice continued throughout the seventeenth century when punishments varied according to the institution which dealt with the illegality. In such cases women were fined, imprisoned, whipped, and sometimes they were banished from the town. Offenders who disturbed community stability were subjected to shaming rituals. In Cheshire, for example such transgressors were 'proclaimed' at the cross.[11] There was a separate form of punishment for perceived scolds. The cuckingstool was used to punish scolds in Lancashire and Cheshire. Where cursing involved the death of a person, a women could be hanged.[12] Cheshire scolds were punished by use of the 'thewe' or 'cuckingstoole.' The 'cuckingstoole' was an instrument of punishment which subjected women to downright public humiliation. It was erected close to the most public arena in the vicinity, where the locals jeered and heaped humiliation on the offender. On occasion, some vehement individual might be tempted to throw rotten vegetables or rubbish at the unfortunate victim, or worse still, they might throw filth at her from the local cesspit. In 1590, the Court Rolls of Nantwich, remark on the construction of one such 'cuckingstoole' near 'cartlake' in High Town near the site of an old market:

> we present yt we want a cuckingstoole and we request yt Sir Hugh Cholmely, a cuckingstoole to be made and erected and a fine new cage were both made and set up at the proper costs of Sir Hugh Chomley.[13]

Soon after building this instrument of torment, Elizabeth Crew, Anne Kyneston, and Margery Beel were reported: 'for Comon Scoulds very turbulous scoulding people to the great disturbation of their neighbours.'[14] While there was no record of a fine for this incident or of punishment by the 'cuckingstoole' there was evidence to demonstrate an imposition of a considerable fine in 1632, when Ellen Walley and

Margaret Stockton of Cholmston were presented for 'skowlds,' and each was fined two shillings and threepence 'a peece.'[15]

Defying the Law: Voices of Agitation in Manorial Court, Portmoot, and Liverpool Town Books

The records of Prescot Court Leet demonstrate that verbal violence was consistently met with punishment in this particular area. For example, John Eccleston and 13 gentlemen jurors on 9 June 1531 issued an Amercement against Jane Smith. Jane Smith, a local wise woman, who was accused of incantation and sorcery. They asserted that she had transgressed 'good faith' but it is not evident whose good faith she offended, nor who it was that she had charmed. What is certain is that she was a wise woman as the following statement will confirm: 'Jane Smeth, for delyng with charms and sorcores contrary to gud ffaith, and callis her a wise womon.'[16] Jane Smeth received a fine, but the amount she had to pay is not verified.

In addition to claims of ritual incantation, scolds were subject to punitive measures and the equipment applied for the punishment of scolds was kept in good repair in Lancashire. Here, the 'cuckingstoole' was a most common instrument for the punishment of scolds. In Lancashire, this device was used specifically for the regulation of scolds and the cost of its maintenance was borne by the members of the community.[17] Edward, Earl of Derby, Deputy Steward of Prescot court on 9 June 1542, ordered Prescot townsfolk to pay for a cuckingstool. The court recorded the details of the preparation of other shaming instruments referred to as stocks which were also manufactured in readiness for any anticipated lawbreakers as is described by them during the 'midsomer' interval. On October 30, the day before All Hallows Eve, The Liverpool Town Books correspondingly record the details of how the local assembly of the common councils of the town of Liverpool in 1578, arranged for a cuckingstool to be made and paid for by a levy imposed upon the locals.[18] The instrument was in need of repair, but whether the requirement for the renovation was owing to over- or underuse is not certain. As was the case with Prescot township and the anticipation of lawbreaking during the midsummer time, perhaps it was the case that William More and the other elected officers of the assembly were expecting brisk business, because they issued a similar order to have the instrument of punishment overhauled as the following statement confirms: 'Wee ffynde yt necessarie that the cuckingstoole shal be repared.'[19] Prescot Court Leet delivered a similar form of punishment for spoken violation and the records of this court similarly demonstrate that it maintained its instrument in good repair.[20]

Scolds were typically widows. In Liverpool, for example, in 1589, three women, two of them widows, Mrs Lathom and Mrs Harrington, were each fined 12d for scolding and causing a commotion as the following statement will demonstrate: 'The late relicte of Thomas Lathom, the wife of Edward Glover and the late relicte of James Harrington, are comon brawlers and scoulds, and hurtfull to theire neighbours.'[21] Some women had gained a reputation for scolding and chiding. Mrs Alice Wilson, for example, had gained a reputation as a transgressor for her part in verbally disrupting the common peace and she was accused of chiding as well as scolding: 'Alice, the wyef of Edward Wilson, slater, for a comon chider.'[22]

Not only were women censured for this type of verbal violence, but so too were those with whom they associated. For example, John Corbett on 15 November 1593, was fined eight pence for associating with undesirable characters. The Court voiced their disapproval of his association with verbally inconstant women and 'lodging in his house light and unchaste women and other evill disposed persons.'[23] An alehouse keeper, on 25 October 1591, was also fined twelve pence for a verbal violation. The charge read: 'we find fynable Roger Smyth for retaling ale and for kepynge a woman of evil conversation in his house, twelve pence.'[24] Liverpool Town Books confirm similarly that, on 23 October 1592, a woman was fined the sum of six pence for providing accommodation for a woman who had been accused of a verbal infraction: 'Anne Monely [is] fineable for harbouring and succouring one Mary Sakey in her house being a woman of evil converccacion.'[25] Similarly, Tugar Bolde, of Liverpool, in 1597 was fined six shillings and eight pence for his encounter with a scold. The charge against him was: 'for keeping a woman of evill conversaccion in his house.'[26]

By the late sixteenth century, scolding and chiding appeared to cause even more concern. The statement below is illustrative of the legal machinery of governing authorities and the punitive measures that had been put in place to systematically punish scolding and chiding. Several authorities penalised women whose language or behaviour was at odds with others in the community and there was a consistent regulation of female language and behaviour. The mayor advised the Liverpool Assemblies to put an end to the increasing problem of verbal violence. In 1597 they agreed upon the imposition of much sterner measures for the punishment of lawbreaking by scolds and chiders by imposing a fine of ten shillings and imprisonment. Such offenders who were found to cause a disruption to the common peace were vulnerable to further consequences as the statement below confirms:

> Concerninge scolders and chiders to the nusance of theire neighbours, yt is ordered and agreed as above, that all suche as shall from henceforth be founde offenders in that behalfe shalbe punished as ensueth, viz. everie offender aforesaid, duelie approved and founde by sufficiente testimonie of witnes, shall either paye the somme of tenne shillinges in money, or else to have and suffer inprisonment by the space of tenne dayes withoute baile or mainprice, at the descreacion of the maior of this towne for the tyme beinge or his deputie. And that there shall not be anie wyne, beare, ale, or other kinde of drincke brought or conveyed to anie such prisoner or prisoners during the tyme of theire imprisonement, excepte onelie theire due and ordinarie meales, which shal be sufficient for theire ordinarie diett, and not otherwise, upon suche penalties as therefore shall be imposed and assessed by mayster maior or his deputie upon the bringers and senders thereof, and this order to have continuance from henceforthe.[27]

Casting Spells and Charms: Elizabeth Crackelow and Margaret Linke's Cunning Craft

Amid periods marked by uncertainty and illness, numerous prosecutions transpired across England targeting individuals engaged in the utilisation of popular treatments or remedies. By way of comparison with the later Northwest, the case of Elizabeth Crackelow illustrates how cunning women could be victimised during times of uncertainty during the mid-sixteenth century. Although a comprehensive regional comparison is not within the scope of this book, several significant representative cases are presented providing valuable insights into the perilous circumstances faced by cunning women who ventured into the realm of magical healing.

It has been noted that popular belief in the power of sorcery was strong and continuous.[28] One such characteristic case in the Oxfordshire Diocesan records illustrates the ways in which cunning women became vulnerable to an accusation. The undermentioned court case demonstrates that such circumstances intensified during times of acute adversity. Blesser and charmer, Elizabeth Crackelow, was a well-known cunning woman and healer of the town of Adderbury in the diocese of Oxford whose history comprised the casting of spells. In October 1546 she was accused of sorcery and witchcraft. The specifics of her magical ritual came to light during an event concerning the will of Henry Tanner, which held detailed evidence about the circumstances in which Henry Tanner died of the plague. Tanner, on his deathbed, made a will, shouting the details through the window to his master, Henry Syviar, and to the curate, Sir Robert, who were standing outside the window of Syviar's house. When witnesses were examined on 9 October and 16 October 1546 to ascertain the circumstances of Tanner's will, the wise woman, Elizabeth Crackelow of Adderbury was arraigned and an inquiry was empowered to decide whether, in making his will, Elizabeth Crackelow had unduly influenced Tanner. Many members of the community were called as witnesses. The court wanted to know whether Crackelow had cast spells to influence the direction of the will, or whether Robert Harres, who, it was alleged, had an interest in the will, went into Syviar's house before Tanner died. As with so many cases, the outcome of this case is not known.[29] However, the court records confirm that cunning woman Elizabeth Crackelow had knowingly put her own life at risk by attending to nurse Henry Tanner, who was dying of the plague, when others would not even think of entering the house. Not only was she jeopardising her well-being, but also, in doing so she risked losing her home. Precisely why her actions attracted such punishment are not clear. She was, however, aware of the fact that she may have been jeopardising her future. She did express concern that she might lose her home in Adderbury, either because she had been in a house where there was plague, or because she was accused of improperly influencing the dying man in creating his last will. Whether she did lose her house or not is not apparent. However, the confiscation of the property of women accused of verbal crime such as sorcery was a frequent punishment in seventeenth century Northwest England. Women healers often found their property and goods were at risk, even though they were performing an essential service that nobody else could, or would, do. On the matter of property in the Crackelow case, the court is imprecise about whose expectations were disappointed by the outcome of the will. What is clear, however, is that Crackelow was brought under suspicion for being a wise woman. Interested parties were given the opportunity to censure her for manipulating Tanner by supernatural means and this was how she later came to be accused of using supernatural or magical powers to influence individuals.

A similar situation of pronouncing charms to that of Crackelow occurred in Abingdon, Oxfordshire, in 1618, when a cunning woman called Margaret Link was accused of performing love-magic and sorcery.[30] However, the depositions of several witnesses disclose that the cunning woman had 'nothing to answer' (not guilty) when accused of sorcery. It was found that Foulke Hart of Chelgrove, when 'in conference with Margaret Linck,' told the cunning woman that he needed help to assist his son who was in love with a maid called Mistress Anne. He asked her to 'use means to bring the young maid to the waterside to carry her away.'[31] Thomasina Linck told the court that 'his purpose was to use sorcery to contrive a marriage.' She also claimed that 'widow Linck was reputed a cunning woman to help men with cattle, no powder, spice or drug, no skill in any such business for all she knoweth [she] does not bewitch.' The deposition of John Link, of Aston Rowant, dated 23 January 1618, confirmed that he overheard 'Goodman Fulke of Chalgrave when he came to the house of Margaret Linck his Mother and told her that his sonne and a mayde were in love together' and said 'yf you can bring her but to the water syde I will give you twenty shillings.' Further, he stated, that 'he did hereby understand that Fulke was purposed to make use of sorcery for the obtayning of the mayde for his sonne and did conceade that his mother had skill to worke by sorcery and inchauntements.'[32] Although the judgment of 'nothing to answer' is ambiguous, the depositions of those who knew Margaret Linck disclose that the cunning woman was innocent of sorcery. The neighbours' depositions bring to light the knowledge that Goodman Fulke was the offender, for he sought to procure love-magic with the intention of kidnapping Mistress Anne. Nevertheless, this case discloses the fact that speaking enchantments could be dangerous and this finding has much in common with cases of the later period of 1630 to 1640 in the Quarter Sessions of Lancashire.

Women and Cursing: A Cultural Perspective

Just as the court records of the Manorial Court, Portmoot, and Liverpool Town Books reveal the context of scolding and chiding, depositions and lawsuits are informative about communicating the finer points about the circumstances of cursing and the female sphere of influence. The depositions of the witnesses who were involved in relating their experience of cursing are indicative of the level of discontent that existed in the townships. They are valuable in explaining the circumstances in which ritual cursing was issued and why it was that cursing was perceived as such an odious crime by the community. In contrast to the consistent, even rhythm of prosecutions against women for scolding and cursing in the sixteenth century, as shown above, the numbers of accusations that were brought to the attention of the Chester Consistory Court rose sharply during the decade of 1630 to 1640. This is a significant period because it is the interval of the build-up to the Civil War. As discontent in the community grew, so accusations of cursing arose. The agitation which led to the Civil War also found expression through the court and provoked much litigation. The records indicate that arguments over land and property were the main areas of contention, especially in cursing cases. They indicate that female vocal misconduct through cursing very often stemmed from unease about lack of financial support and potential destitution.

Ellen Pemberton's Curse

Despite the fact that women resorted to cursing in dire situations, the primary intention behind issuing curses was to cause harm to one's adversary. The underlying reasons that led to the issuance of curses and legal action were typically rooted in disputes over personal property, possessions, livestock, and other material belongings. Numerous lawsuits indicate that a significant number of women accused of cursing had experienced abandonment by their spouses and families. Ellen Pemberton's curse is a prime illustration. This curse is intertwined with a 1633 libel case that unveils a correlation between a grievance concerning provisions, an individual defamed as a promiscuous woman and witch, and the contention that she had been subjected to a curse. In addition to the more common and predictable supernatural context of cursing, matters of violence against Ellen Pemberton surfaced that indicated public threats, extortion, and thieving. The details of the cursing were heard by Edmund Mainwaring of the Chester Consistory Court in 1633.[33] Ellen Pemberton who was brought before the court for cursing and banning her former fiancé.

The courtroom was likely filled with speculations and murmurs when Ellen Pemberton was charged with casting a curse on her ex-fiancé, Richard Bradley. But as she spoke, it became clear that this was not a case of cursing; it was, rather, a matter of property and money. Ellen explained that Richard had acted on her behalf, attempting to collect money owed to her by debtors. When he failed, he abandoned her for Margaret Leigh, with whom he had had a previous relationship. In a fit of anger and betrayal, Ellen had cursed Richard, but it was not a supernatural curse. It was a curse of anger and frustration, of a woman who had been wronged. The accusations that were levelled at her were thinly disguised matters of property ownership and a dispute about money. Ellen Pemberton's deposition put into words that she and the plaintiff, Richard Bradley disagreed vehemently when they argued about the money, property, and goods that existed at the heart of the cursing. Richard Bradley claimed that he had acted on behalf of his previously betrothed, Ellen Pemberton, when he attempted to extract money from her debtors. When he failed in his attempts to reclaim Pemberton's money, he then reneged upon his contractual obligation to marry her. Ellen Pemberton said that she was subsequently abandoned for a Margaret Leigh, with whom Bradley had been involved in a previous relationship and who was named in the deposition. Margaret Leigh subsequently became Mrs. Bradley shortly before the case was heard. Richard Bradley argued conclusively that Ellen Pemberton was cursed. He deposed that her being cursed was the reason for concluding his relationship with her. Pemberton, supported by her friend Janet Rothwell, avowed that she was contracted in marriage to Richard Bradley but was then forsaken by him in preference for Margaret Leigh. Margaret Bradley was assisted by Janet Rothwell who accused Ellen Pemberton of attempting to kill Margaret Bradley with a knife. Pemberton's ill-spoken curses were recorded as follows:

> Richard Bradley is a whoremaster and a foresworne raskall, Margaret Bradley is a whore and Richard Barnsons whore, and should be banned, and said Ellen Pemberton and Jane Rothwell or both or one of them would kyll her with a knife.[34]

Much of what was said at the hearing related to the marital contractual agreement between Bradley and Pemberton. The charge of 'whore' forced the newly betrothed Bradleys into taking the matter to the Church court, but it appears from the substance of the case that Ellen Pemberton was not to blame. This cursing disguised bigamy. According to the court, Richard Bradley was contractually bound to Ellen Pemberton. Abraham Partington and his family witnessed the 'marriage' between Ellen Pemberton and Richard Bradley. In addition, Janet Rothwell as witness swore that she was present at the ceremony. What further emerged concerns sordid details of extortion which confirmed that the cursing allegation was in fact an excuse to be rid of Ellen Pemberton. The situation was further clarified when the court heard of Richard Bradley's attempts to extort money from individuals who had owed money to Ellen Pemberton. The court heard that he terrified her debtors. In circumstances of extreme violence, he threatened to have them thrown into prison if they did not repay to *him* the money that they owed to Ellen Pemberton. Ellen Pemberton, who at the time was apparently unaware of these violent interventions, put forward the view that she had permitted her creditors to repay their debts at length and in their own time. The evidence of Ellen Pemberton's deposition was heard and subsequently exposed the newly married Bradleys as culpable of extreme violence. Nevertheless, it was Richard Bradley, who, although 'defamed,' was guilty of bigamy, extortion and attempted murder. The court, however, did not record his sentence and there were no further particulars entered on the court records.

A closer examination of Ellen Pemberton's curse provides further confirmation of the challenges faced by women in their efforts to safeguard their honour, reputation, and address issues of property theft or abandonment. The social circumstances and the outspoken characteristics of women who cursed, such as Ellen Pemberton, did much to distinguish the women who were typically vulnerable to charges of cursing. For the most part, women were habitually presented to the court for having first been suspected by local townsfolk of cursing a family which had simply encountered illness or bad luck. It followed that when a woman was suspected of cursing, or when she had a history of cursing, or indeed had an association with one accused of cursing, that she would inevitably find herself charged with cursing. When a cursing incident reached the harsh Puritan Justices of the Quarter Sessions, a woman who had been accused of cursing might then be in danger of losing her life. So, it was important for women such as Ellen Pemberton to legally defend themselves. Often, soon after indictment on suspicion of a cursing confrontation, a woman might then be presented for bewitchment. There is an obvious connection between cursing and scolding which is often underscored by deprivation and destitution. Although cursing charges were directed at the wealthy, such crimes were not restricted to the poor starving old lady living on the margins who cursed the very rich. They were habitually aimed women at the middling sort, and in some situations were directed by the desperate poor at the marginally better-off poor. Most of the evidence from the Chester Consistory Court records supports the view that cursing was directed more often at the middling sort. Most clear, however, in the evidence is the set of circumstances that demonstrate that the crime of cursing belonged as much to the material world as it did to the symbolic world.

In certain cases, the failure to adhere to the regulations imposed by religious authorities, particularly in matters of governance, was identified as a contributing factor leading to charges of cursing. In some cases of cursing, one or two cases might involve a defendant's husband as an accomplice in the crime, but even in situations where men *were* involved, it was *always* women who were charged with cursing because it was believed that the potency of their words whether uttered in anger or desperation were a most powerful weapon in bringing down a supernatural judgment on members of the community.

The manuscripts pertaining to cursing display considerable discrepancies in terms of the level of detail they offer. While some manuscripts provide only basic information, such as the names of the individuals implicated, others provide limited glimpses into the identities of the accused and the underlying causes behind the charges.

Despite the brevity of the information, what was recorded in the following brief matter from 1594, reveals the importance of the role of hearsay or irresponsible talk that was communicated between the townsfolk. This case concerns Richard Masterton, who in his deposition, told the court that it was malevolent hearsay that was responsible for drawing negative attention to him through his wife, for 'there was much talke.'[35] While the specific outcomes of these cases are absent from the recorded documents, it is evident that in 1594, Anne Masterton invoked a curse upon an unidentified individual in the town, using the words 'a plague of God light upon you.' This curse led to both Anne and her husband being summoned before David Yale, a registrar at the Chester Consistory Court. Likewise, in 1588, Katherine Lawton faced a more severe accusation of cursing, as it was alleged that her words possessed the potential to cause the death of a gentleman, Richard Massey. Katherine Lawton was vulnerable to the charge because she had not been to church to receive holy communion. The matter arose out of a bitter personal disagreement between Katherine Lawton and Richard Massey. Although there was little recorded evidence in the case to support this view, when Richard Massey died, the court ultimately blamed the cause of his death upon

Katherine Lawton's curse.[36] The broader community was involved in the situation, as it is noted that Richard Massey's friends, described as 'two men of credit,' were sent to reconcile the disagreement, but to no avail. Katherine was perceived to possess an exceptionally potent ability to wield verbal power, and her curse against Massey was regarded as particularly egregious. The curse invoked a fate of a shameful and swift death upon Massey, compounded by the absence of religious solace, as indicated by the following words:

> Katherine Lawton, contrary to gods commandement, and contrary to Christian charity, as thy most wicked and malicious minde, and diabolicall stomacke, hast sundry and many tymes in most detestable and exercurable manner cursed the foresaide Richard Massy gent. wishing a suddayne death and shameful end to fall upon him and that god so only do wronge upon him and quitte him.[37]

While Katherine Lawson faced accusations of cursing, this case stands out as an exception, as it was her husband, Robert Lawton, who faced charges of a crime. Robert Lawton was ultimately found guilty by association with Katherine. His crime was not one of cursing, it was in *allowing* Katherine to execute the curse and failing to take action to *prevent* Richard Massey's death.[38]

Some instances of cursing arose out of sheer desperation, exemplified by a noteworthy case in Manchester in April 1601. Margaret Cheetham, who had previously faced accusations of cursing Ellis Prestwyche, resorted to making claims of paternity against him. After the death of John Cheetham, her husband, Margaret gave birth to a son. Despite uncertainty about his parentage, she named the child Samuel Cheetham. Margaret told the court that Ellis Prestwyche's recent 'good fortune' was brought about by magic. Prestwyche claimed she cursed him by speaking the words below:

> Thou Ellis Prestwyche, art a foresworne man, and thou hast foresworn thyself for two years and thou hast given thy soul to faireies, and thou hast gotten thy goodes with it and the fairies have brought thee thy goodes.[39]

Margaret Cheetham faced charges for uttering a ritual curse, but upon closer examination of the matter, it became apparent that her curse was, in fact, an act of self-preservation and a veiled attack against Ellis Prestwych.

It was revealed that Ellis Prestwych was, indeed, the father of Margaret Cheetham's child, shedding light on her motivations behind the curse as a means to protect herself from destitution. In was in the dire circumstances of poverty that Margaret claimed that Ellis Prestwyche was 'forsworn' and 'bewitched' and concluded that he had made a deal with the fairies. Her declarations were rife with the emotions of bitter irony and resentment. She cursed him for abandoning the family. Through her curse, Margaret Cheetham scornfully rebuked Ellis for his neglect of responsibilities and denounced his failure to provide financial support for their child. In a bitter irony, she suggested that he might engage in a Faustian bargain with the fairies, even contemplating the possibility of selling their own child as a commodity:

> beckoning or pointing towards Samuel Cheetham sonne of John Cheetham's deceased, being yours, is thy sone, take him awaie for you shalt have him, for he is thyne, ... meaninge that the said Ellis Prestwyche was father of the said Samuel Cheetham...these words were spoken in the parish of Manchester.[40]

The curse uttered by a grief-stricken Margaret Cheetham exposes her profound concern regarding the challenges she faced in sustaining her family without a provider. Such instances of cursing frequently illuminate the struggles experienced by women in their endeavour to support and protect their families, compelling them to resort to extreme measures. Margaret Cheetham's testimony substantiates that the case had little to do with sorcery but revolved entirely around the issue of child support. Margaret Cheetham's curse against Ellis Prestwych was delivered with a potent mixture of anger and disdain, stemming from his perceived lack of responsibility. Subsequently, the curse was swiftly followed by a legal action, as she initiated a paternity suit against him.[41]

Transgressors: 'Knaves, Whores and Chyders'[42]

Testimonies from the sixteenth century shed light on the regulation and control imposed upon female speech and behaviour. The commonalities observed in both the Chester Consistory Court and the Oxford Church Court cases are examined in greater detail below. The involvement of friends and associates of women accused of being notorious scolds or cursers often led to charges and subsequent condemnation. Instances of women's participation in burglaries and allegations of receiving stolen goods were also documented. In such cases, male partners associated with women charged with immoral behaviour could become entangled in legal proceedings. The concept of guilt by association played a significant role in these circumstances. Accusations of robbery or extortion lodged against females were frequently intertwined with moral judgments regarding their sexual conduct. Female behaviour in general, particularly sexual conduct, was subject to the steady scrutiny of the legal authorities. The vigilant monitoring of women's activities creates the perception of constant supervision and moral regulation imposed upon them. Women who transgressed societal norms were occasionally labelled as prostitutes, further stigmatising their behaviour.[43] There is a pattern of continuity in the regulation of female sexuality and its connection with spoken offence which is established by many examples from the Church court records in the mid-sixteenth century. The moral authority assumed by the Church courts resulted in the imposition of regulatory measures specifically targeting women. These measures are observed to have intensified in the seventeenth century, particularly in the regional context of Northwest England. As a consequence, an increasing number of women faced prosecution in Church courts for verbal transgressions and infringements. The following cases serve as representative examples of the activities that underwent scrutiny and contributed to a consistent increase during the early seventeenth century. This pattern of rising cases persisted throughout the seventeenth century, with a notable surge in litigations occurring within a ten-year period from 1630 to 1640.

Social and spatial control was exerted through the control of female sexuality. Social and spatial control in the early modern period encompassed the regulation of female sexuality as a means of exerting control. Sexual immorality, often entangled with the ritual of cursing, was closely associated with these efforts. Over the course of the century, there was a gradual increase in the prevalence of regulations targeting this female sexuality.[44] In one case, a woman was cited as behaving in a 'lewd' way and cursing. Similarly, a woman was apprehended for cursing and described as a 'Jesebel.' In another case, the same woman was cited for behaving immorally, for associating with undesirables, for drinking, betting, and for attending cockfights. In 1592, a clear manifestation of female social and spatial control can be observed in a specific case involving Cicilia Collinge from Prestwich. She was accused of engaging in actions that were considered immoral, and the case was heard by David

Yale, who served as the deputy registrar of the Chester Consistory Church Court at that time. This serves as an example of the mechanisms through which control was exerted over women during that period. During the proceedings, Arthur Collinge, Cicilia's husband, provided evidence and presented an unnamed witness who testified based on personal experience about what they asserted to be Cicilia's immoral behaviour: 'She is a lewde and naughte woman, for that I myself have had carnall dealing with her dyverse times.'[45]

In this instance, it is noteworthy that Cicilia Collinge was accused of engaging in 'lewde and naughte' behaviour, while her male partner did not face any charges. This asymmetry in the accusations highlights a gendered disparity in the treatment of individuals involved in the case.

Parlance of the ribald kind was principally related to the functions of the female body. It was sometimes linked to the circumstances of childbirth. Sexually explicit terminology was long-established in arguments about adultery, bastardy, divorce, prostitution, and a succession of issues about the sexual goings-on of people. Allegations of prostitution were frequently made. In 1683, Maria Bostocke brought a complaint to the court, alleging that she had been subjected to verbal abuse by Anne Warburton of Welsh Rowe in Nantwich. Warburton was alleged to have said to Bostocke: 'she was never fuct for a strike or lent her cunt out as her grandmother [had].' Warburton admitted however, that: 'when she was drunk, she showed her cunt to John Rowe and Richard Lewes,' but added: 'she never sold hers to any as her [Bostocke's] Grandmother did.'[46] Such bawdy discourse was common in the courts of the seventeenth century. Events disclose that some women, like Anne Warburton as in the case above, habitually referred to their fellow citizens in such earthy terms.

While some women executed verbal indignities; others were casualties of allegations that proclaimed them as whores. In 1567, Petronilla Vernon accused Anne Homes of uttering malicious words, claiming that she engaged in promiscuous behaviour and went 'whoring.'[47] The following year, both male and female were in trouble for sexually improper conduct. Richard Wilkes and Sara Wilkes each complained to the court of being called respectively 'knave and whore' and acted against the offender.[48] Similarly, in 1572, Anne Holland summonsed Anne Harris to answer charges of defamation.[49] The following year, in 1593, a woman was referred to as 'a married man's whore.'[50] A few years later in 1596, another woman took legal action for having been referred to as a 'rambeaten whore.'[51]

Accusations of bastardy were frequent. They were littered with a phraseology that denigrated women by referring to the female lower body. Townsfolk favoured language that implied carnal frenzy or excessive libidinous engagement. In one such case in 1597, Marie Barrowes was referred to as a 'burnt-arse whore.' Her accusers suggested that 'she was naughty with Randle Harrison' and that the liaison produced a 'bastard child.'[52] The origin of the dispute can be traced to allegations of bastardy. The statement of a witness noted the words: 'one of Marie's children (named Richard) was and is a bastard.'[53] It was after this cause, that Marie's husband, Richard Barrowes, at that point accused her of adultery.[54]

As women were accused of improper conduct more often in the seventeenth century, their conduct was progressively associated with drinking, adultery, producing 'bastards' and prostitution. In 1600, for example, Elizabeth Wright cited Anne Kerry proclaiming that: 'Elizabeth Wright is a whore, an arrant whore, and she hath been delivered of two red herrings instead of children.'[55] Another woman, in 1601, who did not approve of excessive drinking, referred to an individual as 'a drunken pisspot.'[56] The following year in 1602, a woman brought a libel suit against a person who referred to her as a 'whore.'[57] Two years later, a woman sued an individual in the court who said she had 'a disease (presumably venereal disease) worse than the plague.'[58] Again in 1606, a woman was accused of adultery.[59] The steady rhythm of accusations of improper conduct indicates that though women were exposed to patriarchal regulatory pressure, they too denounced those whose language they found offensive. Their statements show that women often vindicated themselves from similar verbal attack. Both genders were equally litigated against for reproaching the sexual piety of their neighbours. The foregoing information demonstrates that while women were referred to as 'whores,' there was an equivalent term of abuse for males, who were termed 'knaves.'

Both men and women sought the justice of the Church court to solve issues of paternity. Matters of divorce were heard at the court in 1608.[60] In 1609, however, Jacob Hulme and Anna Smith locked horns over a paternity suit which was subsequently referred to the High Commission.[61] Similarly, in 1615, Ann Brassie forced John Rydsey to appear in court for saying he was her 'better' and for referring to her as a 'bastard.'[62] Issues arising from marriages gone sour occurred frequently.

In 1620 a woman complained of being referred to as a 'brazenfaced whore.'[63] The registrar's office in the same year called William Cleve to answer their enquiries about a matrimonial issue.[64]

While some women found some terms of reference offensive, others were spiteful in their attempts to seek legal retribution. Some pursued male offenders vociferously to make them take back their words or have them pay compensation. One such incident arose when Elizabeth Street made John Kilmer suffer for referring to her as a 'runagate queane.'[65] Unrequited passion was at the heart of some allegations like the one in 1628, when John Haslehurst and Margaret Cumberbach argued in court over Hasleshurst's euphemistic allusion implying that she requested that John 'garth her butter tubb.' However, he claimed Margaret was perturbed by his reply that 'he should garth her butter tubb when butter came out of Ireland.'[66] Accusations that women were 'whores' were fought out in the court in 1630.[67] Similar accusations were flung about again in 1631.[68] The following year saw yet more women struggling to clear their names of slander.[69]

Several mothers were expected to conform to a standard of conduct that was predetermined by men. However, patriarchal pressure sometimes failed to impose its standards on women. In 1635, for example, Elizabeth Colly was admonished by her father for her refusal to conform to his idea of appropriate conduct for a female. He brought a legal action against his daughter to make her yield to his will. According to his allegations, she 'kept unfittinge and unfashionable company' whilst leaving her children, whom he described as including 'one very younge' at home alone.[70] He reported her for irresponsible behaviour on her children's part, and had her booked for going to cockfights, gambling, and drinking. Elizabeth's father additionally accused her of perpetrating adultery with Thomas Wildinge of Grappenhall. Robert Colly, her husband, whom her father described as 'a silly man,' was reputed to have been with them. The evidence implies that her husband was aware of Elizabeth's conduct and condoned it. Her father's hostility to the situation was recorded by the court. He was said to have spoken 'in great anger and great perplexity of mind.' He repudiated his daughter, and 'asked her whether her town of Cheshire was not big enough to play the whore in, but she must travel to Staffordshire for a lewd companion.'[71] The incident illustrates that some women, notably Elizabeth Colly, did not conform to the patriarchal model of wifely conduct. Moreover, Robert Colly's awareness of the behaviour of his marriage partner, implies that 'adultery' may simply have been friendship. Moreover, gambling, and drinking were entertainments that were enjoyed equally by both women and men but whether Elizabeth Colly was a 'good' mother or not is, however, open to question.

Certain members of the community were effective in imposing and enforcing standards of conduct specifically on women. They were able to exert influence and ensure adherence to societal expectations and norms regarding women's behaviour. Many incidents of adultery were reported to the court. In 1636, two controversial instances involved women: one was a case of adultery, and the other was a case of cruelty.[72] Further instances of adultery emerged in 1637 and again in 1640, while in 1638 the court heard a case of a 'prohibition of marriage.'[73] Also in 1638 a woman defended her reputation after having been referred to as 'a drunken queane.'[74] The following year, actions were brought against one angry woman who defended herself from indictments of 'fornication.'[75]

A case of cursing that is representative of the close relationship between female cursing, sexual matters, and sexually immoral conduct occurred in the parish of Manchester in 1611, when four women, Elizabeth Whitlowe, Margaret Ratcliffe, Elizabeth Jackson, and Maria Rose came together to attack the status of Alice Brook. Their depositions confirm that there was a consensus amongst local townspeople that Alice Brook was a whore; more particularly, a 'millers' whore.'[76] It was quarrelling amongst these neighbours that was later to lead eventually to a charge in which Alice Brook was accused of cursing. It was said of her that she produced 'lewde speeches, cursings, magic and other words.'[77] The situation was indeed so dangerous that Alice Brook's evidence confirms that she was confined to her home for fear that she would be attacked. The records disclosed her anguish: 'if the plaintiff durst come oute of her house the dept. [deponent] would beate her.'[78] Thomas Jackson, aged 28, gave support to Alice Brook's evidence. In Manchester he was present to hear Alice Brook maligned as 'a witch, a whore and an arrant whore, and the miller's whore.' Jackson, however, spoke in favour of Alice Brook and denied such allegations were true. He argued that the opposite was true, that the plaintiff was an 'honest poore woman.'[79]

The connection between female sexuality, intense speech, and magical practices is apparent in various instances, as exemplified by cases such as that of Alice Brook. These examples underscore how a woman's sexual behaviour could be negatively interpreted and became closely intertwined with different types of verbal transgressions. The confluence of these factors contributed to the complex dynamics surrounding women's conduct. Alice Brook was accused of being a 'whore and a witch,' mixing 'lewde speeches' with 'cursings' and 'magic.' Female promiscuity was subject to stringent control and as societal attitudes deemed female sexual activities as improper, such behaviour became closely associated with actions that were more readily perceived as unlawful, leading to increased indictments and legal consequences. The regulation of female sexuality was intertwined with the broader framework of moral expectations and legal standards of the time. The charge of being a 'witch' sometimes appeared with the description of 'whore,' the charges of 'scolding' or 'railing' appeared more commonly with the description of 'whore.' It was also common for a 'witch' to be charged with cursing. At times, the terms of witchcraft and cursing were used interchangeably, indicating a certain overlap or fluidity between the two concepts and cases varied from 'crude name-calling to extraordinary fantasy to direct, dangerous accusations of maleficium.'[80] Some were straightforward attacks on character, some consisted of incidental insults, and some were smear tactics of guilt by association.

Insults, guilt by association and dragging one's character through the mud is often confirmed in the records encompassing cursing. For example, in some instances, the term 'thiefe' might also be thrown into the mix, together with the terms of whore and witch. In the case of Elizabeth Boude, from Rostherne near Chester, which was heard by David Yale, in the Chester Consistory Court in 1617, the court was acquainted with details of the accusations that were made against her. She had been reproached her for prostitution, thieving, and witchcraft. She protested that the incident damaged her reputation and honour and she presented such a convincing case that the court noted that she was libelled and 'publicly defamed as a thiefe a whore and a witch.'[81]

The Curse of Joane Elderson

As previously discussed, the regulation of female sexuality was a significant aspect of social control during the early modern period. Female promiscuity was tightly monitored, and such behaviour became closely linked to activities that were deemed unlawful, resulting in heightened indictments and legal repercussions. The control exerted over female sexuality was an integral part of the prevailing moral and legal framework. As is common in cursing, women who were vulnerable to insults, slanders and other denigratory accusations were often those who were seen to occupy social spaces that were deemed undesirable for a woman of guiltless character. This was especially the situation for women who managed an alehouse or who were otherwise involved in the retailing of ale. Women who sold ale were spatially out of bounds and accused of transgressing the limits of respectability. In consequence, female alehouse keepers were prime targets of distrust. The following case is illustrative of the way in which the evolution of one charge culminated in a charge of cursing. The history evolved from thief, to prostitute, to curser.

Running a brothel was the first in a chain of denunciations against alehouse-keeper, Joane Elderson, of Ashton, Lancashire, who, in 1636, was the proprietor of a popular alehouse. The prevailing belief was that Joane Elderson had a longstanding reputation for impropriety. Her alehouse was a known den of iniquity, and she had been accused of running a brothel and receiving stolen goods. But it was the charge of cursing that really marked her downfall. The townsfolk had always distrusted her, but when rumours began to spread that she had cursed a young child, they turned on her with a vengeance. She found herself in deep trouble and was inculpated for several transgressions that began with running a brothel and continued with receiving stolen goods. These initial accusations mark the onset of several similar allegations, which eventually concluded with her being indicted for cursing. The accusations against Joane grew more outlandish with each passing day. Some claimed that she had made a deal with the devil himself, while others whispered that she had been born with a cursed soul. But Joane knew the truth. She was a woman who had been dealt a bad hand in life, forced to scrape by in a world that offered her few options. And, as she awaited the outcome of the case against her for the crime of cursing, she knew that her fate was sealed. The following statement reveals the negative sentiments that were held by the townspeople:

> the wyffe of John Elderson of Asheton hath of Longe tyme kept a most badd and dispoesed [sic] house receivinge and recettinge into the house all the knaves whores and Chiders in the cuntrie and all the stolen goods that came to her house soe that noe honest man can come to her house but in great danger of his lyffe.[82]

Elderson's neighbours laid blame on her for extortion and of obliging the local criminal element in harbouring those who were ill-spoken and of immoral conduct. She was later found culpable for keeping a brothel and further, of exerting a bad influence over the male population of the Ashton community. Her neighbours asserted that she kept 'mens sons and servants' from more productive endeavours:

> Alsoe she doth continually kepe in her house Lewde and light women of theire bodyes to the great undoinge of mens sons and servants that dwell neare unto her.[83]

Along with charges of keeping lewd and light women, the alehouse-keeper was censured for soliciting. In one such example of this conduct, John Wally and friend agreed to pay Elderson in return for the services of a prostitute.[84] The evidence tells of honest maids who trembled for fear of falling into Elderson's evil ways. A maid, who was accused of innocently delivering bread, divulges the details of one particular occasion when Elderson suggested she could earn more money as a prostitute.[85] At that point Elderson's neighbours approached the Justice of the Peace with a petition. Their petition held the details of why they wanted to see her alehouse closed. The petitioners, in the statement below, claim that the alehouse and the miscreants it encouraged would put their personal property at risk and would be a bad influence on children and servants:

> and if there be no course taken for they Reforminge of these badd demeanours noe neighbour can live neare her butt in great perill of their lyves theire children and servants and the lyffe of their goods.[86]

The incident involving Joane Elderson's accusation of cursing had significant consequences, particularly in later years. This curse, which was believed to be responsible for the deaths of several children in Ashton, became a more serious charge against her.[87]

The enduring animosity towards the alehouse proprietor and the various charges of immoral conduct, harbouring criminals, and defamatory speech levied against Joane Elderson played a significant role in the accusation of cursing. The unexplained deaths of children attributed to cursing were specifically mentioned on 13 July 1636, during the allegations made against Elderson. The allegations emanated from several different informers. Elderson, who was sometimes referred to as Jane, or Jeney, it was proposed, allegedly cursed Elizabeth and Thomas Baxter of Newton. When the Baxter family subsequently experienced sudden inexplicable illness and bad luck they then made charges of cursing hostile to Joane Elderson. A neighbour, Ales Jackson, deposed that she had overheard an argument between Elderson and Elizabeth Baxter. Ales Jackson also appeared as a court witness to give details of the curse. Jackson claimed that shortly after the time that the argument took place, the Baxters' children 'fell into trances' and died soon after. Later, the Baxters claimed that their children had been cursed. The charge of cursing received support from Elizabeth Higgonson, Ralph Sytherland, Dorothie and Robert Taylor, and Thomas Darrow of Newton. They appeared as witnesses to give evidence relating to the curse. Ales Jackson's deposition recalled the quarrel between Elderson and Elizabeth Baxter, which initiated a succession of unlucky events:

> Elizabeth Baxter (wyef of Thomas Baxter of Newton aforesaid), Whitesmith, was at Newton Milne winnowing groats upon the Milne hill where Joane Elderson was goeing to Elizabeth Baxter for malte. Thomas Blackeburne being neere the Milne and passing by Joane Elderson and Elizabeth fell at words concerning Elizabeths children that were lately dead, before the second day of June ... Joane Elderson did say unto Elizabeth Baxter she would not leave her mouth a groate.[88]

Dorothie Taylor who also offered the specifics of the cursing to the court confirmed that, after the disagreement, Elizabeth's children, languished and died:

> That she hath seene Charles Baxter sonne of the said Thomas Baxter many tymes in trances for halfe a year together at severall tymes before his death but what the occasion was shee knoweth not.[89]

However, some witnesses did not directly accuse Elderson of cursing. For example, Whitesmith, Thomas Darrow, claimed that he did not suspect anyone and did not specifically name Elderson speaking only of the child's illness: 'He saw him in dangerous trances often but knoweth not the cause neither can suspect anyone for it.'[90]

Other allegations were more damning. They related evidence of Elderson's power and confirmed her reputation as a renowned curser. For example, Elizabeth Higgonson, spinster, of Newton told how she heard servants say that Elderson's touch meant certain death:

> She hath seene the children of the said Thomas Baxter often tymes in trances and hath heard Ralph Sytherland a servant liveing in the house of

> the said Thomas Baxter with this informer say that after Joane Elderson had touched the child he never after had health.[91]

Ralph Sytherland was also called to appear as a witness. He did not explicitly accuse Elderson of cursing, but he did depose that he saw her 'touch' a child. This touch, it is claimed, was to prove fatal, when shortly afterwards, the child became ill and then died as Sytherland's statement below confirms:

> Joane Elderson the first Thursday in lent last did pass by the child of the said Thomas Baxter being an infant and as soone as shee passed by she turned againe and asked whose child it was and the girle which held the child said it was Thomas Baxters whereupon the said Joane Elderson said shee would kisse her cosen and did so where upon the same night it was taken with a stopping and upon the Tuesday night after it fell into trances which never lefte it till it died.[92]

The witnesses interpreted Elderson's words as expressions of curses. At her touch children fell into trances, languished, and died. Goods were spoiled. Property was lost. People feared starvation. Witnesses who then spoke of Elderson's lethal touch expressed fear and confirmed that they were reluctant to identify her further for fear of the cursing reprisals that might be issued against them. In their testimony they allude to at Elderson's involvement in the death of Elizabeth Baxter's child. However, only Elizabeth Baxter was brave enough to accuse her outright of cursing. The reluctance of Ashton folk to directly accuse Elderson indicates that they were sure to be afraid of meeting the same fate. When a child suddenly became ill, Elderson was held responsible. A kiss from her lips was certain death; even a single word of tenderness was then perceived as a curse. However, this case did not end as so many others did with victimisation and prosecution. As Elizabeth Baxter's fortune fell into a decline, she took legal action. The evidence, however, is indefinite. What is clear is that Elderson retaliated and threw herself into an almighty legal battle. The ensuing litigation, which is examined further below, sheds yet more light on the situation that so often lay behind the allegations. In Ashton, 14 members of the community subsequently became involved. Four Justices of the Peace: Thomas Bridgeman, John Moore, Henry Ogle, and Henry Ashcroft were each consulted, as was a gentlewoman,

Elizabeth Unsworth, who was sent to the Elderson household to arbitrate in the controversy.[93] Elizabeth Unsworth made the claim that she was unable to get through the door of the alehouse because of a fight, however. A carpenter, John Rogerson, told the Justices of the violent quarrel between Elizabeth Leadbeater and John and Joane Elderson:

> Elizabeth, Joane Elderson and John Elderson and this informer beinge in a Chamber together over theire heads came downe into the roome where Joane Elderson and Elizabeth Leadbeater were. And as soone as he came thither (beinge the last one lefte in the chamber) hee sawe John Elderson and Joane Elderson, scrytchinge, beateinge, and pushinge Elizabeth Leadbeater violently in the doore of the roome, and heard the said Gerard Johnson speake aloude, of the house, and give very foule and threateninge words against Elizabeth Leadbeaters in Elizabeth Unsworths Information, hee was upon occasions in the house of John Elderson of Ashton aforesaid, and was there when the said Elizabeth Leadbeater came into the same.[94]

A further confrontation occurred on 8 May 1636 and yet more Ashton folk became involved in the dispute. In this instance, Thomas Coster, Whitesmith, gave a close account of the incident. He said that all hell was let loose when Joane Elderson refused to serve Elizabeth Leadbetter with a flagon of ale.[95] On 16 May 1636 the Justice issued a recognisance to legal officials about the incident.[96] When Elderson then took countermeasures against the Ashton folk, it emerged that she was the victim of a storm of terror. Her property was at risk and the deposition indicates that she was afraid of Elizabeth and Jefferey Leadbeater of Ashton:

> Joane the wife of John Elderson of Ashton within the said County, husbandman, hath personaly come before us and hath taken her corporall oath that shee is affrayde that Elizabeth Leadbeater the wife of Jeferey Leadbeater of Ashton, husbandman will beate wound murther kill or burne her houses, and hath thereupon prayed safety of the peace against the said Elizabeth Leadbeater.[97]

As a result of the investigation, Elizabeth Leadbetter was bound over to keep the peace and warned she would end up in jail if she did not. She was also commanded to appear at the next Quarter Sessions.

On 11 July 1636, Anne Fielde, of Ashton in Makerfield, told Justice Thomas Freeland that the house in which Joane Elderson lived was sold by Thomas Blacke, son of James Blacke to Thomas Baxter for five pounds.

The discussion about Elderson's house was said to have occurred during a drinking session when Thomas Baxter discussed the prospect of having more children with his wife, Elizabeth. From this statement, it becomes obvious that the matter pertaining to Joane Elderson was without a doubt at its source a dispute about property. The evidence shows that Joane Elderson was previously married to James Blacke of Ashton, who had since died. When her son Thomas sold her house, Elderson then attacked him and demanded money:

> Joane Elderson now wife of John Elderson, and here before wife to James Blacke of Ashton, deceased, and mother to Thomas Blacke, came into this Informers house and upon a suddaine insaulted Thomas Blacke, and struck him and spoke a loude in words that is to say, 'Ah Rascaell, ah rogue, thou shalt take me namely from Thomas Baxter of Newtown, but if thou wilt fell thy rights of his house, I'll procure the money.[98]

Although Thomas Blacke accepted money for the house, Elderson begged to be allowed to keep the tenancy. She claimed she wanted to give it to her younger son, John Blacke. Thomas's cold-hearted response was to say that the house now belonged to the Baxters and that the house would not be passed down to John but would go to the Baxters' children. This is the point at which Elderson was to reply and this reply was subsequently reported as a curse:

> Thomas Blacke replied and said, that is to say, 'Mother handle you contente for Elizabeth Baxter wife of Thomas Baxeter of Newton aforesaid, is a younge woeman and may have Children.' Joane Elderson replied and said that if Elizabeth Baxter had twenty Children, they should none of them live to enioye Thomas Baxters house, but that (meaninge John Blacke sonne of the said James Blacke and brother to the said Thomas Blacke should have it).[99]

Thomas Blacke, on the 7 July 1636, gave evidence to Justices Thomas Freland and Edward Bradsman and, on the 16 July, both he and Robert Hulme, who was a labourer, received a summons to attend the court and they were required to give evidence about the incident. Thomas Blacke admitted that he accepted five pounds from Thomas Baxter as payment for Joane Elderson's house. He said that when Charles Baxter 'sonne of Thomas Baxter of Newton Whytesmith was liveing they were together in his father's house' and Thomas Blacke said he was to 'have taken five pownds from the said Thomas Baxter of Newton aforesaid in consideracion of his and expectation of children.'[100]

There was some confusion about precisely who owned the property. Since Charles and Phillip Baxter were both dead, Joane Elderson argued the house belonged to her. Elizabeth Baxter insisted that it was for this reason that Joane Elderson had cursed her sons and, in doing so, had caused their deaths. Baxter implied that she cursed her sons so that she might keep the house. Elizabeth Baxter's petition provides a history of ownership of the house. Her mother Ellen Keinon, of Newton in Makerfield, upon being widowed, legally ensured that the house would be inherited by Elizabeth Baxter:

> That Ellen Keinon widow late wiffe of John Keinon late of Newton in Makerfeild within the County of Lanc deceassed, and mother of the said Elizabeth Baxter did show unto two Justices in trust all her mesuage and interest and being in Newton for some of fourscore and neenteen years and she lives in the originall house soe long doe continue to and for the use and profitt of the said Elizabeth her assiquie or assiques during the naturall liffe of the said Elizabeth.[101]

What emerges from the deposition is that the house was conditionally *leased* to Joane Elderson. The disclaimer was that she would vacate the premises when Elizabeth had children. However, Elderson argued that she would not leave the house because Elizabeth Baxter's sons died and because Baxter in fact then had no children that she could not evict her. The five pounds which passed hands between Thomas Baxter and Thomas Blacke was given to procure their good will when it was presumed that they would then leave the house. However, Joane Elderson did not leave with good will. In place of vacating the property, it was claimed that she exchanged harsh words with the Baxters. When Elizabeth Baxter's sons died afterwards, Elizabeth Baxter then accused Elderson of cursing them. The source of the curse stems directly from the enmity between Elderson and Elizabeth Baxter about Elizabeth Baxter's childlessness and Joane Elderson's right of tenure to the property. Elderson then argued that her sons ought to inherit the home as Elizabeth Baxter had no children to leave the property to. Elizabeth Baxter was convinced she had bought out their rights of ownership, but Elderson remained resolute:

> Now be it was that this Elizabeth Baxter was married some 15 years or there about and never had any child in all that tyme. Thomas Baxter her husband did offer unto the said Thomas Leech five pounds for his good will of the said tenement, which hee would have taken, but that his mother would not suffer him to doe but since that tyme shee given her sonnne three pounds in consideration of the said house toe a younger sonne.[102]

It was when the Baxter's children died that they recalled the details about Joane Elderson's physical proximity to their children. Subsequently, they held Elderson responsible for their children's deaths. Elizabeth Baxter complained bitterly to the Justices that she was afraid for her life and assets. She was afraid she would lose everything because of Joane Elderson's curses:

> It pleased God to send to your petitioner twoe fine boyes which boyes are both dead, and your petitioner will take her oath of it if it please your good worshippes shee may bee sworne for the kinge that the said John Elderson was the cause of there deathes by reason that shee touched them they never were well till they were dead, and lykewyse your petitioner will take her oath that shee is afraid of her owne liffe besydes if it please God to your petitioner never so many children shee is afraid they will none of them live if not some course is taken with her all soe your petitioner hath of her goods and is afrayed shee shall lose most of all shee hath.[103]

The Quarter Sessions records usually provide only minor details about such matters, but, in this instance, they provide a significant history of cursing offering greater insight into the complex social circumstances which provoked the allegations of. As with so many others, the cursing phenomenon had a protracted history. It involved a large group of people. The deeper concerns that underlay this long-running case of cursing in Ashton in Makerfield reveal that there was a hidden agenda and the fact that cursing allegations were dispute about the ownership of property connected with the deaths of family members. In most cursing cases in the communities of the Northwest, sickness and premature infant deaths were similarly revealed to be at the heart of the allegations. Joane Elderson was resolute in her decision not to relinquish the property which she argued belonged to her. Elizabeth Baxter, grief-stricken over the loss of her children, blamed the deaths of her sons on Joane Elderson and she was adamant that the house belonged to her. No recorded outcome is available for this particular case. Nonetheless, the case serves as evidence of a prevalent popular belief in the efficacy of curses to cause harm, leading to women being held responsible for the misfortune experienced by others.

Not all instances of cursing exhibited such a lengthy historical background, nor were they connected to a complex series of offences. Simpler and more straightforward ritualistic curses were not uncommon, often serving as expressions of social discontent and reflecting common grievances. In some cases, there is no history or background information available. However, in each case, the names of those involved, the place, date, and details of the curses which were spoken were recorded. For example, in Clitheroe, in 1607, Anne Jenning cursed a local man's goods, and wished an evil illness would descend upon him and cursed all his actions with plague and trouble. The curse she uttered was 'the plague or curse of god take him and I pray god that with nothinge thou do any tyme will come to good.'[104] During the winter of 1608, Elizabeth Booth from the parish of Alford was accused of cursing John Leigh, despite suspicions surrounding her husband. The outcome of the case and Elizabeth Booth's guilt or punishment remain unknown, as no evidence regarding these details is available. However, the evidence implies that curses had inordinate impact when spoken by a woman. Elizabeth's curse, called forth a religious supernatural power, and for this reason her words offended 'Christiane charite,' when she invoked the wrath of God against neighbour, John Leigh and his family. Although the outcome of the matter is not recorded the curse consisted of of the following words:

> I praie to god that all the plages of god maie light upon thee and thy children [and I] praie god that John Leigh maie rot in prison and I hope God to see John Leigh to rott in prison....[105]

A case from 1616 highlights the varying responses of the courts when it came to allegations of cursing involving both men and women. This suggests that the legal treatment and outcomes differed based on gender in such instances. During a 'public interrogation,' David and Elizabeth Rogers of Holy Trinity, Chester, were accused of cursing the mayor, Robert Jure. David Rogers claimed that he was forced to defend his wife from Robert Jure who had victimised her for years. Robert Jure told the court of 'scandalous and opprobrious speeches uttered unto him by David Rogers.' He said that the Rogers family cursed him by pronouncing the following words:

> Robert Jure art or is a raskal, a false knave, a tainted knave and was a wasted drunkard in Aldersoyt house where he was Maior, and thy tonge should have an ende of thee, thou art a dissemblinge knave, curse thou Robt. Jure, thou art fortified, thou art solitious, thou art an asse and a fool, thou art a base fellow, a curse on you and yours.[106]

Interestingly, the specific accusation of cursing was not levelled by Jure against David Rogers. Instead, Rogers accused Jure of engaging in deceit, perjury, and libel. This highlights the complex nature of their dispute and the variety of charges brought forth, indicating that cursing was not the sole focus of the legal conflict between them.[107] Interestingly, while Jure's words were deemed severe in terms of cursing, it appears that the curses uttered by his wife, Elizabeth Rogers, were considered even more potent and thus more incriminating. This can be attributed, at least in part, to the duration and persistence of her curse over a significant period of time. The narrative suggests that the extended duration of her curse contributed to its perceived potency and its impact on the individuals involved. It was said that she consistently cursed Robert Jure from 1615 to 1616. Obviously, the duration of the curse was as important as the severity of the words spoken. Furthermore, Elizabeth's testimony unveiled that Jure had physically assaulted her, a claim that aligned with her husband's testimony. Her words reverberated with fear and a profound animosity fuelled by a longstanding hostility between them. The curse, reflective of her intense emotions, was repeated within the court proceedings, emphasising the significance and impact of her words on the case as indicated below:

> What thou forsworne man, thou villaine, I hope to see hellish divelles to steale awaie thy soule when thou art deade. May god looke upon Robert Jure and poore thy plague upon him for he hath molested me and troubled me this manie yeares.[108]

While both members of the Rogers family faced charges of defamation, it was solely Elizabeth Rogers who faced the specific accusation of cursing. Surprisingly, the mayor's own misconduct went unpunished, despite evidence suggesting that he, too, had uttered curses. This case highlights the disparity in treatment, indicating that women accused of cursing were more likely to be charged than their male counterparts. This discrepancy may be attributed to the prevailing belief that a woman's curse held a potent and deadly power.

Unravelling the Tangle of Curses, Grief, and Petitions from 1630 to 1640

The underlying motivation for ritual cursing was often rooted in the fear of poverty and starvation. In many cases, women resorted to cursing out of the fear of being left homeless. Additional concerns included the potential loss of property, threats to their families, abandonment, and the risk of jeopardising their essential livelihood or small businesses. These issues formed the core of the disputes that troubled the community, highlighting the desperate circumstances and significant challenges faced by women in their daily lives. The aforementioned conflicts often reached a high point in the form of a formal curse. The existence of such discontent highlights the dynamics of animosity and ill will that ultimately led to charges of cursing in the Northwest region. These cases reflect the deep-seated tensions and conflicts within the community, underscoring the significance attributed to the act of cursing and its consequences within the social fabric of the region. The distress that lay behind ritual banning is manifest and articulated in the depositions and narrative of the women who were accused of cursing. The cursing allegations which are revealed in the court cases frequently reveal a deep emotional torment that arose from sickness, material loss, poverty, or the untimely death of family members as the following legal actions will demonstrate.

On 24 September 1630, Sybill Lingard appeared before the Chester Consistory Court accused of cursing and of having an 'abusive tongue.'[109] However, the depositions soon reveal that Sybill Lingard was desperate with grief at the death of her child. She became an object of mistrust when she did not turn up for church. Sybill Lingard had always been a devoted wife and mother. But when she lost her child, she felt as if a part of her had died with him. It was a loss that she could not bear to speak of and so she withdrew from society, finding solace in her solitude. But her absence from church soon made her the subject of suspicion and gossip. The townsfolk whispered about her, accusing her of cursing her own family and causing their deaths. They did not understand her pain and they did not want to try. In their eyes, she was guilty and there was no other explanation. Sybill wanted to defend herself, but her grief was too great. In the courtroom, Sybill was reluctant to speak of her dreadful situation. After much questioning she reluctantly disclosed that she was ashamed to be seen in public because her husband was involved in a love affair with their neighbour, Cicily Pointer.[110] Subsequently, Sybill described a situation where, throughout the affair, her husband locked away her clothes and forced her to stay indoors.[111] She said that she felt so humiliated by these events that she withdrew from society to the extent that she did not attend church. Later, her husband became ill and, soon after his death, Sybill's child died. Even after suffering the loss of her husband and child, her absence from church made her more susceptible to accusations of cursing. She was later charged with cursing her own family and causing their deaths.[112] Although Sybill Lingard categorically denied having cursed her husband and child, the depositions disclose that she was prepared to accept the punishment of the court. However, the court records are not explicit about the kind of punishment that was imposed on Sybill and gave no indication of the outcome of the matter.[113]

Such events highlight disturbing family problems and affairs of the heart and what was then regarded as adultery. Most situations of cursing attest to a passionate reaction to occurrences of sickness or to the deaths of loved ones. By far the most recurrent disaster in situation of cursing was the death of children and child mortality was high. The community harboured doubts whenever an alleged curse was linked to the loss of a child. Cursing a pregnant woman was deemed especially reprehensible. In 1632, Elanora Patrickson was accused of cursing Maria Robinson, who happened to be pregnant at the time. The act of cursing a pregnant woman heightened the perceived severity of the offence, as it was seen as not only an attack on the individual but also on the unborn child, symbolising a malicious intention to harm both mother and baby.[114] Elanora Patrickson was required to answer charges to the allegation in the Chester Consistory Court before Thomas Staffords.[115] She was questioned by Thomas Staffords about the ritual curses she allegedly pronounced on Maria Robinson who was in labour. The circumstances of the curse involved 'Mary Robinson being in her owne house in extreme paine and travell of childbearing.' Her husband, Thomas Patrickson, was also present. Elanora Patrickson carefully timed her curse to coincide with the most challenging phase of Maria Robinson's labour, amplifying the perceived malevolence of her actions. This account is supported by the testimonies of two witnesses, Dorothy Cowpland and Jenett Sittledall, who provided detailed descriptions of the specific elements involved in the execution of the curse. The intricate 'performance' of the curse, as outlined below, shed light on the calculated nature of Patrickson's actions and the deliberate intent to inflict harm on Maria Robinson during her difficult labour. The curse was delivered dramatically, in the ritual manner, on bended knees, with the hands and eyes raised upwards. Two neighbours, Dorothy Cowpland and Jenett Sittledall who were near neighbours and were present at the cursing. They gave evidence to the court as follows:

> the one assaid the other, how Mary Robinson did, and the other replyed, very sicke, and more like to die than live, or to that effect, and you the said Elanora Pattrickson hearing these speeches, held up your hands and prayed, or rather cursed saying 'I pray God shee may never goe otherwise.'[116]

There is no indication of whether Maria Robinson lived or died but the Robinsons were appalled by the curse, and afterwards brought the matter to the attention of the court. Since legal action was usually taken as a preventive or as a retaliatory measure against the fulfilment of some dreaded scenario, the most likely outcome was that Maria Robinson's child died. The recorded narrative of this action, as with many others, is not clear about whether the allegations were found to be true or false. They do illustrate, however, the fact that cursing was regarded more seriously when it involved the deaths of children. The lawsuits involving cursing delve deeper into the association between curses and the unfortunate deaths of children. These legal cases provide a closer examination of the circumstances surrounding the curses and their alleged connection to the demise of young lives. By exploring these specific instances, a clearer understanding emerges of the belief system that attributed such tragedies to the power and malevolence of curses. The lawsuits shed light on the complex interplay between supernatural beliefs, societal perceptions, and the legal framework in addressing these distressing occurrences.

Lawsuits of cursing provide compelling evidence of the belief that women possessed the ability to inflict misfortune through their curses. Sybill Farclough was one such woman with reputed expertise in the practice of cursing found herself entangled in such a predicament. The lawsuit unravels the perception of her as a powerful figure capable of invoking harm upon others through her mystical abilities. This case highlights the societal inclination to attribute blame to women who were believed to possess the capacity to wield curses as a means of inflicting suffering. Sybill Farclough of Orrell, Lancashire, during the years 1634 to 1638, was accused of causing illness, crop failure, and held responsible for multiple afflictions and unlucky events. Along with various other charges, she was accused of practising cursing several times during that period. Sybill Farclough may well have been a woman of great power, but her power was not well respected. Her words were feared, and her touch was avoided. She lived alone in a small cottage on the edge of town. Her reputation had preceded her, and the townspeople whispered about her, accusing her of invoking supernatural spirits and causing death and destruction. But Sybill was not the monster they made her out to be. She knew that she was a woman who had been blessed with a gift that allowed her to communicate with the spirits of the earth. She used her gift to heal the sick and to bring life to the dying crops. She knew the power of words and the strength they held. But the people were afraid of her, and they did not understand. They accused her of cursing them, of bringing harm to their families, but Sybill knew the truth. She knew that the only harm that came from her was the harm that the people themselves had created. Townsfolk continued to express concerns about her conduct and speech. They described her manner of speaking as 'lewd' and, critically, it was alleged that she had procured several deaths in the neighbourhood by cursing.[117] Her appearance in any domain was reason to suspect disaster. It was broadly understood that wherever she went she created havoc. Even when she looked too long in one direction she was quickly accused of a 'bewitchment' or of 'magick.'[118] She had, like many women who were accused of cursing, a contentious past marked by frequent conflicts with relatives and neighbours. However, when a series of unfortunate events unfolded, resulting in the illness and deaths of local children, she became the focal point of blame. Multiple charges were brought against her, accusing her of directly causing the death of a child. These allegations tied her closely to the tragic events and reinforced the belief that she possessed the power to bring about misfortune through her alleged cursing abilities. The case exemplifies the serious implications and consequences associated with the accusations of cursing, particularly when linked to the loss of innocent lives. Sybill's cousin, Margery Ireland, who brought one of several proceedings against her, believed that Sybill had access to a very particular and destructive supernatural power. Her words indicate that it was common knowledge that Sybill Farclough's curses were potent. It was alleged that with a few well-chosen words she could bring about the death of her enemies and that Sybill could, by 'magick' ensure that her enemies' lives were ruined. On 22 July 1638, Margery Ireland and her Orrell neighbours presented a petition to the Justices of the Peace to remove Sybill from the community. The petition recorded some details of the incidents which had taken place and included Ireland's request that the Justices deal with Sybill:

> may itt please your goode worshippes to take into your consideration your poor petitioners case and by some speedy meanes to take such courses with the said Sybill that your poore petitioner may live quietly and without feare of her life and goods.[119]

Ireland complained, in the statement below, that whenever she met with Farclough, she had borne Sybill's curses and verbal violence. She deposed the following:

> Sybill Farclough being a very wicked lewd and malicious woman hath dyvers and sundry tymes with violent and wicked speeches meeting your poore petitioner threatened her in that regard and her husband.[120]

Sybill's reputation and alleged activities quickly spread through hearsay among her neighbours, reaching the ears of others in the neighbourhood. The petition reveals that the local community was going through challenging times, marked by sickness and worsening fortunes. In such dire circumstances, people began to recollect and attribute their misfortunes to the curses that were believed to have been cast by Sybill Farclough. The memory of her alleged curses became intertwined with the hardships faced by the community, strengthening the perception of her as a source of malevolence and misfortune. The petition they drew up acquainted the Justices with the elements of cursing and the magic that they believed was brought to bear on them. Sybill Farclough, it was said, unrelentingly cursed the Ireland family. They recalled that it was soon after they were cursed that their children became ill. When they were taken with 'strange and sudden diseases' the unfortunate turn of events was attributed to Sybill Farclough's 'cursing,' 'violent and wicked speeches,' 'magick,' and 'wicked and malicious tongue.'[121] The petitioners recounted the following:

> Dyvers of your petitioners had fell into strange and sudden diseases and some of them dyed as alsoe shee threatens her father with the like speeches, and shortly after shee had been, a child dyed in regard whereof your poore petitioner is putt into a continuable and dayly fear both of her lyef and goods by that wicked and malicious tongue of hers.[122]

Soon after the above petition was presented, Sybill Farclough was arrested and charged with cursing. She did not give evidence to the Justices, nor are there further details about her circumstances, only the elementary details that were given to the Justices are presented. What the evidence does reveal is that between 1634 and 1638, a significant number of people, especially children, were dying very suddenly. It was at such crucial times as these that cursing women were held responsible. The petition does not provide specific details regarding the reasons for Sybill Farclough's frequent conflicts with her close relatives and neighbours, nor does it explain her motivations for cursing them. The implications of her curses and the reasons for the perceived threat she posed to those around her are also left unaddressed in the manuscript. However, the evidence from the petition does shed light on the broader context of the community in Orrell during that period. The mention of death, sudden diseases, and concerns about property indicates that these were common issues faced by the community. It suggests a backdrop of hardship and uncertainty, which could have contributed to tensions and conflicts within the neighbourhood. The prevalence of such challenges may have heightened the fears and suspicions surrounding Sybill Farclough, leading to a perception that her alleged curses held the power to cause harm and misfortune to those she targeted. While the manuscript does not delve into the specific dynamics of Sybill's personal conflicts or the motivations behind her curses, it underscores the overall atmosphere of distress and anxieties prevalent in Orrell, which may have influenced the perception of her actions. The testimonies given by Sybill's neighbours provide a striking portrayal of the extensive distress encountered within the community. The fact that Sybill's cursing episodes occurred consistently over a four-year period indicates the existence of a notable crisis in the Orrell community. The prevailing themes of loss and illness that underlie the act of cursing, as documented in the Lancashire Quarter Sessions records, find further confirmation in the extensive evidence found in the records of the Chester Consistory Court and the Quarter Sessions of Cheshire. These recurring patterns of distress and misfortune are indicative of intermittent acute crises occurring in specific towns and villages throughout Northwest England between the years 1630 and 1640.[123]

The curse of Sybill Farclough highlights three significant and recurrent themes pertaining to cursing. First, it illuminates the prevalent association between the deaths of children and accusations of cursing. The belief that curses possessed the power to cause harm to innocent lives, particularly children, was deeply ingrained in the collective consciousness. Second, the case underscores the pervasive fear surrounding women who were believed to possess the ability to curse. Women, in particular, were often associated with a perceived potent and deadly cursing power. The attribution of such power to women reflected broader societal anxieties and stereotypes surrounding female agency and the supernatural. Third, the case provides insights into the adverse social conditions that accompanied situations involving cursing. It reveals the interconnectedness between cursing and accusations of witchcraft in certain regions. The fear of curses and witchcraft was often intertwined, reflecting a climate of suspicion, superstition, and a search for scapegoats during times of distress. Overall, the case of Sybill Farclough sheds light on these enduring themes, emphasising the complex interplay between curses, the perception of female agency, and the social and cultural context in which such accusations and beliefs arose.

The instance of Jenet Wilkinson in Ellel, Lancashire, exhibits a striking resemblance to the observed pattern in cursing cases, and to that of Sybill Farclough. In both instances, a protracted history of neighbourly dispute precedes the allegations of cursing. In the case of Jenet Wilkinson, the cursing incident transpired over a span exceeding ten years, commencing in 1629. The extended duration of the case implies the presence of deep-rooted animosity and ongoing conflicts within the community. This suggests that the disagreements and tensions among neighbours were not easily resolved, prompting the utilisation of curses as a means to express grievances and seek retribution. In the case of Jenet Wilkinson, it becomes evident that cursing served as a manifestation of long-standing disputes and resentments, highlighting a breakdown in social relations and a failure of alternative methods for resolving conflicts. The protracted nature of these cases points to the persistence of contentious relationships within the community and highlights the significance of cursing as a form of retaliation or expression of discontent in such circumstances.[124]

The circumstances surrounding Jenet's curse diverged somewhat from those of Sybill Farclough. The curse's inception can be traced back to a specific dispute regarding property ownership. In contrast to the broader themes of illness and loss associated with Sybill's curse, the central focus in this case revolved around the contentious matter of determining the rightful possession of a particular property. The property dispute acted as a catalyst, intensifying tensions and conflicts between Jenet and the individuals involved. As the disagreements intensified, the use of cursing emerged as a means of exerting power, expressing frustration, and influencing the outcome of the dispute. It highlights the intricate relationship between property disputes and the resorting to cursing as a form of aggression and coercion within the context of legal battles and interpersonal conflicts.

Cases like Jenet's offer insights into the specific factors that could provoke incidents of cursing, underscoring the importance of property ownership disputes as a catalyst for invoking curses. It underscores the intricate interplay between legal conflicts, personal grievances, and the manifestation of curses as a means of exerting control and seeking resolution in complex social dynamics. The individuals central to the case were identified as landowners, highlighting their significance in the context of the property dispute. They were Anne and Thomas Harrison, a Freemason, John Wilson, and Ellen and John Clarke. The circumstances relating to the charge make evident the connections that existed at the time between women and cursing, property ownership, and guilt. The initial incidents from which the dispute grew provide a classic example of how rising tensions in the community might often result in accusations of cursing against women such as Jenet Wilkinson. This cursing was brought to book in October 1629, when Thomas Covell, Justice of the Peace in the county of Lancaster, heard the details.[125] The initial conflict revolving around property, possessions, and finances escalated to the point where Jenet Wilkinson was forcibly evicted from her residence. The owners of the property expressed feelings of unease and remorse over their actions towards her. Subsequently, when they encountered misfortune, they attributed it to Jenet Wilkinson's curse upon them, holding her responsible for their unfavourable circumstances. The dispute about the property served as the fundamental cause of distress. Anne Harrison's deposition revealed that peculiar events started to unfold shortly after Jenet was instructed to vacate the house:

> About nyne or tenne years agonne, Jenet Wilkinson of Ellel, widowe, takinge some displeasure against this Informer and her husband by reason shee was debarred of dwellinge in a house of theires, shee the said Jenet Wilkinson came to this Informers husbands house And Cursed this informer and her husband verie bitterly sayinge unto Thomas Harrison, 'hearest thou, hearest thou (clappinge her hands together) if thou and I live together this shall bee fortie pounds losse to thee.[126]

According to the testimonies of the petitioners, Jenet Wilkinson was a malevolent individual who derived much pleasure from cursing others. The clapping and chanting that accompanied her curse painted a damning picture of her as a wicked villain relishing in the misfortune she invoked. Allegations emerged that shortly after Jenet's curse, the Harrison family's cattle mysteriously perished one by one. Additionally, Anne Harrison claimed to have experienced eerie phenomena, even during her sleep. She asserted that she was haunted by the presence of Jenet Wilkinson, with the face of Jenet appearing before her in her dreams:

> that yearly since the said Thomas Harrison had dyvers of his goods that dyed, which seemed to bee bewitched, amongst which was an heffer three kyne and foure oxen, one of which oxen this Informer caused to bee burnd, And sayth that in the night whylest the said oxe was in burninge, shee was soe troubled with the said Jenet Wilkinson that shee could not rest in her bedd shee still thinckinge the said Jenet was at the bedd syde disquieting her, whereupon this Informer fell to her prayers.[127]

Elizabeth Gervis was an eyewitness to her father's curse and shared the belief that Jenet's curses were accountable for the misfortune that befell their family:

> Elizabeth the wyfe of Edward Gervis upon her oath Informeth that about Nyne or tenne yeares since Jenet Wilkinson aforesaid came to the house of Thomas Harrison aforesaid this Informers father And there Curssed the said Thomas and his wyfe saying if I live this shall bee Fortie pounds losse to thee, And further Informeth that the said Thomas Harrison hath since that tyme had great losse in his goods through death of them.[128]

Other individuals, such as John Wilson, a Freemason residing in Ellel, also experienced a reversal in their fortunes and encountered the haunting presence of Jenet Wilkinson. Despite the absence of specific details regarding any prior dispute between them, Wilson expressed fear about Jenet's alleged magical abilities and the potency of her curse. He firmly believed in her possession of destructive powers, asserting that she had the capability to inflict bodily harm upon him through the assistance of supernatural forces. His testimony confirms that even in his dreams he believed that she could tear him to pieces:

> Who upon his oath Informeth that about three weekes before the takeinge of this Informacion hee this Informer fell sicke, And that about Eight or tenne daies after hee began with the said sicknes hee did see one Jenett Wilkinson of Ellill aforesaid widowe, or the shape of her the said Jenet, come three severall nights together to him this Informer being in bedd, And that hee then verily thought shee the said Jenet did teare him in peeces.[129]

Wilkinson's wife, believing him to be 'forsworne' appealed for a counter-bewitchment, and subsequently went to see a cunning woman to search out a cure for the curse. However, in fear for her life, nothing would induce the cunning woman to assist. She refused to offer a counter-spell for fear of the consequences, as the words below will illustrate:

> And thereupon this Informer suspectinge hee was bewitched hee sent his wyfe twoe severall tymes to a woman whose name hee knoweth not who dwelleth in Morton, which was holden to bee a skillfull woman, which woman tould this Informers wyfe the latter tyme that hee this Informer was forespoken, And tould his said wyfe that shee trusted to mend him, And further sayeth that this Informers said wyfe tould him this Informer that shee asked the said woeman who had forespoken him which woman answered shee would not tell for a thousand pounds, And further hee hath taken his corporall oath that hee is affraide of bodily hurt to bee donne to him this Informer his wyfe or his goods by the said Jenet Wilkinson.[130]

In the testimony provided by Ellen Clarke, the widow of John Clarke, she asserted that the curses issued by Jenet Wilkinson were not only potent but also fatal. Ellen Clarke recounted the circumstances surrounding Jenet's cursing of her husband to the Justices. Although no specific details regarding any dispute or relationship were disclosed, Ellen Clarke claimed that her husband was entirely affected by Wilkinson's curse. As he fell ill, the curse took its toll. His health never regained stability, ultimately leading to his premature demise:

> that about foure yeares since her said late husband beinge at the Plower, Jenet Wilkinson, widowe came by the draught and held up her hand and said 'speed,' (as her said late husband tould this Informer) whereupon the said John Clarke fell sicke presently, And came home where he languished for a month or thereabouts and dyed, And sayeth that dyvers tymes in his sicknes hee complained that the said Jenet Wilkinson was still in his mynd, and that hee verily thought shee had bewitched him.[131]

The supernatural aspects concerning Jenet Wilkinson's curse reveal an intriguing psychological element inherent in the act of cursing. This psychological dimension, intertwined with financial hardships, played a significant role in most cursing cases. Jenet Wilkinson's case highlights the distinct sense of guilt and anxiety that accompanied these disputes among neighbours, particularly concerning financial struggles and property ownership uncertainties. The underlying emotional and financial strains likely fuelled the intensity of the cursing episodes and added depth to the overall narrative. In the case of the Harrisons, Jenet Wilkinson's curse is a case in point that typifies the argument that underlying community tensions often resulted in strong sensations of guilt, for example, the guilt arising in the minds of property-owners who had refused aid to a needy widow.[132] When further difficult situations occurred, local people reacted suddenly and vigorously to incidents that had occurred over ten years before. To explain their own situation, the Harrisons recalled a time when they had forced Jenet Wilkinson out of doors and to leave their property to which they claim that she had reacted with curses. The ensuing loss of their goods, cattle and money is well documented. The dramatic 'burning' of an ox, the feverish and ghostly apparitions of Janet Wilkinson in the night. On three consecutive nights 'the shape of Jenet Wilkinson' appeared in the small hours to terrorise the Wilsons. The fact that John Wilson sought assistance from a cunning woman is yet more evidence of his physical and psychological torment. The locals believed that Jenet's curse would work because the Harrisons felt guilty. The Harrisons certainly, and perhaps the others mentioned in this case, had refused charity to a widow. They had turned her out of doors. As their misfortune increased, so they perceived their association with bad luck, which became more intense and progressively more serious. The cursing allegations against Jenet Wilkinson gradually evolved into a formal court case, spanning over a decade. The Harrisons and Clarkes, who accused Jenet of causing the deaths of their livestock and bewitching their cattle, eventually escalated the accusations to the level of cursing people to death. Their belief in the immense power of Jenet's curse was so strong that they feared she could end the life of John Clarke simply by uttering the word 'speed.' The significant time delay in bringing the case forward to the Justice of the Peace underscores the gravity and complexity of the accusations, as well as the underlying fear and belief in Jenet's deadly supernatural abilities.

The occurrences of cursing, exemplified in the cases of Jenet Wilkinson and Sybill Farclough in the two decades preceding the civil war, highlight that disputes surrounding possessions, land, and property ownership were primary catalysts for such controversies. However, the accusations levelled against Jenet Wilkinson were of a particularly grave nature. Unfortunately, the manuscript does not provide information regarding the ultimate fate of Jenet, leaving her outcome uncertain. Nevertheless, it is worth noting that if it could be substantiated that a woman's curse led to the death of another person, cursing within this context might be deemed a capital offence. Justice Thomas Covell, the Governor of Lancaster Castle, was reputed for his severe handling of such preternatural cases. The reputation of Justice Covell did not bode well for women like Jenet Wilkinson. Whether Jenet was released or met a similar fate to the Lancaster witches who were hanged for witchcraft in 1613 remains unknown.

The discordant incidents that arose within families had the potential to indefinitely disrupt relationships. Petitions filed against accused wrongdoers were frequently brought to court by individuals of various social positions, including yeomen, landowners, husbandmen, and tenants. A comparable case involving cursing, akin to that of Jenet Wilkinson, pertained to the utterance of alleged 'vile and evil curses' spoken by Elene Poole of Ormskirk. This case not only offers intriguing insights into the nature of cursing but also provides information regarding a confession to the crime, the expenses incurred during the legal proceedings, and the fine imposed on the defendant. On 25 June 1635, the court heard the specific details of Elene Poole's cursing directed at Edward Simkins and his family.[133] Simkins complained of her 'very bitter and grievous curses.' Witnesses Thomas and Jane Rookwood supported Simkin's statement and said they heard Elene Poole 'offer very bitter and grievous curses' that besought cruelty and godly retribution and further, invoked 'gods hounds come down and light upon him and his meane wife and family as long as shee lived' and 'bid the divill take him, confounde him, and hoped to see some evil end befall him.' Poole pronounced this curse it was said in full view of the world at large and publicly cursed the couple, as it was confirmed that she 'being in the open street in Christchurch,' declared 'evil and wicked curses' and said 'she will curse them whilst she has ever to live.' The cursing case involving Elene Poole was a protracted legal affair, spanning over a year. The proceedings associated with this case incurred significant expenses, amounting to three pounds, ten shillings, and ten pence. Eventually, Elene Poole confessed to the accusation of cursing, leading to a guilty plea and a fine of ten pence. Elene Poole confessed to the charge of cursing, she was issued with a fine of ten pence arising from a guilty plea, which was legally referred to as a 'confession.'[134]

In 1635, Catherine Sproston of Rosthern found herself in a predicament where her reputation was at stake. She defended herself against the accusation made by William Leigh, who allegedly referred to her as 'a cursed woman known as Jesebel.'[135] This case highlights the potential consequences of being labelled a curser and the concern it caused for the accused individual.' Leigh was asked to respond to Sproston's charge and was asked whether he said 'cursed jesabel' 'in any malicious or angry manner.'[136] The outcome of case however is not recorded.

During the year of 1642 in the Chester Consistory Court there were few cases. From 1643 to 1660 there were none. Of course, this is explained by the closure of the courts during the years of the Civil War and the Cromwellian Commonwealth. Some lawsuits, however, went before the Quarter Sessions at Lancashire. These were mostly petitions brought by women, who sought to clear their good name and who had been imprisoned for cursing or for witchcraft and who were appealing to the Justices to provide for their families while they were serving time in prison. Such confirmation from Lancashire and Cheshire Quarter Sessions suggests that the long-held traditions of cursing most likely continued throughout this period. In general, what the above instances of cursing demonstrate is that imprecations were not merely a matter of public ritual with supernatural associations that sought to invoke the wrath of God. The fact of poverty, eviction from the home, hunger or violence was ever present in the narrative of women. The difficult circumstances they encountered when involved in establishing the paternity of a child cropped up regularly in the records of numerous townships. Petitions concerning paternity or requesting poor relief were presented regularly to Quarter Sessions and were most often granted.[137] Cases of cursing disguise a variety of specific and complex social grievances. Lawbreakers were most often those who transgressed religious and social norms and values, and such acts as avoiding church, or indulging in fornication, or acts of violence such as bullying, or victimisation lie behind many cases of cursing. Spatial control was important to building up a case against a curser. Prostitution as well as adultery appeared often in the records as is demonstrated by some of the cases that are examined here. Although the surviving records relinquish a small amount of information such as the charge and the personal details of those involved, what they reveal more substantially is that cases of cursing went on for months and some for years. Depending on the manuscripts, some court cases contain only one or two lines relating to a charge whilst others continue for scores of pages. The evidence presented above highlights a significant pattern. Women were prominently implicated in each of the cursing indictments. Interestingly, even when men were involved in a particular incident, it was the women who were singled out and charged with cursing. This disparity raises questions about the gendered nature of cursing accusations. Furthermore, the underlying social dynamics behind these instances of cursing provide valuable insights into the nature of cursing itself, as well as the social and material circumstances that greatly impacted the lives of women in the regional Northwest. Exploring these concealed social dimensions can offer a key to an understanding of the prevalence of cursing and its implications for women in that context. It is evident that the social and economic conditions prevailing during that time played a pivotal role in fuelling disputes and exacerbating conflicts that led to cursing incidents. The struggle for property, livelihood, and financial stability created an environment of discontent and desperation, ultimately contributing to the occurrence of cursing cases. Overall, the investigation of these social and economic conditions serves to enhance an understanding of the underlying factors that contributed to the prevalence of cursing during that period and its impact on the lives of women in the regional Northwest. A deeper exploration of the intricate interplay of social and economic factors that were at the very heart of cases of cursing are investigated in further detail in the following chapters.

Notes

1. Cheshire Record Office, Ecclesiastical Records, Chester Consistory Court (henceforward CRO) EDC5/1616/12, Chester, Holy Trinity, Cursing.
2. See, for example, K. Thomas, Religion and the Decline of Magic: Studies in Popular Beliefs in Sixteenth and Seventeenth Century England (London, 1971), p. 600. Joanna Westhide of Herefordshire, in 1617 cursed the churchwarden John Smith 'in words he could not understand.'
3. F. G. Bailey, *Gifts and Poison: The Politics of Reputation* (Oxford, 1971). This study examines the function of gossip in communities. See also A. Clark, 'Whores and Gossips: Sexual Reputation in

London 1770–1825,' in A. Angerman, G. Binnema, A. Keunan, V. Poels and J. Zirkzee (Eds.), *Current Issues in Women's History* (London, 1989). Further literary studies of female spoken issues refer to the representation of female speech on stage and in performance. However, they do not offer an intensive historical analysis of female spoken crime in the community. See, for example, K. Stavreva, *Words like Daggers: Female Speech in Early Modern England* (University of Nebraska Press, 2015) and F. Dolan, *Marriage and Violence: The Early Modern Legacy* (University of Pennsylvania Press, 2009).

4. See, J. Sharpe, *Crime in Early Modern England 1550–1750* (London and New York, 1984), p. 2.
5. K. O'Brien 'Petitioning, Sexual Impropriety and the Dynamics of Ill Will in Daily Urban Life.' *Urban History* 43, no. 2 (2016): 177–196.
6. D. Underdown, 'The Taming of the Scold: The Enforcement of Patriarchal Authority in Early Modern England,' A. Fletcher and J. Stevenson (Eds.), *Order and Disorder in Early Modern England* (Cambridge, 1985).
7. In the same period, in Devon, numbers of female ale-house keepers decreased. There was also an increase in defamation cases involving sexual slander of women. See J. A. Thompson, *"Her Good Name and Credit": The Reputation of Women in Seventeenth Century Devon* (University of Cincinnati, 1984), p. 103.
8. F. Young, *Magic as a Political Crime in Medieval and Early Modern England: A History of Sorcery and Treason. International Library of Historical Studies* (London, New York, 2018).
9. C. R. Chapman, *Ecclesiastical Courts: Their Officials and Their Records* (Dursley, 1992), p. 17. Chapman argues that 'From at least the mid-twelfth century the ecclesiastical courts in England and Wales operated at four levels in increasing seniority from archdeaconal, diocesan and provincial to papal, presided over originally by an archdeacon, bishop, archbishop and the Pope.'
10. C. B. Herrup, *The Common Peace: Participation and the Criminal Law in Seventeenth Century England* (Cambridge, 1987), p. 2. See also, J. Sharpe, *Crime in Seventeenth-century England* (Cambridge, 1983), R. B. Shoemaker, *Prosecution and Punishment: Petty Crime and the Law in London and Rural Middlesex, c.1660–1725* (Cambridge, 1991), and M. Ingram, *Church*

Courts, Sex and Marriage in England, 1570–1640 (Cambridge, 1987).

11. The Consistory Court papers record numerous cases where offenders were punished in this way.
12. For further information about the legal proceedings regarding the execution of women accused of cursing children, see Chester City Records Office, Town Hall, Chester, Extracts of Fines (QSPE) Rolls of Offences, Gaol and House of Corrections, (QAG) 1575, and see also J. P. Earwaker, *The History of the Church and Parish of St. Mary on the Hill, Chester* (London, 1898), p. 28.
13. See, for example, J. Hall, *Nantwich* (1899), p. 72.
14. Ibid.
15. See, for example, the Countess of Warwick Fee, Nantwich 23 October 1632, in D4059/30 James Hall's notebook, Cheshire Record Office. Hall wrote: 'they were not put on the ducking-stool.' He claimed that there is no proof such an instrument of punishment for this liberty existed, but also notes that there was one in Nantwich.
16. F. A. Bailey (Ed.), *Prescot Quarter Sessions Records, 1447–1600*, The Record Society of Lancashire and Cheshire, Volume 89 (1937), pp. 80–81. An 'amercement' was the term used to describe a judgment.
17. Ibid. pp. 96–97. A note read: 'a payne of xxs. upon the inhabitants of Prescott for makinge of a cuckestool before Michelmas next to be levied from the goods of the tenants.'
18. All Hallows Eve became a significant date in witchcraft folklore.
19. J. A. Twemlow, (Ed.), *Liverpool Town Books, Proceedings of Assemblies, Common Councils, Portmoot Courts, 1550–1862*, Volume II, 1571–1603 (Liverpool, 1935), p. 308 and p. 423. 'Also, we fynde that the lord shuld make a payre of stocks, and a kucstole.'
20. F. A. Bailey, (Ed.), op cit. p. 106.
21. J. A. Twemlow, (Ed.), op. cit. p. 600.
22. Ibid. p. 600.
23. Ibid.
24. Ibid. p. 635.
25. Ibid. p. 635.
26. Ibid. p. 740.
27. Ibid. pp. 530–531.

28. J. Callow, *The Last Witches of England: A Tragedy of Sorcery and Superstition* (London, 2022).
29. Oxford Record Office, MS Oxfordshire Diocesan papers, 1546 ff. 73v, 74, 74v, 75, 75v, 76, 76v, 83v, 84, 84v, 85, 85v, 86v, 87, 87v.
30. Oxford Records Office, Depositions of Thomasina Linck, 1616–1620, Oxon, c.118–f223, Wydowe Linck.
31. Ibid.
32. Ibid.
33. CRO EDC5/1633/60.
34. Ibid.
35. CRO EDC5/1594/18. Richard Masterton, Anne Masterton, for cursing.
36. CRO EDC5/1588/2.
37. Ibid.
38. Ibid.
39. CRO EDC5/1601/7 Parish of Manchester, diocese of Chester. Margaret Cheetham, Ellis Prestwyche.
40. Ibid.
41. K. O'Brien, 'Intimate Worlds: Kinship Relations and Emotional Investment among Nantwich Women 1603–1685.' *Journal of Family History* 41, no. 2 (April 2016): 131–143; K. O'Brien, 'Companions of Heart and Hearth: Hardship and the Changing Structure of the Family in Early Modern Townships.' *Journal of Family History*, 39, No. 3, (2014).
42. Lancashire Record Office (henceforward, LRO) QSB1/170/55. The term 'knaves, whores and chyders' is derived from a transcript of a case that came before the Lancashire Quarter Sessions in 1630.
43. LRO QSB1/170/58.
44. See for example, CRO EDC5/1635/72. In this case a woman is cited for cursing and for behaving in a 'lewd' way. See also EDC5/1637/27 with reference to cursing and 'Jesebel.' Also see EDC5/1635/87 where a woman is cited for associating with consorting with those who were prone to drinking, gambling, and for attending cockfights.
45. CRO EDC5/1592/35. Cicillia Collinge of Prestwich named as a 'lewde and naughte woman.'
46. CRO EDC5/1683/37 Nantwich.

47. CRO EDC5/1567/19 Nantwich.
48. CRO EDC5/1568/3 Nantwich.
49. CRO EDC5/1572/5 Nantwich.
50. CRO EDC5/1593/24 Nantwich.
51. CRO EDC5/1596/71 Nantwich.
52. CRO EDC5/1597/76 Nantwich.
53. CRO EDC5/1597/76 Nantwich.
54. CRO EDC5/1597/76 Nantwich.
55. CRO EDC5/1600/14 Nantwich.
56. CRO EDC5/1601/2 Nantwich.
57. CRO EDC5/1602/14 Nantwich.
58. CRO EDC5/1604/38 Nantwich.
59. CRO EDC5/1602/14 Nantwich.
60. CRO EDC5/1608/50 Nantwich.
61. CRO EDC5/1609/102 Nantwich.
62. CRO EDC5/1615/33 Nantwich.
63. CRO EDC5/1620/26 Nantwich.
64. CRO EDC5/1620/27 Nantwich.
65. CRO EDC5/1621/46 Nantwich.
66. CRO EDC5/1628/41 Nantwich.
67. CRO EDC5/1630/55 Nantwich.
68. CRO EDC5/1631/15 Nantwich.
69. CRO EDC5/1631/81 Nantwich.
70. CRO EDC5/1635/87 Nantwich.
71. CRO EDC5/1635/87 Nantwich.
72. CRO EDC5/1636/9 Nantwich (Adultery), EDC5/1636/10 (Cruelty),
73. CRO EDC5/1637/120 (Adultery), CRO EDC5/1640/72 (Adultery).
74. CRO EDC5/1638/99 Nantwich.
75. CRO EDC5/1640/73 Nantwich.
76. CRO EDC5/1611/27.
77. Ibid.
78. Ibid.
79. Ibid.
80. J. Simpson, 'Witches and Witchbusters.' *Folklore* 107 (1996): 5–18.
81. See CRO EDC5/1618/45, Elizabeth Boude, Rostherne, Chester, which contains the words 'thiefe whore and witch.'

82. LRO QSB1/170/58.
83. Ibid.
84. Ibid.
85. Ibid.
86. Ibid.
87. See LRO Quarter Sessions records, QSB1/170/60, QSB1/170/55 and QSB1170/64, which contains details of accusations against Joane Elderson that she cursed children to death.
88. LRO QSB1/170/55.
89. Ibid.
90. Ibid.
91. Ibid.
92. Ibid.
93. LRO QSB1/170/60.
94. Ibid.
95. Ibid.
96. LRO QSB1/170/64. A substantial case involving many groups of townsfolk in dispute about a house and money. This case is also connected with QSB1/170/55.
97. Ibid.
98. Ibid.
99. Ibid.
100. Ibid.
101. Ibid.
102. Ibid.
103. Ibid.
104. CRO EDC5/1607/25 Cursing Libel, Clitheroe.
105. CRO EDC5/1609/27 Aldford, Elizabeth Booth and Robert Booth. 1608 and 1609.
106. Ibid. Deposition of Robert Jure.
107. CRO EDC5/1616/12 Chester, Holy Trinity, Cursing
108. Ibid.
109. CRO EDC5/1630/50.
110. Ibid.
111. Ibid.
112. Ibid.
113. Ibid.
114. CRO EDC5/1632/32 Cursing of a pregnant woman.
115. Ibid.

116. Ibid.
117. LRO QSP/1634–1638. Sybill Farclough.
118. Ibid.
119. Ibid.
120. Ibid.
121. Ibid.
122. Ibid.
123. C. B. Phillips and J. H. Smith, op cit. p. 11. See also Wrigley and Schofield, op. cit. p. 651, C. D. Rogers, *The Lancashire Population Crisis of 1623* (Manchester, 1975), and A. Appleby, op. cit. p. 147. These studies support the view that there were a number of spasmodic local crises in the Northwest, especially during the 1590s, 1620s, and 1630s. See also R. Houston, *Social Relations and Economic Life on Landed Estates, 1600–1850* (Routledge, 2014) and for a close study of poverty in Lancashire, see J. Healey, *The First Century of Welfare—Poverty and Poor Relief in Lancashire, 1620–1730* (Boydell and Brewer, 2014). For a broader exploration of law and the relationship between law and religion in the communities of England see J. Bogiato, A. Green, M. Lobban, *Law, Lawyers and Litigants in Early Modern England* Essays in Memory of Christopher W. Brooks (Cambridge, 2019).
124. LRO QSB1/64/21–23, 1629.
125. Ibid.
126. Ibid.
127. Ibid.
128. Ibid.
129. Ibid.
130. Ibid.
131. Ibid.
132. K. Thomas, *Religion and the Decline of Magic* (London, 1971).
133. CRO EDC5 1635/7.
134. Ibid.
135. CRO EDC 5 1637/27.
136. Ibid.
137. See, for example, S. Howard, (Ed.) Quarter Sessions. *Petitions to the Cheshire Quarter Sessions, 1573–1798*, *British History Online* http://www.british-history.ac.uk/petitions/cheshire [accessed 12 February 2020].

CHAPTER 4

The Interplay of Curses, Social Crisis, and Economic Instability

The socio-economic background reveals much about the context in which cases of cursing occurred. It provides an intimate understanding of the nature of the crisis that lay behind most incidents of cursing. The following inquiry examines the social and economic conditions that gave rise to conflict and a lack of empathy within relationships in the communities of the Northwest region. It investigates the influence of economic volatility on these communities and explores whether there were unique factors that distinguished the Northwest from other regions in England. Some of the earliest pioneering work of the region is based largely on primary sources of various archives of the regional Northwest.[1] In respect of growth and development, the Northwest region of England was certainly different from other English regions and its economy was well developed. The records that incorporate the features of the broad social and economic conditions that prevailed during the period are helpful in providing the social and economic context within which conflict arose in the effort to exert an increase in the control of female speech and activity.

The distinctive economic mechanisms and governance structure of the Northwest region played a vital role in shaping the circumstances that gave rise to cursing, particularly in conjunction with an unprecedented growth in population. This combination set the stage for a significant amount of discord and conflict among the townships. In order to

K. O'Brien, *Cursing, Crisis and Customary Knowledge in Early Modern English Townships*, Palgrave Historical Studies in Witchcraft and Magic,
https://doi.org/10.1007/978-3-031-44045-8_4

gain a comprehensive understanding of the occurrence of cursing, it is imperative to first comprehend the social and economic framework of the Northwest region. A thorough exploration of the complex social dynamics and economic organisation within the region allows for a deeper comprehension of the fundamental factors that contribute to the manifestation of cursing. By examining the interplay between societal structures, interpersonal relationships, and economic conditions, a clearer understanding of the root causes and motivations behind instances of cursing can be achieved.

The Northwest comprises two main counties: Lancashire and Cheshire. Lancashire is the larger area, containing 1,183 square miles and Cheshire contains 900 square miles. The combined total area of the region is 2,083 square miles, representing 5.83% of England's total area of 50,331 square miles. In 1563 the population density of the Northwest was low. The population of the Northwest is estimated to have been 146,000, or 4% of the three million total population in England. By 1664 this number had risen to 240,000 or 4.6% of the 5.1 million total population of England.[2] The population of Lancashire in 1664 was 141,641 and Cheshire was 94,170. The two populations combined were 235,811, representing 4.6% of the 5.1 million total population of England.[3]

In terms of its religious organisation the diocese of Chester was one of the six English dioceses established in 1541 by Henry VIII. Its function was to exercise religious and moral control over the region's population. The Chester Consistory Court was there to exercise moral control over the population. Its territory included Lancashire and Cheshire. The diocese was geographically diverse. Cheshire was a prosperous area, which consisted of flat arable land with pastures, meadows, and large areas of parks and woodlands. Market gardening was an essential part of the economy. Cheshire produced oats, barley, rye, and wheat. Its inhabitants also bred cattle and poultry. Medieval Lancashire, in its southwest, possessed large forests and moorland, however, this land had been cleared, divided, and enclosed by the seventeenth century. East Lancashire, in contrast with Cheshire, was mountainous with some moorlands. Peat mosses and marshes made communications between Cheshire and Lancashire difficult.[4] The diocese of Chester was 120 miles long and 570 miles in circumference. It included 533 churches and parochial chapels.[5] It also incorporated within its boundaries Flintshire parishes, parts of Westmorland and Cumberland as far as Workington, and, in the east, large areas of Yorkshire. The following deaneries were established to make administration easier: Copeland, Furness, Kendal, Lonsdale, Richmond, Catterick, Boroughbride, Amounderness, Blackburn, Leyland, Warrington, Manchester, Frodsham, Wirral, Chester, Middlewich, Macclesfield, Nantwich, Malpas, Bangor, and parts of Flintshire.[6]

The size of the diocese presented difficulties for its proper management. It was described by Bishop Downham, in 1561, as 'a poorly endowed, monstrously large and administratively unmanageable ecclesiastical unit.'[7] As a consequence, religious authorities registered their concern about the region's moral and spiritual welfare. What they regarded as pagan superstition was common practice in the population. In the western parts of Lancashire, Catholicism retained its hold.[8] The irreligious characteristics, notably common in the Northwest, may have contributed to the view that the region was backward. Though the region's population may well have been largely irreligious, it is important to recognise that such beliefs co-existed in a society with a remarkably developed economy and that it was an economic system which for most of the time was able to feed, clothe, and shelter those who lived there. It is interesting to note how wealth was distributed. The communities of Lancashire and Cheshire cannot be classified as wholly rural. Some were rural, some were urban, and some were both. The combination of exceptional pasture and the manufacture of salt made Cheshire a wealthy county. The Weaver valley ran through the heart of Cheshire where the salt towns of Nantwich and Northwich were situated. Salt was extracted from brine-springs and produced an industry that aided the manufacture of cheese, for which Cheshire was famous. Salt-making in the three 'wiches' ('wic' being the old English term for trading place) of Nantwich, Northwich, and Middlewich had taken place since Roman times. Details of the salt industry were included in the Domesday Book. Nantwich, a market town in southeast Cheshire, was involved in the salt industry, but did not become important as a salt town until Anglo-Saxon times. Christopher Saxton's map of Cheshire illustrates the lie of the land and the distribution of parishes in 1577.[9] According to John Speed's maps of Cheshire and Lancashire, in 1627 there were 123 settlements in Cheshire and 70 settlements in Lancashire; a total of 193 settlements in all.[10]

Mortality Crisis and Social Structure in Lancashire and Cheshire

Given the close association between cursing and hardship or poverty, it is crucial to obtain an accurate understanding of the social conditions that underlie cursing phenomena. The examination of Hearth Tax returns proves valuable in assessing the extent of poverty within a given community or region. By analysing these records, insights can be gained regarding the economic struggles and social challenges faced by individuals and households, shedding light on the context in which cursing incidents occur. The years 1563 and 1664 are significant for the estimation of the region's population. In parochial returns of 1563, families were counted by chapelry and parish, and grouped into rural deaneries. The Hearth Tax returns for 1664 list the names of heads of households in townships of hundreds.[11] Because many poor households were listed as 'tax exempt,' with the very poorest excluded from some records, the 1664 Hearth Tax returns provide ***minimum*** figures for the population. According to the parochial returns of 1563 there were 12,703 households in Cheshire and 17,314 in Lancashire. The returns counted only the male head of the household, and ignored the rest of the family, so there is no definite population figure.[12]

Because it was unusual for parish population sizes to change notably in the short term, a large short-term increase in the number of deaths is an indication of a rise in mortality.[13] High levels of mortality are indicative of disease and famine. The distribution and chronology of burials over deaths varied in the region, with growth measurable up to the late 1580s, after which losses followed. There were fluctuations again to the mid-1620s, followed by a resumption of growth that halted in the 1650s. Crisis levels of mortality were scattered among the parishes. In Cheadle in 1587 and 1589 deaths increased by a third. In southeast Cheshire, Nantwich had burials of 114 and 117 in 1623 and 1624 respectively. These represented increases of 40% and 43% respectively on the decennial average. Another peak occurred in 1629, when 134 people were buried.[14] In Lancashire, studies show that famine, and probably famine fevers, were responsible for the excess mortality in 1623. It was found that there was crisis mortality throughout the North, but it was more desperate in Lancashire where famine swept through the townships.

Nantwich Township: Turmoil and Discord

Records from the Cheshire Inquisitions Post Mortem,[15] Cheshire Quarter Sessions,[16] and Chester Consistory Court, reveal substantial information about the discord which existed in seventeenth-century Nantwich. Seventeenth-century Nantwich was a much-troubled town and there are many indications of this discord. Some townsfolk who were employed by local gentry refused to work. Neighbours were at loggerheads with the Nantwich Churchwardens who repeatedly found themselves the targets of hatred. Churchwardens were the recipients of much foul speech and violent acts. Neighbours fought each other over trivial matters, while some clashed in church, pushing each other out of pews, anxious to maintain their status in the church hierarchy which accurately reflected the social order of the town. Nantwich nurses were forced to look after plague victims and were then cheated of their pay. They had their complaints heard by the Justices of the Peace at Nantwich Quarter Sessions. The starving, 'maymed soldiers' of the 'Scotch' invasion, appealed for justice as did the many widows of Nantwich soldiers who died in the wars. The records are full of details of the social conflict which arose from hardship imposed upon Nantwich at the time of the Civil War. During this period, women began to be dealt with more harshly. Some women, who were accused of verbal crimes were publicly whipped. Some were imprisoned for slander. Certain townsfolk were incarcerated for stealing a few shillings. Some people could not tolerate the harsh conditions which their employers imposed on them. For example, Justices Richard Wilbraham, Thomas Delves, and George Cotton in 1627 heard how Randle Hampton abused the Churchwardens. The Churchwardens complained: [Hampton] 'will not work on highways and gave ill language bidding us do the worst we can for he will neither work nor pay.'[17] In similar fashion, in 1630, widow Mary Bressy of Willaston, refused to work for 'Cheny house ground.' It is likely that either she was not paid according to her expectations, or she was expected to work too hard for too little. It is not made clear in the records what happened to Mary Bressey. The evidence from several sources reveals hostile popular attitudes towards the Churchwardens. The records make it abundantly clear that they were the least popular people in the town. When, in 1627, Churchwarden Thomas Sparrow reported Nantwich labourer, Thomas Harrison, who had accused him of being responsible for having three men executed, Harrison responded violently. The Churchwarden responded by seeking revenge through the Justices for his intemperate conduct in Nantwich church.[18] Harrison was accused of abusing the bellringer who, according to the report, was 'then Ringinge for the funeral of Ladie Lee.' Harrison 'violently' grabbed the rope from them, and 'walking up and down the church in a most abusive manner reproaching and revyling him with many opprobrious and malicious speeches, saying viz; thou art a basse fellow, a home bred Rogue, a whyte lyvered rascall and hathe hanged three men.'[19] Thomas Sparrow asked the Justices to 'inflict some punishment.'[20] It is more likely than not, that Sparrow was punished. Similarly, on 24 February 1653, Sir Thomas Mainwaring, heard how Richard Jackson, shoemaker, attacked the Churchwardens 'with a great logge of wood' and refused to pay a church 'Ley' [tax] of sixpence.[21] Mainwaring issued the Churchwardens with a warrant for Jackson's arrest.

'All These Late Warres'[22]

In the aftermath of the Civil War, the details of conflict and poverty were often relayed to the Justices by ex-soldiers. For example, in 1650, Thomas Oulton and Denis Brayne, both of Nantwich, were forced to request a pension to keep them from begging and starving. These two soldiers had fought on the side of Parliament during the civil war. Oulton, a soldier in the 'Trayned Band' of Nantwich, said that he was in service for 26 years. He was shot through the left leg and disabled. He told of the efforts of Lord Capel's forces from Nantwich who fought at the bridge in 1644, and of the two assaults made by the Parliament forces during which he was wounded and literally 'left for dead on the ground.'[23] Denis Brayne described himself as 'a maymed soldier in the service of Ireland against those Monsters the rebells of Ireland under the command of Sir Charles Vavasour.'[24] His responsibilities included 'keeping out such persons as should come to this town from any place infected with that heavy visitation the Plague.' It was during this time that an 'Irish rogue' fell upon him and swore to 'bite off his nose.'[25] Oulton was paid 40s per year, which was to begin 'next Lady Day.' There is no record of what Brayne received, but it is likely that he received a similar pension.[26] Comparably, 'private soldiers' from Nantwich in 1651 told Justices Mainwaring, Delves, and Croxton that they were fighting on the side of Parliament and 'inlisted in the regiment of Colonel Croxton [and] to serve for the town.'[27] They were promised pensions which they did not receive. In the same year, certificates were produced which identified some of the Cheshire men who served under the command of Thomas Malbon and were wounded during the Scottish invasion. They considered themselves to be 'very poore.'[28] William Walley, Richard Ellyson, and Robert Lowndes each were wounded when they fought under Captain Malbon, in an 'expedition against the Scots.'[29] The Justices ordered that the soldiers be given 50 shillings and another 50 shillings when cured.[30]

Widows, Orphans, 'Maymed' [sic] Soldiers

Women and children suffered similarly from the effects of war because their marriage partners were either disabled or killed. Women who nursed the sick were often underpaid. Sometimes they were not paid at all. The records demonstrate that Nantwich had problems with the devaluation of currency. Two Nantwich nurses, Margaret Walker and Ellin Danham, were sent for by the Constables of Middlewich to nurse plague victims in Manchester in 1649. They travelled at great inconvenience to and from Manchester but were paid with money they could not spend. They were forced to petition the Justices when they received 'clipt money' and were out of pocket 'having spent more than they have received.'[31]

Besides losing a beloved partner, widows of the wars were reduced to poverty and found that the process of applying for a pension was fraught with difficulty. Their petitions disclose that they sought to negotiate the terms by which they were expected to prove the deaths of their husbands.[32] Recent research also shows that they suffered significant hardship.[33] In 1651, Anne Merryman, Elizabeth Crowther, Katherine Peake, and Anne Parke, who was described as 'a very poore woman,' appealed to the Justices for a pension because their husbands were killed in service in Scotland. The women did not receive pensions immediately. Overseers of the poor were ordered to provide for them until the next sessions.[34] It took until 1661, immediately following the Restoration, for the Justices to issue an order to widows, orphans, and maimed soldiers to appear before them in relation to the payment of pensions.[35] The order, which was issued to respective head constables within their hundreds, included the following words:

> Whereas there hath been a great number of Maymed souldiers widowes and orphans within this county ... and seeing that several Souldiers were maymed in his late Ma'ts service and some slayne who left widdowes and

orphans in great distress and penury it is therefore thought fitt and ordered by this court that there shall be a general review of all pensioners.

Poverty and Mortality

By exploring townships, researchers and scholars can gain insights into the economic, social, and religious dynamics that shaped the region and influenced patterns of poverty and infant mortality. In the investigation of poverty levels and infant mortality in the Northwest region, Nantwich serves as an illustrative example of a prosperous market town in Cheshire, comparable to Manchester. Nantwich was characterised by its economic advancement and a prominent non-conformist presence, sharing similarities with Manchester. Additionally, Nantwich had substantial trading connections with London, further contributing to its economic development and prosperity. By examining such towns, we can gain insights into the economic, social, and religious dynamics that shaped the region and influenced patterns of poverty and infant mortality. This township offers a microcosm of the prevalent poverty situation that existed throughout the Northwest region. First, Nantwich was geographically well located at a strategic communications point at the centre of two main arterial routes between the north and south. On the whole, it was a wealthy town, and had strong trading links with London, and it experienced significant conflict during the period from 1660 to 1670. The prevailing economic and social conditions of the town were important determinants of the levels of female independence within the domestic sphere. In practice, some women played an important role in household management, the domestic industry, agriculture and in the professions of midwifery and nursing. However, it is clear from Nantwich's 'Buglawton Rent that poverty was widespread.'[36] The Poor Rate Assessments indicate that the children of impoverished parents were often forced into work due to dire economic circumstances because they attracted family support from charities if working.[37] In this way, children contributed to the upkeep of families that, for much of the time, lived in conditions of desperate hardship. Communities took their grievances to the legal institutions which were bursting at the seams to accommodate a highly litigious society. Such activity occurred against a background of fractured religious organisation in a society that was adapting itself to the pressures of the competing religious and economic ideologies. The process involved in this ideological struggle is explored in more detail below.

As with Northampton society, which was matriarchal because marriage to a widow conferred freeman's status on the male, it may well have been in the interest of the male population to promote marriage and with it female dependency as an imperative.[38] The distribution of wealth amongst the population of Nantwich and the disharmony which often arose from the social hardships, illness, poverty, and, above all, episodes of high child mortality in the town are registered in Wills and Inventories. These, with the Nantwich Hearth Tax records, provide a key to understanding the distribution of wealth in the town, and provide a portrait of the town's resources.[39] Nantwich women's wills convey their financial independence. The representation of Nantwich provided by the wills shows that, at the very least, women were often in control of their own lives, and, in many cases, they were also intimately involved in the lives of those they employed. In most cases, the extent of their wealth is indicative of their success in several avenues of trade and business which was a world often dominated by the skilled and the competitive, and clearly, Nantwich women contributed significantly to this world.[40] Information from the 1664 Nantwich Hearth Tax is supported by information from the Nantwich parish registers to reflect the population and its distribution throughout Nantwich, and the numbers of birth, deaths, and marriages that took place. Emphasis is placed upon the numbers of children who died during this period, particularly those in infancy.

Detailed sources that shed light on the lives of the lower socio-economic strata are scarce. However, the Buglawton Rent emerges as a crucial historical document that offers valuable insights into this often-overlooked segment of society. Specifically, the source provides information about the impoverished residents of Hospital Street in Nantwich. By utilising this data, a more comprehensive and balanced perspective of the town can be achieved, considering the experiences and conditions of its less privileged inhabitants. An investigation into the origins of social antagonism that triggered a significant prevalence of female spoken crime, and the subsequent overwhelming response, during the period from 1660 to 1670 in Nantwich, requires an examination of the affluent and powerful individuals, those of middling status, and the impoverished members of the community. By closely analysing these different social groups, it is possible to unravel the underlying factors contributing to the heightened level of female spoken crime and the societal reactions it elicited during that specific timeframe.[41] The county of Cheshire Hearth Tax for which there are no available Hearth Tax studies, provides intimate details of charity, health, hardship, credit and debt, and the accompanying struggles that were played out in the social sphere as the family configuration changed often according to fluctuating socio-economic circumstances. The wills, inventories, probate records, deeds, poor accounts, and parish records provide an insight into hardship through a close study of all the poor in one street in 1664. This reveals that poor children worked hard and, when apprenticed, were also compulsorily separated from the family home, and that child mortality was equally high among rich and poor people in early modern Nantwich townships.[42]

Infant Mortality

The occurrence of cursing and its connection with social hardship was certainly true of the 1630s and the 1640s in several places in Lancashire. The connection was particularly evident in the case of Nantwich during the years from 1660 to 1670, when a notable increase in litigation was observed. Nantwich shared much in common with numerous other townships, where social difficulties were often expressed in litigation that arose from cursing, which was often provoked by the hardships of the material world. Investigation of the circumstances connected with cursing finds that many of the Nantwich townsfolk involved were in debt. Women who were caught up in the dramas of cursing often expressed their concern about midwifery practices, and some gave evidence of the details which tell of the circumstances of infant and child mortality. The loss of infants, or anticipation of such loss, drove some women to take extreme measures. There was acute social stress related to infant deaths in Nantwich in the decade from 1660 to 1670. It is noteworthy to draw attention to a variation in the distribution of Nantwich families between 1660 and 1779 that was found in a study of Nantwich and the surrounding parishes, and further analysis is called for to explain this distribution.[43] It is crucial to examine the numbers of children that were born in Nantwich during the period from 1660 to 1670. The following investigates evidence about child mortality, that is, the data which points to the deaths of small children through cyclical illnesses, such as fevers, measles, and smallpox. Firstl, it is important to consider the numbers of births. The Nantwich Parish Registers of Saint Mary's Church recorded a total number of 1017 baptisms in Nantwich between the years 1660 and 1670 and, as 37 children were children born outside Nantwich and baptised, this meant that 980 children born in that decade were born in the parish of Nantwich. According to the Nantwich Parish Registers, there were on average 98 children born every year from 1660 to 1670. Two typical years can be shown in more detail. From 1 January 1662 to 31 December 1662, there were 88 children baptised. Of these, 85 children were born within Nantwich, while three were born outside Nantwich. In this year there was only one illegitimate child baptised. Between 25 March 1663 and 24 March 1664, a total number of 91 children were baptised at Nantwich church. Of this number, 88 were born in Nantwich and three were born outside Nantwich. There were three sets of twins baptised, and four illegitimate children were baptised.[44]

In Nantwich there was a cyclical pattern of burials of children. The numbers of children buried doubled every six years from 1650 to 1699. Wyatt argues that 'At age 1–4, six parishes had more female infant mortality between 1650 and 1699, one had less, and one had the same.'[45] Although this is a slightly later period than the one under analysis, there is no evidence to suggest that things would have been much different during the period 1660 to 1670. The Nantwich study reflects an increase in adult burials as well as children. The study found that there were cyclical epidemics of smallpox, measles, and other infectious diseases. Young children were more likely to die from infectious diseases than were older children. Many of the peak mortality years followed a seasonal pattern. Measles occurred between September and July, peaking at the end of March and was concentrated in a few months. Children aged between one and four years were most likely to die. It was found that 'many women would not live to the end of their child-bearing period.'[46] Similarly, it was suggested that 'most of the burials of women dying within one month of the baptism of her child, and practically all those within one week would be because of traumatic childbirth.'

Scholars have put forward the idea that 'something restricted women from having as many children as they might have done.'[47] A study of the Nantwich people traced from marriage to burial shows that the biggest group were those with no children, and next were those with only one child. No doubt women dying in childbirth accounts in part for these figures.[48] Bad midwifery practices were also considered to be a cause, but more research is needed in this area to support this claim. The petition of cursing presented against midwife, Anne Knutsford of Nantwich discussed below, for example, illustrates how she legally protected herself against the evidence in depositions given by her neighbours, who accused her of being drunk while attending a birth.[49] The evidence of the Anne Knutsford case relating to accusations of cursing and poor midwifery confirms that deaths of new-borns were likely to be because of disease rather than the dangers of childbirth. The petition attesting to her skill is broadly supported by women of the town of Nantwich, moreover they agreed that most midwives in Nantwich were proficient in their profession.[50]

Archival evidence substantiates the presence of numerous contradictions within towns like Nantwich during the period from 1660 to 1670. The wills of affluent women reveal that certain female residents possessed substantial wealth, while those at the lower end of the social hierarchy experienced extreme poverty. Infant mortality was high in Nantwich and children born to poorer families faced a life of hard work. The laws governing the births of illegitimate children were severe, as was the punishment of so called 'bastard-bearers.' Paternity petitions were often presented by women. In addition, during cycles of illness, particularly epidemics such as measles, young children lost their lives at a higher rate than usual. At certain periods, an entire family might be wiped out. As set out above, most families in Nantwich were touched by the loss of at least one child. The distress caused by such loss, together with the scarcity of essential services, such as midwives and nurses, the sorrow of those who were impoverished by previous wars, rising tension about social status, property disputes, gender divergence, and territorial squabbles over social space come together to make the communities within towns of the Northwest extremely volatile.

Evidence from the 1660s confirms that the middle strata of Nantwich, who were upwardly mobile lived in the shadow of debt.[51] Some of those families, according to the evidence, were even forced to compromise their ideals of respectability to survive. Such people lived in fear, and were, during the period under question, found to be constantly in conflict with each other. Such circumstances, when considered alongside the periods of life-threatening illness, had a devastating effect on the children. What each member of Nantwich society shared was the fact that his or her children were in danger of being struck down. Fevers, measles, and smallpox took the lives of many children, and all mothers, even wealthy ones, such as Maria Wilbraham, risked their lives in childbirth. The decade from 1660 to 1670, and particularly the year 1663, stand out as a period of an unusually high rate of prosecutions in Nantwich.[52] Archival evidence discloses with great certainty the fact that Nantwich was a deeply divided community during the time in question. Some wives, even those of gentlefolk, were forced to imperil their good names when harsh conditions forced them to offer landlords sex instead of money.

In general terms, the investigation of Church court records discloses a colossal wide-ranging legal struggle which was related to moneylending, property ownership, and overwhelmingly concerned with maintaining one's status in the fluctuating circumstances. The desperate social and economic circumstances that were present in towns throughout the region were more acute in Nantwich where the familiar themes of sickness, money shortages, and concerns about property, surfaced regularly.

The numbers of children which women bore was affected by social status. Upper-class women married at an average of 20 years of age in the late sixteenth century. By the end of the seventeenth century the average age at marriage was 22.[53] London daughters of wealthy tradesmen married at age 20, migrant women at age 24.[54] Undoubtedly, women accumulated childbirth and child-rearing experience over their lifetimes and across generations, leading to the transmission of a substantial reservoir of societal knowledge and wisdom. On average they bore a child every two years. They ceased giving birth around age 40 and were responsible for children until they were in their 50s. Grandmothers helped daughters with maternal responsibilities. However, profound differences in practices between the classes were discernible. Contemporaries observed how large families were produced by 'poore people': 'the poore do most of all multiply.'[55] One-third of the population was poor. An increase in family numbers could 'drop a woman below the poverty line.'[56] The wage-earning capacity of women was reduced by pregnancies and childcare responsibilities.[57] Some women turned their maternity skills to an advantage by helping in nursing and child-rearing. Poor relief varied from parish to parish. Certainly, the numbers of impoverished increased in the seventeenth century.[58] Women gained knowledge through the experience of childbirth and child-rearing but the issue of 'How this experience was evaluated by themselves, and their society remains to be assessed.'[59]

The social and personal tensions that were created by the fateful events of pregnancy and childbirth were often intense. Baptist congregations sometimes coerced men into marrying women who became pregnant by them.[60] Quarter Sessions records contain much information about such illegitimate maternity. It has been noted that giving birth might be regarded as a 'female rite of passage par excellence.'[61] Midwives provided women with support, through knowledge and skill. On the other hand, the midwife took an oath to divulge the names of illegitimate fathers and she could be called as a witness in infanticide cases, which led to much tension in the community. The circumstance of childbirth raises many issues. It has been noted that women depended upon midwives and often expressed their loyalty to them. Some women bequeathed belongings to their midwives in wills. In difficult pregnancies more than one midwife attended. Male physicians were called only in dire circumstances to perform Caesarean sections, and in these cases many women died. Mothers became more inclined to allow male participation after the introduction of obstetric forceps. This innovation is said to have changed attitudes to male participation in childbirth during the seventeenth century.[62] However, it has been noted that there was 'a strong body of female opinion in favour of female attendants.' Women disliked 'groaping doctors whose fees were too high.'[63] Labouring women procured talismans, pronounced charms, and resorted to prayer. The 'eagle stone,' known as aetite, was believed by many to have made childbirth easier. The letters of gentlewomen, and the diaries of their husbands, record the details of the trials associated with births of their children.[64]

The pressure of patriarchal ideology took a secondary role to another force which 'shaped the changing social context in which women gave birth.'[65] The importance of motherhood itself offered 'women an important personal and social role.'[66] The many circumstances surrounding childbirth in early modern England were dominated by women and sometimes when men intruded upon traditional women's business as medical 'experts' opposition arose. The world of midwifery was sometimes troubled with controversy about who was professionally qualified enough to carry out the role of midwife. The conflict which surrounded the role of the midwife is present in the Church court records relating to Nantwich in 1663 and is explored further below.[67]

The Turbulent Decade of 1660–1670: A Chronicle of Loss, Hardship, and Curses

As with the decades from 1590 to 1610 and from 1630 to 1640 there was an increase in the incidence of cursing presented to the Chester Consistory Court during the decade from 1660 to 1670. This period was also a very active for legal action against women accused of scolding in Lancashire and Cheshire. The court records disclose that community strife occurred more often. In addition during this decade, cursing cases involved higher numbers of contestants and the upheavals precipitated by cursing and scolding were increasingly more public.

Throughout the decade from 1660 to 1670 the Chester Consistory Court proceedings heard the familiar themes of loss, death, and hardship. Cases that were presented in the Lancashire Quarter Sessions appeals were also comparably associated with occurrences of female spoken contraventions. Disputes about reputation and honour took place more often. In the winter of 1667 in the parish of Greater Neston, for example, a cursing ritual took place when two women, Margaret Lowndes and Alice Bridges, were alleged to have been involved in a cursing ritual that was also accompanied by an incident of scolding. Margaret Lowndes who, it was believed, was 'a woman of good carriage and behaviour and good repute,' was accused of scolding and of cursing which was alleged to have brought harm to adolescents by supernatural means. It was alleged that Alice Bridges, in return, pronounced imprecations against Margaret Lowndes. The curse took place in front of neighbours, who, it was alleged, 'were within hearing of the said words.' Mrs Lowndes' witness related the details of the incident as follows:

> Alice Bridge in a very passionate and scolding manner in Neston open towne gate and speaking to Margaret Londes who was standing in her owne doore, sayd to Mrs Lowndes thou old witch my children nevere comes neare thy doore that he dares or thrives but he is worse for it.[68]

The Bridge and Lowndes cursing instance was heard at Chester Consistory Court on 1 June 1668 before John Wainwright. It was a substantial proceeding that encompassed more than 20 members of the community of Greater Neston. The origins of the curse were traced to Margaret Lowndes' first, in words that maligned Alice Bridge as an 'oyster carrier.' More insidious, however, were the words that prophesied her an evil end

to her life, and this curse was voiced publicly, 'uttered in a railing manner in the open street.'[69] It was alleged that Margaret Lowndes said the following: 'Alice Bridges art or is a Billingsgate scould, hang thee, thou Chester carrion and I shall see an ill end of thee, thou wilt be hanged for thy husband or thy husband for thee.'[70]
The case disclosed that the conflict was long-standing and the enmity persisted throughout the entire winter. On 10 February 1668, Alice Bridges in front of a large crowd of people publicly defamed Margaret Lowndes as a 'witch mother damnable.' Her statement alleged that Margaret Lowndes had executed the cursing of a child and a horse. The details were put before the court as follows:

> Alice the wife of John Bridges before all, in a scolding and disgracefull rayling manner did call Margaret Lowndes a witch and mother damnable and sayd that she had bewitched a mare and her child and it never thrived or prospered since.[71]

However, all members of the community were not united in their condemnation of the curse. A close reading of the witnesses' statements confirm that the neighbours of Greater Neston were divided into factions. For example, Edward Emerson, Joseph Emerson, and Edward Johnson were character witnesses for the Lowndes.[72] Edward Johnson gave evidence to the court testifying that he had heard Alice Bridge call Margaret Lowndes a 'witch mother damnable' and was present to hear her say that she had caused the death of a mare, having come in contact with it while bringing it back from Chester. Even more deadly there were the suggestions that young children were at risk from her curses:

> At the time of the words and difference betwixt the aforesaid plt. [plaintiff] and deft. [defendant], Alice Bridge called the interrogant a witch and mother damnable and said that she got rid of a mare from Chester one time in Margaret Lowndes her company, and her mare never thrived after or to that purpose, also said she had noe mind that she should meddle with her children for they never thrive after or to that purpose.[73]

Joseph Emberton, a 30-year-old nailer of Neston, gave his version of events as follows:

> Alice Bridge without any occasion that this deponent either heard or could perceive given unto her, did come in a very uncivill and scolding manner

> from her owne house or doore to the plaintifs doore in Neston and there in the open street in such scolding and railing manner called Margaret Lowndes a witche, and mother damnable and said that she had bewitched of her the said Alice's children soe that it never prospered or throve after or to that purpose and gave her many other uncivill words in a very bitter manner ... there were severall other persons in the street but where they were this deponent did not much heed.[74]

Edward Johnson gave Margaret Lowndes moral support and testified to her good character. He affirmed that he was aware that she possessed a virtuous disposition and further gave evidence of her unsullied reputation. Bridgitte and Hugh Ball gave conflicting evidence about the dispute. They claimed to have heard Margaret Lowndes' confession during which time Lowndes admitted that she would not have been sorry to be rid of Bridgitte. Margaret Lowndes, upon examination, confessed to the court that she had said the words of which she was accused. She subsequently received the heavy bill of costs of four pounds and ten shillings which she was required to pay.[75]

In cases of cursing, the support of neighbours was important if such charges were to be successfully deflected. Once again, behind the charges were the themes of loss or damage. Also, in this case the theme of illness and the precarious existence of children is most prominent. The degree of detail on punishment is exceptional for few documents deriving from lawsuits include the close details of the fines and penances that were associated with cursing and verbal transgression. However, this case is instructive in several respects. The participants were relatively wealthy, and they were able to pay the fine. Had Alice Bridges been without the support of the community, the court may well have come to a different conclusion. In conclusion, Margaret Lowndes' confession resulted in her having to pay substantial costs.

A similar confrontation explicitly associated scolding and cursing with a dispute over a personal estate. This case of cursing that came before the Chester Consistory Court on 16 July 1664, took place in the familiar domain of transgression, the alehouse when innkeepers Peter and Hanna Durringe accused Susan Wilcocks of scolding. They referred to Hanna Durringe as a 'forsworne whore' in a 'scoulding and railing manner.'[76] Susan Wilcocks however, contested the charge of scolding, with witnesses Alice Pownall and her 73-year-old, widowed mother Margaret present at court to defend her social standing. Hanna Durringe alleged that

Wilcocks labelled her as a companion of sex workers and had subsequently cursed her. Margaret Wilcocks gave evidence which told a different story:

> the plt. [plaintiff] and dept. living in the same house together in Minshill, some angry words passed betwixt them and amongst the rest this deponents daughter said she could not be quiet in her owne house for a company of harlots.[77]

Wilcocks' neighbour, Peter Ormrocke, to whom she referred as 'baldy pate,' repeated her words and he afterwards invited her to repeat them before a Justice of the Peace:

> then the said Hanna asked if she meant by her whereupon the sd. Susann Wilcocks replyed noe but 'baldy pate' (meaning as this dept. thought by one Peter Ormrocke) called her a forsworne whore before a Justice of the Peace.[78]

Susan Wilcocks was later to say that she heard 'baldy pate' refer to Hanna Durringe as a 'foresworne whore' before a Justice. In fact, as later evidence revealed, the impetus for the charge came not from scolding or cursing, but rather was instigated by Peter Durringe's enclosing of common land which was forbidden:

> the originall of that falling out concerned was about the taking in of a peece of ground on the back side of the house which the said Hanna's husband was about inclosinge and then did then inclose, which he ought not to have done.[79]

This cursing episode discloses that it was the dispute about land and property which directly led to conflict about the ownership of common land. Such incidents as these that came before the court from 1660 onwards and most could often be traced to disputes about public and private space, property, and land.

Female Spoken Transgressions and Sexual Activity

The control of female language and behaviour by court and community intensified during the period from 1660 to 1670. During this period there was a greater tendency to communicate an unfavourable account of those women who displayed independence in their sexual behaviour. At the same time, spoken crime and sexual activity were unacceptable for a woman who was deemed to be of good social standing and were increasingly associated with cursing and scolding. Similarly, the definition of female vocal transgressions throughout the period from 1630 to 1670 was extended to include social activities such as alehouse drinking and gambling. Popular meeting places progressively came to be further regarded as centres of drunkenness, adultery, prostitution, depravity, and sedition. As demonstrated by such as Joane Elderson of the Ashton alehouse, women were troubled by their neighbours who were imposing their standards of proposed respectability. The charges of immodest behaviour were also extended to barmaids and alewives whose presence in the alehouse was seen by the virtuous as a sign of their moral depravity. The evidence discloses that those who consorted with them were often also vulnerable. Throughout the period from 1630 to 1670, some communities of the Northwest imposed a legal regulation that was focused carefully upon female social space. The testimony of the townsfolk often establishes that drinking in the alehouse, innkeeping, and any such complementary social activities which women had naturally enjoyed during the sixteenth century, became less well tolerated as the seventeenth century progressed. At the same time, there was certain pressure to conform to the required standards which intermittently intensified during the periods of 1590 to 1610, 1630 to 1640, and 1660 to 1670.

The Curse of Anne Knutsford

> You, Anne Knutsford, are ordinarily much addicted and given to lyinge sweringe and cursinge, and for a woman so vitiously disposed, you have been and are amongst your neighbours and such as know you commonly accompted reputed and taken.[80]
>
> Hugh Delves, his wife was as arrant a whore as ever turned tale to hedge, and Randle Mottershead got her last child and fuckt her a hundred times up the house and down.[81]

A 'Public Bawd'

The townships were undeniably characterised by volatile social relations. This is evident in the substantial number of legal actions that unfolded between 1660 and 1670. Among these cases, one instance of cursing action stands out. In 1663, the distressed community of Nantwich brought a cursing case against Anne Knutsford, who was an active midwife in the town throughout the tumultuous decade of 1660 to 1670. This particular case of cursing serves as a poignant reflection of the prevailing disharmony within the community during that period. By the year of 1660 she had already been a midwife for 15 years. She practised far and wide. Her practice took her beyond Nantwich to Wybunbury, Wrenbury, Wigsbaston, and Acton.[82] Her house was in 'Baron's Fee,' which was the largest district within the hundred of Nantwich. Her husband Thomas Knutsford was not as skilled as his wife as he was an unskilled labourer. Thomas Knutsford paid Hearth Tax on two hearths in 1664.[83] Anne Knutsford's house on Pepper Street, was nine doors away from her neighbours, who were Hugh Delves, Thomas Proudman, Richard Illidge, and Richard Yoxall. Anne Knutsford was midwife to the wives of each of these neighbours. In 1662, however, troubled circumstances surfaced that were to highlight the disturbed nature of the relationships that existed between these neighbours. These disordered circumstances formed a fractured social context out of which there was a turn of events that ensured that Anne Knutsford's nearby neighbours became her adversaries.[84]

Before examining the particulars of the events that took place in that year, it is worth establishing some further particulars about Anne Knutsford herself. The details of Anne Knutsford's age are uncertain. She was born in Nantwich and was the daughter of Raphe and Margery Elcocke.[85] In the 1630s her family were reasonably well-to-do. Her grandfather and her father were both named Raphe. Raphe was well known and respected in Nantwich. Knutsford had three sisters who were named Bridgett, Sarah, and Ellen. Ellen was married to John Cowper, who was a shoemaker, lived in Pepper Street and enjoyed a warm relationship with Anne Knutsford. Knutsford had three brothers who were named Ephrain, Raphe, and Samuel. Her family had once owned property in Mill Street, but ownership of the property was in dispute in the 1660s. It was the disputed ownership of this property that led to a long-running quarrel over social status. As the pew space designated social position, the much-disputed social order was reflected in the arrangement of the pew space at Nantwich church. Anne Knutsford married Thomas sometime between 1640 and 1644. There were 13 children, born between 1645 and 1677 that were recorded under the name of Thomas Knutsford and were baptised in Nantwich church. However, it is unlikely that Anne Knutsford gave birth to all these children. Some of the children listed were probably the children of her eldest son, Thomas, who was born in 1645.[86] Thomas who became a tanner in later years was, in fact, her only surviving son.[87]

The multiple upheavals that occurred between 1660 and 1670 in which Anne Knutsford and her neighbouring residents were embroiled, offer a detailed and intimate portrayal of the prevailing opinions and beliefs. The inherent essence of this societal unrest serves as a testament to the attitudes, convictions, and customs held by the inhabitants of Nantwich during that time. Moreover, the expressed opinions vividly underscore the sentiments harboured by the townspeople regarding the prescribed conduct of women. A close reading of the townsfolk's depositions to the court brings to light their preoccupations, fears, and anxieties, and illuminates many undisclosed dark secrets. Within the fabric of litigation, numerous webs of conspiracy emerged, seeking to exert control over women like Anne Knutsford, who wielded the power of curses to further their own objectives. This analysis looks into the lives and experiences of individuals within a town that, despite its efforts to reconcile its conflicts, remained profoundly divided. By shedding light on these dynamics, this reading uncovers the intricate complexities and power dynamics at play within the community, providing insight into the struggles and divisions experienced by its inhabitants.

'Husht, Negative and Averse'

Instances of cursing were heard by the Chancellor, John Wainwright, in the Chester Consistory Court of the 1660s. The administration of the court was undertaken by deputy registrar William Wilson, and the details of the case were recorded by the Clerk of the Court, Henry Prescott. Henry Prescott later succeeded William Wilson when he later died in 1689.[88] Henry Prescott wrote in his diary that most of the business of the Chester Consistory Court took place in the 'better inns of Chester.' The inns he described in detail were the Falcon, the Calf's Head Club and the Fountain.[89] If Henry Prescott was true to his word, the administrators would have spent many hours drinking wine and ale in the Chester inns. Henry Prescott, whose diary was written at a slightly later date than the period under investigation, provided an insight into the ways in which the functionaries of the court perceived the population at large. People of the lower orders were described by him as 'the Mob.'[90] On another occasion he referred to ordinary folk as 'vulgar spectators.'[91] The attitude of the townsfolk to the functionaries of the court was one of suspicion. On one occasion, Henry complained about the cool reception he and the Chancellor, John Wainwright received when they approached the diocesan town of Wigan, which he described as being 'husht, negative and averse.'[92]

It was two hours' journey by road from Chester to Nantwich, where lived Anne Knutsford, who worked out her strategies to deal with her legal business in Blossam's Inn. Midwife, Anne Knutsford, generated a great deal of paperwork for the Chester Consistory Court. In the 1660s she was involved in ten separate official instances of litigation, and six unofficial instances.[93] Numerous additional incidents were reported during that period, involving a significant number of people. The townsfolk that were involved, numbered more than 100 and were of varying social backgrounds. Some were artisans, shopkeepers, and tradesfolk. Several complainants were of 'gentle' status, and two petitioners were high-ranking members of the community. When possible, additional information about the individuals involved in the cursing incidents has been gathered from their wills and inventories, providing valuable insights into their backgrounds and allowing for a more precise placement of the information within a social context. Details such as the births of their children, baptisms, and marriages have been sourced from the Nantwich parish records, contributing to a more comprehensive understanding of their lives. The examination of this data has revealed the intricate details of a monumental legal struggle primarily revolving around property ownership and money lending. Moreover, it has become apparent that maintaining one's social status posed challenges amid the ever-changing circumstances in Nantwich. The participants involved in the accusation, both through their statements and omissions to the Court, as well as the information they disclose in their depositions, provide valuable insights into the hidden facets of female spoken offence. These insights shed light on the underlying social and economic factors that contribute to the dynamics of ill will and ultimately propel such accusations. By closely examining the perspectives and motivations of those involved, a deeper understanding of the complex interplay between social dynamics, economic conditions, and the driving forces behind these accusations can be understood.

To give a feeling of the circumstances of this cursing it might be best to begin with the events which took place in February 1663, when an unusually large number of Nantwich townsfolk organised a petition that was brought against Anne Knutsford, a local Nantwich midwife Nantwich for cursing. In this instance, 19 people initially signed the petition, then 30 more appeared in court to give evidence. Later still, however, a further 93 people were involved indirectly. The petition was primarily directed at the midwife for 'misbehaviour in the office of midwifery,' but, in addition, numerous other charges of cursing and spoken violence were also laid against her. Almost immediately, upon receipt of the petition, John Wainwright, 'Doctor of Lawes' and the 'Bishop of Chester,' acted against Knutsford by issuing an interim order that was based on the petition. Wainwright issued Anne Knutsford with a Prohibition of Practice, which is set out below:

> Anne Knutsford, whereas we are sufficiently informed by very good testimony of your scandalous life and under carriage and misbehaviour in the office of midwifery in revealinge the secretts of women, and in other things, we have thought good to suspend you from any further practice or expense of that office untill you have cleared yourself unto us and we do hereby inhibit and command you not to proceed any further in the execucion [sic] of that office as you will answere the contrary at your peril notwithstanding any Licence or Despensation [sic] to you by use, or any other, either by Authority from or under the lordshippe of Yorke, or any other person, under the seal of our office on the 5th day of February, 1663.[94]

According to the processes of the Chester Consistory Church court, signatories to a petition, such as the one which involved Anne Knutsford, were required to attend court as witnesses. Cursing at this level was not felonious. It is notable that certain cases that initially commenced at the Church court eventually progressed to the Quarter Sessions or Assize courts, where the potential penalties for guilt were significantly more severe. This transition from ecclesiastical to secular jurisdiction underscores the gravity and perceived seriousness of the offences in question. The shift in legal proceedings highlights the potential consequences individuals faced when accused of cursing or related crimes, emphasising the increasing severity of punishment as cases advanced through the legal system. The witnesses, or 'deponents' as they were called, were required by the court to give evidence about 'Items,' which consisted of a list of charges. The charges were declared publicly and were read out aloud in the court. Subsequently depositions were given that could throw light on the charges. Often, the verbal accounts of witnesses, or 'depositions,' were found to be contradictory. In this case a close investigation of these inconsistencies reveals details of concubinage, concerns about 'bastardy,' concealed debt, stealing, lying, and sexual impropriety. Among the numerous charges levelled against Knutsford, is one notable accusation that she divulged sensitive information pertaining to improper conduct, thus bringing to public knowledge details that many witnesses would have preferred to keep undisclosed. This allegation highlights the potential breach of confidentiality and the exposure of private matters associated with Knutsford's actions. It suggests that the revelations made by Knutsford had the potential to disrupt social norms and expose individuals to public scrutiny, further complicating the case and adding to the gravity of the accusations against her.

To fully understand the sudden surge in litigation and the heightened concern about cursing in Nantwich between 1660 and 1670, it is important to look into the reasons behind the townsfolk's profound preoccupation with Anne Knutsford's curse. Additionally, it is crucial to explore the implications stemming from the accusations of cursing levelled against the midwife, and to examine how resentment was fostered in Nantwich through hearsay. Lastly, a thorough examination of the depositions in the case of Anne Knutsford is warranted to uncover the underlying issues that witnesses deliberately sought to conceal. By addressing these aspects, a deeper understanding of the social dynamics and motivations surrounding the surge in litigation and concerns about cursing during that period can be achieved.

As is indicated in the cursing cases discussed above, a reputation for cursing gathered momentum slowly over a long period of time. Nantwich was no different to other localities in this respect. Resentment and tension existed in Nantwich long before accusations were made. In some cases a period of years was involved. The litigation involving Anne Knutsford, however, matured into a full-blown accusation within three years, but the initial momentum behind the circumstances, that is, the conversations that were involved, and the incidences involving affront and offence were generated in Nantwich ten years before the petition which led to Anne Knutsford's presentation in court in 1663.

The depositions of the townsfolk lay bare the details of several levels of conspiracy. The most important stratagem to stop the midwife from speaking was initiated by landowner and notable, Captain Richard Walthall. On the surface it was orchestrated by Walthall as a campaign of hostility against a midwife with a 'scurrilous tongue.' It was organised by a network of notables whose activities, were questionable in a town conscious of maintaining high levels of moral behaviour. Some people who were of 'good credit' were in debt, and some, such as Sir Philip Egerton and Richard Walthall, were involved in extramarital affairs with females, a few of whom were prominent members of Nantwich society. When these relationships produced children, they became anxious since they knew that any midwife was required by law to disclose the identities of the parents of what was then perceived as 'bastard' children. Although she was impertinent and often rude, Knutsford's knowledge of the extramarital affairs of the people of Nantwich, especially local notables, thus made her vulnerable to allegations of scolding and cursing. Critics of the midwife, finding safety in numbers, would join forces and are observed here to give support to each other's accounts especially when they are thrust into the public eye before a court. The neighbours supported each other in their accounts with the deliberate intent of implicating the midwife in spoken offence, especially rumourmongering. Their mutually supportive accounts deflected such rumour away from themselves and onto the midwife. Their public demonstration of solidarity ensured protection from the midwife's words and the security provided by joining forces also shielded them against the negative moral judgements of other more important members of the community.

When the midwife became indicted as the source of ill will, her enemies said that her words and behaviour were antagonistic and disruptive. They complained that she offended public morality and crossed the borders of 'good neighbourliness.' She was rebuked for bad language and was charged with being a 'public bawd' and for being the source of social scandal. Numerous conversations emerged in which the midwife had, over the previous years, implicated high-born townsfolk in improper behaviour. These conversations were repeated by witnesses. The townsfolk, afraid of the stigma they might incur, protested that Anne Knutsford had slandered them. The petition implied that Anne Knutsford's words were pure invention. Her critics hoped that Knutsford's allegations of sexual impropriety, bastardy, insobriety, stealing, prostitution, and concubines would be quashed by a legal battle in the public arena of the court and that they would result in Knutsford being branded as a rumourmonger. Such discourse, however, pointed the finger of moral suspicion squarely at them. Thus, gossip and hearsay—what had been said, what had been heard, and what was said to have been heard and said—was spoken like lines in a script and mouthed by actors in a public drama.

The circumstances surrounding the midwife, Anne Knutsford, provided a useful public forum for releasing the rising tension which had long simmered below the surface. The 'defamed' of Nantwich cried out in a single chorus of public outrage. By bringing a petition designed to discredit Anne Knutsford, and aimed at disallowing her from practising, the witnesses believed they would stop people from taking note of her talk about them, and restore their credit and reputation. However, in this respect, they were very much mistaken.

Although as noted above, the petition brought against Anne Knutsford was first presented in February 1663 and was signed by 19 Nantwich townsfolk, many more people endorsed the inferences of the petition and were adamant in supporting the claims by appearing as witnesses. The inhabitants of Nantwich petitioned against Knutsford's scandalous talk, lying and swearing, and being a common curser. The petition outlined her transgressions in the following words:

> These are to certify whom it may concerne that we whose names are subscribed doe very well knowe Anne Knutsford of Namptwich. And that Anne is a woman of very uncivil language towards her neighbours: and doth comonly abuse and iniure many of them by her scandalous speeches. That contrary to her profession of a Midwife, she hath revealed the secretts of women. That she is ordinarily addicted to Lying, swearinge, and cursinge. And herein (for anythinge we knowe) shee perseveres without the reformation of her manners. Witness our hands.[95]

Many of the signatories of the petition in 1663 appeared as witnesses to give evidence to the court of what they knew in relation to the charges brought against Anne Knutsford. Some signed the petition, but did not appear in court, while some appeared but did not sign the petition. Some claimed in their depositions that they had indeed signed the petition, but in fact they did not. Those who were unable to write made their mark, which was usually the first initial of the Christian name. Those who signed the petition were: Richard Jackson (Minister), William Harrison (Churchwarden), Thomas Burroughs (Churchwarden), Margaret Jackson, Mary Maisterson, Margaret Jeurl, Elizabeth Proudman, Dorothy Delves, Elizabeth Cliffe, Elizabeth Church, Dorothy Hussey, Barbara Croxton, Elizabeth Johnson, Hana Harrison, Elizabeth Harware, Margaret Wickstad's mark, Mary Ellidge's mark and one more name that is illegible and an initial which is also illegible. The court issued a list of 'items' which set out in precise details the spoken transgressions of the midwife as follows:

> You, Anne Knutsford, have been and are a woman of very uncivill language towards your neighbours, and have abused and injured many or some of them who are persons of quality by your scandalous speeches, as the witnesses in the cause to be produced against you can particularly demonstrate.[96]

Further to the allegations of spoken offence, the midwife was accused of behaving 'imodestly.' In this respect her speech and behaviour were construed in a way which reflected unfavourably upon her as a female. Amongst these allegations was one of violating a sacred bond between women. The townspeople voiced their grievances regarding Anne Knutsford's disregard and casual approach in discussing the profoundly personal aspects surrounding women in labour, as delineated below:

> you have imodestly by words not bifittinge a midwife or modest and civill woman rivealed the sicrettes of women who had been in trauell [labour] the particulars whereof the witnesses to be produced are required to declare.[97]

Most female signatories gave evidence about the midwife speaking 'imodestly' and of 'rivealing the sicrettes of women.'[98] However, when most of the women who were asked to provide depositions, they were unable to say that they *personally* were victims of Knutsford's indiscretions. Instead, they repeated what they had heard others say. Knutsford's critics repeated hearsay—what had been said, what had been heard—and what was said to have been heard and said.

Cursing, however, was considered by most petitioners to be the midwife's main violation. However, this cursing was closely related to scandalmongering and verbal infringements which were spoken against prominent members of the community. Evidence was given about Knutsford that confirmed that Knutsford was, in addition, accused of having a malicious nature and a predisposition to the spreading of rumour during her rounds as midwife. Subsequently she was accused of having a vicious nature and of maliciously hurting people with lies, swearing, and curses, as is described below:

> You, Anne Knutsford, are ordinarily much addicted and given to lyinge sweringe and cursinge, and for a woman so vitiously disposed, you have been and are amongst your neighbours and such as know you commonly accompted reputed and taken.[99]

The authors of the document operated under the presumption that the individuals who affixed their signatures had experienced mistreatment at the hands of the midwife. Given their esteemed positions within the community, these signatories enjoyed a certain level of prestige, which granted them the presumption of respectability. They asserted their own standing as individuals of honourable reputation and character, employing the following expressions to level accusations against Knutsford, citing instances of offensive language and impropriety[100]:

> By rieson [sic] of your lewd and civill life and scurrilous disgraceful and immodest language as aforesaid, your neighbours both men and womane, persons of good quality and reputation, are much offended and abused.[101]

The allegations of cursing, swearing, lying, and 'rivealing the sicrettes of women' had previously led to her exclusion from the profession of midwifery in February 1663 when these allegations had been first raised. A long list of wrongdoings presented in court in March 1663, also included a condemnation of Knutsford for practising midwifery when forbidden by the Bishop and Minister from doing so. The following Item records how she continued her rounds despite the ruling of the Court:

> [Anne Knutsford] was privately and personally inhibited and publiquely in the congregation soe declared to bee, [inhibited] But have proceeded to exercyze the office of midwife to the wives of John Pratchett and Johnathan Chones.[102]

In addition to the accusations outlined above, the midwife faced charges of professional neglect. Her adversaries claimed that she selected patients, not out of concern for the well-being of mother and child, but for financial reward which had the effect of making Knutsford appear uncharitable:

> you have been sent for and decided to doe your office of a midwife to some woman or women in or neare the towne of Namptwich, who [was] in trauell of childbirth; and because they were poore you have neglected them and left them, and gone to other women who were past that peril, and

> sayed you must, would, and soe did, doe to others that were richer; and by reason of such neglect such poore woman, or women miscarryed.[103]

The final Items unite the signatories in a common voice of disapproval. The people of Nantwich not only substantiated their allegations, but they also appeared in public to discredit the midwife where they announced that she was a nuisance and that 'all and singular' agreed with the Items brought against her. They subsequently issued the following deposition:

> Anne Knutsford hath been and is a public bawd and has fame in Namptwich aforesaid, as the witnesses to be produced can particularly declare upon their depositions, which they are required to express at large.[104]

But as the following analysis will demonstrate, 'all and singular' did not agree. There was much contention between neighbours and the people who strove to discredit Anne Knutsford, the midwife of Nantwich.

The Curse

> Anne is a very frequent curser and swearer and will ordinarily goe down on her knees and curse people grivously, and this deponent hath seen her doe soe diverse times.[105]

Before turning to examine the depositions of the witnesses that supported the charges against Anne Knutsford, it is worthwhile examining the charges that were laid against the midwife for cursing, lying, and professional neglect. First, let us scrutinise the charge of cursing more closely. Without a doubt the midwife had a distinguished reputation for her use of language. She was imaginative with a choice of ribald expression. She was quick-witted. She launched scathing attacks upon the pretentious. She parodied notions of respectability and exposed hypocrisy in the most colourful language. Her aptitude with rhetorical speech allowed her to expose the pretences of the ostensibly respectable members of the town. She made no distinction between victims of high or low status. However, Anne Knutsford's tongue-in-cheek rhetoric became indictable when it came to include cursing. As the evidence below will demonstrate, she frequently resorted to ritualistic cursing to achieve her ambitions.

Undoubtedly, Knutsford cursed people regularly. Nine members of the town gave evidence against the midwife for cursing. The recipients of her curses were often tradespeople who lived close to Anne Knutsford's home in Pepper Street. Janet Brookett, who was married to furrier, Thomas Brookett, disclosed in her deposition that Anne Knutsford had cursed James Wilson.[106] Barbara Croxton, shoemaker, in her deposition confirmed Knutsford was a curser and added lying and swearing to her complaint when she stated that 'Anne Knutsford is accounted to be addicted to lying and swearing and cursing.'[107] Similarly, grocer Jane Wright alleged that she heard Anne Knutsford 'curse her father.'[108] Margaret Jackson claimed that Anne Knutsford had a propensity for cursing. She affirmed this with the following words:

> Anne Knutsford is a woman very much given to vaine swearing and cursing and lying upon many occasions, for which and other reasons this deponent and the rest, subscribed to the certificate now shewed her the contents whereof are all of them true. And she is much taken notice of for such a one.[109]

Certainly, the above deposition is proof of Anne Knutsford's reputation for pronouncing curses. She was linguistically proficient, scurrilous, and she was certainly inclined to curse. Amongst those she cursed was Margaret Birkerton, a teacher of reading and sewing who had lived in Nantwich for over 40 years. In her deposition she provided extended details of Anne Knutsford's cursings. It is difficult to establish the nature of her association with Anne Knutsford although her evidence suggests that Knutsford may have in the past assisted her as a midwife. Her deposition provides evidence in support of the many Items critical of the midwife. Her report claims that she had allegedly been on the receiving end of Anne's sharp tongue:

> she hath done as much to this depots. selfe to her owne face before severall people of late calling her salt bitch and drunken salt women bitch, and the like, and thou hast a hole I may put my head in.[110]

The teacher illustrated the midwife's tendency to attack without provocation. She referred the court to numerous unprovoked attacks upon the Proudman family.[111] Margaret Birkerton, however, also provided evidence of a very serious nature against Anne Knutsford for cursing. This charge was most serious because the midwife had executed the curse in the formal ritual style in public for all to hear. Knutsford was accused of getting down on her knees, while raising her hands and lifting her eyes dramatically towards the sky and called upon supernatural forces to do their worst. The curse executed in this way was a theatrical display and it was performed with the intention of attracting the attention of as many people as possible. The curse performed this way gave the curser an opportunity to describe their injuries and to elevate to public attention any issues which the 'audience' may not have been aware of. Margaret Birkerton confirmed that she saw the midwife perform this ritual many times. She did not say who this curse was directed at, but she did draw attention to the consistency of the midwife's ritual attacks:

> Anne is a very frequent curser and swearer and will ordinarily goe down on her knees and curse people grivously, and this deponent hath seen her doe soe diverse times. And she is commonly accounted such a one.[112]

Margaret Birkerton affirmed solidarity with her neighbours and stated her familiarity with them.[113] She claimed that she was cursed along with many others:

> the neighbours are much offended and many of them iniured by Anne's base tongue. And the contents of the Certificate inteste this deponent verily believes are all true and she knowes most of them to be true.[114]

Margaret Birkerton did state, however, diverging from the rest of her deposition, that the midwife was a skilled practitioner and that she had a good reputation as such: 'Anne is a good midwife and generally accounted soe to be.'[115]

Further evidence of Anne Knutford's cursing was given by 52-year-old Thomas Proudman, who was a shoemaker and a neighbour of Anne Knutsford. While going about his everyday life, he claimed that he had frequently witnessed the midwife's curses. He asserted that he witnessed numerous acts of callousness. He stated that he was present when Anne cursed members of her own family.[116] He said: 'Anne is much given to cursing and swearinge on any idle occasion' and recalled an occasion when Anne Knutsford cursed her father, beat him up, and threw him out of doors: 'this deponent did hear her one time curse her owne father and bid the divill rid the world on him and he was the basest villane that did get children.'[117]

As Thomas Proudman was a close neighbour and he also claimed that he overheard Knutsford's quarrels and drew attention to an occasion when the midwife cursed her family: 'her sister and brother in lawe both say on several occasions say that she is one much taken notice of to be given to vain cursing and swearing.'[118]

The shoemaker also signed the certificate to demonstrate his loyalty to the community.[119] Anne Knutsford's coarse language had occasion to offend many people in Pepper Street. Janet Brookett, for instance, said that the midwife cursed her and her husband. Brookett referred to a separate instance of litigation involving a 'difference' with the midwife. She deposed that they had since patched up their quarrel.[120]

Similarly, innkeeper Elizabeth Cliffe said she was present when Anne Knutsford cursed Sir Phillip Egerton and Captain Richard Walthall. She also claimed that she herself was a victim of Knutsford's scandal-mongering, but that, when she confronted the midwife, Knutsford had histrionically publicly cursed *herself* in an effort to deny that any such conversation had ever taken place:

> Anne hath very falsely and iniustly raised a scandall upon this deponent and Sir Philip Egerton, as alsoe of Captain Walthall and Samuel Husseys wife and notice thereof being given to Anne Knutsford she came to this deponent one time and fell downe on her knees and grivously swore and cursed her selfe if ever she had reported any such thinge by any of them or ever iniured any of them by her.[121]

Significantly, the Minister of Nantwich church, Richard Jackson, supported the claims of those who had subscribed to the certificate.[122] In his statement he claimed the following 'Anne is too much adicted to lyeing, swearing and cursinge And for such a one is comonly taken and reputed in the neighbourhood.'[123] However, he was unable to provide an example of Knutsford's bad conduct. Similarly, coster William Blundell shared the common view of the midwife as a curser and swearer: 'Anne hath been and is one much given both to lying and cursing and swearing, And comonly taken notice of for such a one and her neighbours are much offended at it in her.'[124]

William Blundell, as with the Minister, referred to hearsay. Blundell did not provide a specific example. He did, however, allege that his wife was the victim of a curse, but he did not say how, and though he declared Knutsford of using 'unhandsome words' he did not make a distinction between cursing or swearing: 'Anne Knutsford is a woman of very uncivill and unhandsome words and language to her neighbours and is apt to iniure them by her tongue as she hath done this deponents wife and others.'[125]

The evidence at hand reveals a collective display of solidarity among the townspeople in their endeavour to highlight the midwife's use of curses. Nevertheless, it is worth noting that certain individuals, including the Minister and William Blundell, were unable to substantiate the prevailing consensus with first-hand information. In their depositions, they disclose that their knowledge of the midwife's behaviour rested solely on hearsay accounts provided by others. In contrast, the case of 76-year-old widow Margaret Wirkstad diverges from the aforementioned individuals. Wirkstad exhibited a heightened sense of urgency to solidify her reputation within the community, primarily due to the midwife's accusation of witchcraft levelled against her. This circumstance compelled Wirkstad to take additional measures to safeguard her standing among her peers: 'And this deponent hath been told that by persons of credit that Anne reported that this deponent was a dun arse and a leather-faced witch, and when she met with her, she had noe luck that day.'[126]

Not surprisingly, Wirkstadt supported the general view of the midwife as a common curser.[127] She stated: 'Anne is much given to idle vaine cursing and swearinge and lyinge, And is ordinarily taken of for such a one.'[128] Although Wirkstadt did not disclose the names of the 'persons of credit' who asked her to appear, it is reasonable to assume that, since she was related to Richard Walthall, she was probably induced to appear by him.[129] Margaret Wirkstad having a keen interest in defending her own reputation, refuted having any such association with the term 'witch.' As widows were sometimes susceptible to accusations of witchcraft by disgruntled townsfolk, it is not surprising to find, therefore, that Margaret Wirkstad was anxious to confirm fellow feeling with the more seemingly respectable Nantwich townsfolk. Wirkstad held that Anne Knutsford referred to her husband as 'an old rotton Rogue.'[130] Nevertheless, she tried to persuade Anne to curb her tongue, but, as her deposition will illustrate, the midwife's response was less than enthusiastic:

> And one time this deponent being in company with Anne was advising her to be fair conditioned amongst her neighbours, and in a familiar way be [sic] laid her hand upon Anne's hand when Anne before all sundry sufficient neighbours answered to this deponent, 'ah! the divill, lay thy hand off me!'[131]

Anne Knutsford was not persuaded to be 'fair conditioned' towards her neighbours. She had no intention of deferring to the respectable folk of Nantwich society. She, ostentatiously and before 'all sundry,' parodied her neighbour's kindly efforts. Margaret's attempts to urge Anne Knutsford to curb her tongue fell on deaf ears. Margaret Wirkstad promptly sought to safeguard her name and position in the community and demonstrated solidarity with those who wanted to put an end to the 'lewd and scurrilous life' of the midwife.[132] She set down her signature on the petition, joined the others and washed her hands completely of Anne Knutsford.

'Rivealing the Sicrettes of Women'

Placed prominently among the accusations levelled against the midwife was the charge of conducting herself in an 'immodest' manner. Anne Knutsford's speech and behaviour were perceived unfavourably by the community, as they clashed with the prevailing societal norms observed in Nantwich. Neighbours asserted that her choice of language cast aspersions on both her role as a midwife and her standing as a woman, deeming it a breach of the sacred trust that exists among women. Specifically, she was accused of divulging the intimate details of the women she assisted in her capacity as a midwife.

When word reached them of the midwife's alleged indiscretions, the women of Nantwich were outraged to find that Anne Knutsford had spoken publicly about the intimate details of the delivery of their children. However, since Knutsford as a midwife was, by law, also required to provide details of the birth of children born outside of wedlock, some women, such as Elizabeth Cliffe, Dorothy Hussey, and Anne Blagg were more outraged than others. Witnesses lined up to give evidence about the charge of immodesty. Many were anxious in their attempts to make public knowledge the midwife's 'imodesty' and her indelicate 'rivealing of the sicrettes of women.' Few, however, were able to say that *they* were victims of the midwife's indiscretions. Instead, they related details about what they heard *others* say about it. Once again in the realm of hearsay.[133] In order to discredit the midwife, some townsfolk referred to victims who were possibly fictitious as these individuals did not sign the petition and neither did they appear at the court.[134]

'Rivealing the Sicrettes': Measures and Countermeasures

Some of the complaints that were made against Anne Knutsford were recorded in detail. Janett Brookett accused the midwife of having shouted: 'Richard Yorksalls wife was rotton and stunke so that she could scarce sit by her for the smell.'[135] Of her client, Mrs Booth, it is alleged that she stated: 'when she went to John Booths wife in bed she found her drunke and with the childe upon the hearth.'[136] In a similar manner, she said of the Minister's wife that 'she took a child from Mrs Jackson that stunke like a turd and came from her in peeces as black as a thrush.'[137] In addition, there were turbulent words exchanged between the midwife and James Wilson, whose wife was Anne's client. It was at a social occasion at the alehouse that somebody asked after *his* good health. In response, the midwife took it upon herself to reply for James Wilson and her words were less than civil. Anne Knutsford made it clear that it was his wife who had recently given birth and not Wilson, and so, she complained, why ask about his good health?

> she answered with an oath that if he were so, [in good health] his wife were not, for she had been twice with her of a child but she bled soe exceedingly at the fundament that she had noe minde to goe againe.[138]

Perhaps it was common for Anne Knutsford to speak in frank and open terms about her profession but people thought her language was offensive and that she went too far. In the social climate of this town, she contravened the regulations that were associated with the kind of language that was expected of a profession and a woman and additionally contravened the expected norms in disclosing sensitive information about the female body. According to the depositions, the details of women's bodies during labour were a private matter to be discussed privately and *only* by women. A prominent member of the community alleged that she heard the midwife contravene this directive: 'Anne Knutsford did report very uncivill and unhandsome things concerning women before men which this deponent was ashamed to heare though she doth not nowe particularly remember them.'[139]

Margaret Jackson did, however, recall Anne Knutsford's conversation about one alleged person that she offended, known as Mrs Milton. It was alleged that Anne Knutsford said:

> Mrs Milton was not soe weake as she reported to be but she had a thigh as big as the maine post of the house and was well enough to give sucke though she included her husband for that her suck run downe her sides and down her thighs.[140]

Contradictory evidence was deposed by women who were as socially prominent as Margaret Jackson. However, their evidence did not correspond with the above accounts. There was one testament to Anne Knutsford's professionalism that was contributed by Elizabeth Walley who had no hesitation in accepting the midwife's denial of the allegations. Moreover, she favoured Knutsford's word above that of others and provided the court with the following deposition:

> She her selfe never heard Anne to be immodest in reveallling the secrets of any woman, though she hath heard something to that purpose, but Anne denyed it be soe, and whether she did soe this deponent can not depose.[141]

Similarly, Elizabeth Brumall found no fault with the midwife's language and said so explicitly in her deposition.[142] She was careful to say that she did not socialise with the midwife, but that she found Anne Knutsford to be of assistance when she needed it. Despite the words of others, she did not wish to condemn Knutsford as indiscreet:

> she having very little to do with her but in time of need either for her selfe or friend, hath heard that some of her neighbours say that they have been much iniured and offended by Annes foule tongue, but whether she were guilty of any such thing this deponent knoweth not.[143]

The 'Sicrettes' of the People of Nantwich: Bastards and Paramours

The evidence arising from this cursing incident indicates that the secrets exposed by the midwife were not exclusively centred around the physiological aspects of childbirth or her use of vulgar language. Rather, the secrets divulged by Knutsford pertained to her knowledge of Nantwich's illegitimate children and illicit relationships, including extramarital affairs. Anne Knutsford's profession naturally put her in a position to know the intimate details of sexual relations in Nantwich. For instance, in her role as a midwife she was consulted by women about the approximate delivery date of the births of their children. According to the depositions, the midwife spoke too freely of delicate matters. Though the matters she spoke of generally were indeed confidential, it was not the details that they complained about that the townsfolk were anxious to conceal. The midwife made public knowledge of Captain Richard Walthall's receipt of payment in kind instead of hard cash, that is, in sexual services, from women who rented properties from him and evidence of the hardship that existed at the time. The women who Anne Knutsford identified that were involved with Walthall were Elizabeth Cliffe, Dorothy Delves, Janet Brookett, and Ann Blagg. The intimate knowledge of these encounters might have remained secret had Anne Knutsford, their midwife, not laid bare the details of illicit sexual conduct before the whole town.

The prospect of financial commitment in support of a child brought forth an army of men into what was formerly a mostly female concern. When the likelihood of an issue of bastardy arose, the men of the town had much to lose. While the petition suggests that the midwife spoke in rude terms of Captain Richard Walthall and Sir Philip Egerton, these prominent and respected members of the community were the subject of hearsay which related the fine points of the torrid sexual encounters with two well-known and properly married women who were Elizabeth Cliffe and Dorothy Hussey. In Restoration Nantwich the conduct of illicit sexual dalliance out of wedlock was unacceptable, first, because the women were 'cuckolding' their husbands, but more importantly, because such sexual adventures raised issues of bastardy, prostitution, and concubines. According to the depositions, the evidence was based upon hearsay. The information relating to Captain Walthall, Sir Philip Egerton, Elizabeth Cliffe, and Dorothy Hussey, for example, had been the subject of scandal in Nantwich for some time. The midwife, owing to her profession, had access to more intimate knowledge than most lay people would. Perhaps she spoke too freely of these issues. However, it was a most serious offence that occurred when, it was alleged, the midwife said that Captain Walthall paid for the sexual favours of Mrs Dorothy Hussey. Knutsford expressed it thus: 'Mr Walthall did give Samuel Hussey's wife 50 shillings a year to occupy her.'[144]

In addition, the midwife was reported to have said that Sir Philip Egerton paid Mrs Cliffe a little less handsomely for the same kind of service: 'Sir Phillip Egerton gave Mrs Cliffe 40 shillings a year to occupy her.'[145]

Dorothy Delves, a prominent figure in Nantwich society, was also embroiled in a sexual scandal. The midwife disclosed the intimate particulars about a relationship between her and wealthy notable Randle Mottershead. This relationship, Anne Knutsford stated, produced a bastard child. Of Dorothy Delves, the midwife spoke in dishonourable terms: 'Hugh Delves, his wife was as arrant a whore as ever turned tale to hedge, and Randle Mottershead got her last child and had fuckt her a hundred times up the house and down.'[146]

The midwife similarly accused Sir Philip Egerton of fathering the child of Elizabeth Cliffe. The midwife, it was alleged stated the following: 'Mrs Cliffe was an arrant whore, and Sir Phillip Egerton got most of her children and she would not care how many children she had for he gave her forty pounds a year.'[147]

Dorothy Hussey, who rented property from Captain Walthall, was accused of behaving improperly with him. This affair, according to the midwife, also resulted in bastardy. Of this relationship, Anne Knutsford had this to say:

> coming to this deponent from Samuel Husseys where she had been laying his wife in bed, [Anne Knutsford] told the deponent that she had been with Sam Husseys wife and had taken her a young Walthall in the world, for she was an arrant whore, and her Landlord Walthall was the father of it, and she kissed out her rent with him for fifty shillings a year.[148]

According to the depositions of the Nantwich townsfolk, Anne Knutsford generated rumours of bastardy and joked about the illegal ways in which some of her clients had made a living. For example, during the lying in of Mrs Leeth, to whom she was midwife, Anne Knutsford demonstrated great dexterity. It was claimed that in the process of delivering a child at the same time as she looked out of the window, and there she spied two people, Mrs Delves and Randle Muttershead, whom she surmised to be lovers: '[Anne] looked out of the window and saw Mrs Delves and Randle Muttershead together at Mrs Delves door.'[149]

The midwife observed the fine points of the tryst and recorded her observation of their first union. In accordance with her profession, she calculated the time and place of a proposed conception of Mrs Delves' first child and linked it to that first observed meeting: 'Look yonder, ugly Muttershead does goe. He has got Mrs Delves first child and kisses her up the house and down, and I reccun'd her for to the very house that he got it, and it was his.'[150]

Edward Blagg accused the midwife of speaking ill, of levelling accusations of cuckoldry, and of spreading malicious rumours about persons of credit. The marriage of an older man, such as Delves, to a younger woman was a classic situation and likely to provoke charivari. It was too tempting to resist for one such as Anne Knutsford. According to Blagg's deposition she said:

> one time seeing John Hussey, since deceased, and his wife, being a young woman, walking together, said to this deponent and others that were there, 'soe howe nowe yonder old foole is of that young whore, he thinks that he marryed a mayde but she has been a whore there seven years to my knowledge, its an easie thing to cozen such an old foole for if I were to be marryd againe I could make a straight comodity and cozen him.'[151]

Margaret Jackson persuaded the Court that it should pay no heed to a similar accusation of Anne Knutsford's, namely that Mrs Walley 'when she was a widow' had been guilty of prostitution and of receiving gold in return for sexual services. Margaret Jackson said:

> Anne is a woman very apt and ready to scandalies and abuse her neighbours and others with her tongue and particularly this deponent heard her say that Mrs Walley when she was a widowe preferred some affection for Mr Massey of Namptwich and inbragled him and got a great bagg of money and plate from him that which weighed her downe all of one side as she carryed it home.[152]

She asserted that the midwife's words had no meaning and that she used such language recklessly without basis in truth or fact:

> And in her ordinary discourse talking of severall people would frequently calle them if they were younge people, young whores, and if old people, old whores and she is generally taken notice of for such an abusive woman.[153]

Not surprisingly, the midwife's talk of bastards, prostitutes, and concubines were not well received by Nantwich society. For speaking in this way, she found herself challenged by yeoman, Edward Blagg. Blagg was intent upon defending the honour and reputation of Dorothy Hussey. In front of all and sundry he publicly upbraided Anne Knutsford, in his words: 'blaming her for it and commanding her modesty of Hussey's wife.'[154]

However, the midwife would not budge about bastardy, and she stood her ground. Unrepentant, she did not retract a word. Indeed, she claimed to possess superior knowledge about prostitution, especially in relation to the conduct of Dorothy Hussey. She answered: 'Hold your tongue she's as arrant a whore as ever turn'd tale to hedge I know more than you doe.'[155]

Edward Blagg gave further information about Anne Knutsford's loose talk, he alleged that he heard the midwife accuse Mrs Leeth, (who did not sign the petition or appear as a witness) 'to her face' of receiving stolen goods. The midwife implied that Mr Leeth, who was an excise man, stole the commodities he oversaw and in so doing made an easy living. The midwife, who regarded the incident as a joke, bantered about the easy way in which Mr and Mrs Leeth obtained their livelihood. The yeoman, however, was not amused. He outright defended the reputation of his neighbour and challenged the midwife. His deposition read as follows:

> This deponent also heard her tell Mrs Leeth to her face that she got all by the exciseman, and then being blamed for it made only a laughter of it, Mrs Leethes husband being an exciseman.[156]

There was certainly no love lost between Blagg the yeoman and the midwife. They were sworn enemies.[157] The Chester Consistory Court had previously heard several cases which heard evidence of the shoemakers, Mr and Mrs Proudman, who were friends of Ann Blagg and Edward Blagg. The court records disclose the fact that Anne maligned the yeoman's wife Mrs Blagg as 'a porky arst whore and called her also in the open street a whore and double whore.'[158]

The depositions of the townsfolk verify the fact that the townsfolk expected that the midwife would be held accountable for creating the destructive talk which then filled the mouths of the people of Nantwich. Their depositions reveal an underlying argument within each of the accusations against Knutsford. The matter always disclosed discord pertaining to ready money. According to Knutsford, the women who were caught up in the matter were concubines who were either 'paid' by Walthall or 'paid' him in sexual services for the rent on their properties. As noted above, according to Anne Knutsford's testimony, Mrs Cliffe received 'forty pounds a year' from Sir Philip Egerton, and Samuel Hussey's wife, received 'fifty shillings a year' from Richard Walthall. Although Anne Knutsford certainly did reveal information which her clients believed was of a private sexual character, she said, in addition, much that was related to the sensitive issues of the ownership of property and wealth. Of course, according to law, those children who are referred to as bastards in early modern Nantwich were born as the result of fornication outside of wedlock. In the common law court fornication was punished very severely.[159] Both offenders, male and female, were subject to the punitive measure of whipping or gaol at the house of correction. Those accused of such an offence had the option of pursuing a suit at the Consistory Court and that is exactly what the townsfolk did.

Bastardy and Richard Walthall's Activities

Despite Anne Knutsford's tendency to divulge sensitive information or speak indiscreetly, Richard Walthall's actions remain questionable. The matter of illegitimate children and Richard Walthall's activities emerges prominently within the context of bastardy. He was undoubtedly the focus of much talk in the town. The midwife's accusation of his involvement with his female tenants was truthful. Elizabeth Johnson's deposition reveals that he paid her, and other people, to appear at the court to speak well of him. In addition, he was implicated in several illicit liaisons, which were vividly described by the midwife. Later, in 1675, he was married 'clandestinely' to wealthy Maria Wilbraham.[160] As with others of high standing in the community, he was deeply disturbed by the midwife's conversation. He took aggressive measures against the midwife not only to stop her from practising midwifery but to stop her from naming him as the father of several the town's children who were described as 'bastards.'

At least four of the deponents who testified against Anne Knutsford were related to Richard Walthall. Most of those who were not related to him had a monetary relationship with him. For example, the Johnsons, were indebted to him and leased land from him.[161] Innkeeper Elizabeth Cliffe, who also rented property from him, was vague and confused in her admission that she was related to him through her 'gratfather [her grandfather so that she and Walthall] were brother and sister as she hath been told.'[162] Although she was vague she was more certain than his other relatives, who could not explain their connection by kin at all. Margaret Wirkstad, for example, said she was related to Richard Walthall but could not say how. In her deposition she said: '[her husband] was neare a kin to [the promoter of the cause, Richard Walthall] but how neare she well knoweth not.'[163] Margaret Jeurl, said that she and Richard Walthall were cousins, but neither was she able to account for the family connection. Of her connection with him she deposed the following: 'Mr Walthall and this respondent doe ordinarily call Cosens but what if kin they are?'[164] Similarly, Elizabeth Church, who was also related to Richard Walthall, could not account for the family association: 'her husband is of kin to Mr Walthall but how neare she knows not.'[165] So, many were related to him, but none could explain the family connection. Some, such as Elizabeth Church, were yet more hostile when she was asked to explain her family association. How was it the those of Nantwich town were related to him? Why was it that they could not, (or would not), own up to the family connection? Was it not possible that the rumoured associations of Captain Richard Walthall and respectable married women of the town were not entirely without foundation? Was it not possible that Captain Walthall might have fathered a few bastards around the town of Nantwich, as had his forefathers before him?

In this respect the evidence given by the witnesses for Richard Walthall and against Anne Knutsford in their depositions reveals several inconsistencies. Much of the evidence they gave indicates a consensus that was reached without basis in fact. While it was true that Anne Knutsford had a scurrilous tongue, she often spoke mean words and certainly she had cursed people frequently, but unlike the situation which was demonstrated in earlier chapters, where victims or their families were damaged in some way by a curse, none of the deponents claimed to have been materially or physically damaged by the midwife's curses. They were largely concerned about the damage she might have done to their standing in society. Most of the evidence they gave to the court was hearsay, it was not fact. If any hearsay was true, then it may well have been the observations made by the midwife about prostitution and the offspring produced by these illicit affairs. But it is not the purpose here to investigate whether the midwife was guilty or innocent. The purpose is to explore the reasons for cursing and to reflect upon the circumstances which underpinned the complaints about the curse. Anne Knutsford was present as an eyewitness on several occasions when various alleged lovers were seen to have met secretly. What is more, she was consulted by each of the women involved to deliver their children. In the capacity of midwife, Anne Knutsford was *required by law* to express any doubts she had about the parentage of the children she delivered. Her disclosure about the towns' bastards necessitated such disclosure and in this it might be said that she was doing what was required of her as a midwife.

Captain Richard Walthall, who was supported by Nantwich allies, reacted immediately to Anne Knutsford's allegations. He approached the court to silence the midwife. He was the principal protagonist in the action to silence Anne Knutsford. Having initiated the earliest petition and sought support from the townsfolk who were in debt to the midwife, at that juncture he then paid them to sign the petition and then offered to pay them to appear in the Consistory Court as witnesses. As noted above, the Minister of Nantwich, Richard Jackson, was commanded by Richard Walthall in February 1663 to publicise Bishop Wainwright's prohibition against Knutsford, to stop her from practising midwifery. Walthall insisted on publicly discrediting the midwife and insisted that the prohibition be placed on the church door for all to see. Walthall instructed the Minister to make his intentions thus:

> the Inhibition was delivered to the deponent and he was required by a messenger sent from Mr Walthall to publish it in the Church where accordingly he did when Anne Knutsford was in the Church and this deponent hath been told by severall persons of credit that after that time she did the office of a midwife to the articulate Pratchetts wife as Pratchett himselfe told this deponent.[166]

When the cause was heard by the Chester Consistory Court on 24 March 1663, among the many other charges levelled at the midwife, the Minister said that she was guilty of disturbing the peace of the neighbourhood.[167] However, the evidence he provides raises a few questions. Why did the Minister in this instance rely so heavily upon hearsay? Why was it that he acted so quickly upon the evidence of Richard Walthall? Why was it that Mr Pratchett, who was referred to in the document, was not called to give evidence? As for Anne Knutsford—curser, revealer of secrets, and 'public bawd'—if she was such a disreputable one, what was she doing at church?

> In the face of the allegations that were made against her conduct and speech, Anne Knutsford ignored Walthall's 'Inhibition,' and continued to practise midwifery.[168] Furthermore, she displayed contempt for the decision of the court, for Richard Walthall, and for his allies. In a symbolic gesture of defiance, Knutsford contrived what was in her opinion the more useful function for the document. In summary of her opinion the Registrar wrote:

> [Anne Knutsford] you have not only contemptuously abused the Authority of this court – when the inhibition was served upon you, you said it should serve to wipe your arse with.[169]

In February 1663, Anne Knutsford openly defied the prohibition on practising midwifery and continued her activities without hesitation. In response to her defiance, Richard Walthall promptly took action to initiate a decisive case against the midwife. A list of 12 articles were produced with the intention of discrediting her and intended to put a stop to her midwifery practice.[170] The subsequent examination of the depositions of witnesses revealed that the midwife's 'lewd and scurrilous tongue' had indeed unearthed some uncomfortable facts about the lives of the townsfolk. Richard Walthall acted to protect his honour and reputation in relation to his associations with Elizabeth Cliffe and Dorothy Hussey. Their appearance at court gave them the opportunity to publicly demonstrate their innocence, which no doubt explains why they agreed to appear for Walthall and to discredit the midwife. Elizabeth Johnson's evidence explicitly demonstrates that Walthall 'secured' witnesses to appear against the midwife.[171] The deponents appeared as witnesses, first, because they were paid to appear by Richard Walthall, and second, because they wanted to conceal that they were in debt to the midwife. Elizabeth Cliffe, Dorothy Hussey, Ann Blagg, and Dorothy Delves could not meet the expense of maintaining a high profile in society, and neither were they able to pay rent to Walthall. When they paid in kind the midwife delivered their bastards. Walthall's allies did not act for the sole purpose of curbing the tongue of the 'lewd and scurrilous' Anne Knutsford: they did so because they were afraid that others might believe her.

Walthall's alliance and Anne Knutsford clashed repeatedly. The details of their battles were to be recorded in the Consistory Court papers across the 1660 s. The more specific issues relating to moneylending, property, sick children, childbirth, and bastardy, which arose in the action of Richard Walthall and that were to involve Knutsford during the 1660 s, were mentioned again in each of the ten separate causes. The problem of moneylending arose most particularly, however, in 1663, when Anne Knutsford took Anne Blagg to court to collect an outstanding debt.[172] Knutsford, perhaps because her reputation for cursing had undermined her credibility, failed to obtain the money owed to her by Blagg. Subsequently, in later years, when it was decided that she should apologise to Ann Blagg for cursing, she opted instead to refer the matter to the high court at York, only to decide against this action eventually when the cost of running the case proved to be too expensive.[173] As the court record for 1668 makes clear, financial considerations loomed large in the case:

> After sentences were given in this court on the behalfe of Edward Blagge and Anne his wife in two causes, Richard Williamson advised Anne to appeal to Yorke, telling her it would but cost her fifteen shillings to prove the cause thither, but shortly after he advised her to agree with Blagge which she forthwith did, and paid Blagge in compensation £4, and had his peleace [word] for the same.[174]

The details of Ann Knutsford's long-running pursuit of Ann Blagg were provided by witness, Foulke Harte, who appeared in court to support Anne Blagg's action. In his deposition, he claimed that Anne Knutsford had vociferously pursued Ann Blagg for the money she owed her.[175] The background behind a further long-standing antagonism, that between Elizabeth Cliffe and Anne Knutsford, was also revealed in the Blagg case of 1664. Anne Knutsford had long asserted that Elizabeth Cliffe was guilty of producing bastard children. Further evidence came to the fore through the lawsuit against Anne Blagg, which claimed that it was in reaction to the continuing claims of prostitution that Anne Knutsford raised against her that Elizabeth Cliffe was compelled to clear her name. Knutsford apparently scattered her accusations of prostitution in numerous conversations. She alleged that Cliffe was 'nought [naughty] with John Egerton, and Dorothy Hussey parded out her rent with Richard Walthall, her landlord.'[176] The persistence of these allegations, and the repetition of the claims in the subsequent lawsuits, eventually forced Elizabeth Cliffe to pay, what Knutsford described as a 'iourney,' [a fee for swearing one's freedom from guilt], and to swear her innocence before a Justice of the Peace.[177]

To understand the accusations piled against Knutsford in 1663, and the motivation of her enemies, it is important to understand that the case had a strange prelude. Further investigation of the documents reveals that Knutsford herself had launched proceedings against Barbara Croxton in 1662, in a case which anticipated many of the features of the major cursing case of 1663. In March 1662, Knutsford had summonsed Barbara Croxton for slander for saying that she had revealed indiscretions during the private business of childbirth.[178] It was Anne Knutsford, however, who took exception at Barbara Croxton's report about her client, Mrs Bromall. Croxton was alleged to have said:

> You, Barbara Croxton did report and say of Anne Knutsford, when you were in labour and in extremity of paine that you had occasion to say that Anne Knutsford bidd you shitt or do your business in her hands, for Mrs Bromhall, (one who Anne Knutsford is midwife unto) did shitt or do her business in her hands, and most of her children were brought into the world that way.[179]

Again, in 1664, in yet another lawsuit, Knutsford had Barbara Croxton arraigned for saying that Knutsford's techniques of midwifery had endangered her child. It is clear from the evidence above that Croxton was offended by the Knutsford's technique 'of having her shitt in her hands.' Knutsford also denied having spoken of Elizabeth Bromhall indiscreetly. Croxton's evidence inadvertently puts on record Knutford's 'hands off' approach which gave women in labour greater freedom by allowing them to decide for themselves the precise time at which to go to a 'birthing stool.'[180]

'A Powiful and Ready-Handed Woman': The Vindication of Anne Knutsford, March 1663

In March 1663, Anne Knutsford won the battle against Richard Walthall and his Nantwich alliance's attempts to stop her from practising as a midwife. A notice was issued by the Chester Consistory Court which declared 'Anne Knutsford's innocence of the charge of revealing the secrets of women.'[181] In addition, 21 women came to Chester, not only from within Nantwich, but also from the neighbouring areas of Acton, Wybunbury, and Wrenbury, to sign a petition which affirmed Knutsford's 'great skill and judgment.' The petition read as follows: 'There is none whatsoever in these parts of the country so apt and fit for the execution and performance of midwifery as Anne Knutsford.'[182]

> What is more, the court proved Walthall's alliance to be 'without just cause' and came out in favour of Anne Knutsford, deciding that she had proved her innocence. In the Registrar's words: 'the information mentioned in [the] Suspension or Copy of [the] Suspension now written, was maliciously and without just cause devised and given against Anne Knutsford.'[183]

Clearly, the town was divided when it came to losing the service of such a proficient midwife. Walthall's pressure to discredit Anne Knutsford was rejected. The women, who had originally supported Walthall against the midwife, formed an unlikely alliance of female solidarity, albeit one which was born of self-interest. Women who had previously given evidence against Anne Knutsford for cursing, when forced to speak of her expertise as a midwife, had second thoughts when they realised that she was going to lose her licence—and they were going to lose a midwife. Nantwich's women, who had previously signed Walthall's petition, now testified in favour of reinstating Anne Knutsford. The women who changed their minds about Anne Knutsford were Jane Wright, Elizabeth Cliffe,[184] Margaret Birkerton,[185] Janet Brookett,[186] Elizabeth Proudman,[187] Elizabeth Johnson,[188] Barbara Croxton,[189] and Maria Elledge[190] As in the case of Margaret Jackson, although the female members of Walthall's alliance cited evidence against the midwife for verbal crime, they were unable to prove fault against her as a midwife. Moreover, a further five women were explicit in their belief that they found the midwife to be a superior practitioner. One of these was apothecary Elizabeth Walley, who had a high opinion of Anne Knutsford. She flatly contradicted the evidence of Knutsford's enemies and denied having heard the midwife speak abusively of women but did say that she had heard them speak ill of her. In contrast to the 'vitiously disposed public bawd' cited by others, she knew her to be a highly skilled professional.[191] She drew attention to Knutford's charitable side and spoke of her success in delivering safely from complicated childbirth.[192] Elizabeth Walley was the head of an all-female coalition which denied the charges of professional incompetence, preferential treatment, and neglect. All the women changed their minds, contradicted their former statements, and supported Elizabeth Walley. Elizabeth Walley explained that she had signed the petition only to obtain an opportunity to speak in support of the midwife.[193] While she believed that the others who had signed the petition were good and creditable individuals, she believed it was in the interest of the public to protect Anne Knutsford, and she was not prepared to join them in their condemnation of the midwife. She stated:

> The onely cause of this deponent subscribing [the petition] was to testify her knowledge of Anne's ability and dexterity in her profession, and for her readiness to help poore people, and that she might be continued in her imployment.[194]

Elizabeth Walley's view found equal support from two women of 'gentle' status. One was Elizabeth Church, and the other, her daughter, Elizabeth Bromhall. Their evidence declared that Anne Knutsford had been midwife for over two generations. The first, 32-year-old Elizabeth, who was married to mercer Thomas Brumall, said that Anne was midwife to her upon six occasions.[195] Her mother, 54-year-old Elizabeth Church, also pronounced that she had first-hand experience of Anne Knutford's skills:

> Anne is a very good midwife and one of the best thereabouts and is reputed soe to be. Anne Knutsford 14 or 15 years agoe having done the office of a midwife and taken a childe of this deponent into the world soe long since.[196]

Elizabeth Church's daughter, Elizabeth Bromhall, refused to sign the petition against Anne Knutsford. She highlighted the midwife's assiduity in attending to women experiencing troubled labour. Indeed, she said Anne Knutsford came to the aid of women when other midwives refused.[197] Margaret Jackson whose deposition did much to injure Anne Knutsford about cursing, could not denigrate her ability as a midwife because Anne Knutsford had delivered each of her seven children.[198]

A further 21 women signed a petition requesting that Anne Knutsford's suspension be revoked. The petition highlighted the desperate conditions of some of the women she tended, and underlined Knutsford's willingness to assist with the problems they faced. The women put their signatures to the following statement:

> In regard whereof and of her great skill and judgement in the execution and performance of midwifery and especially her readiness to assist and helpe poore women not onely in the performance of the office, but also in sending and furnishing them with money, clothes, and other necessaries in their straites.[199]

Anne Knutsford, after a long and expensive legal battle, was finally victorious. In the succeeding years, she resorted to, and was the recipient of, a series of charges and counter charges by which she intended to make her enemies sorry for denouncing her. Throughout the rest of the decade, she issued citations almost as often as she did curses.

Cases of cursing illustrate most emphatically that verbal power, though it was not distinct from popular belief in the supernatural, neither can it be wholly attributed to it. Cursing and scolding had an especially pronounced social dimension. Cases of cursing from 1630 to 1640 and from 1660 to 1670 disclose that it was often owing to an act of down-to-earth impulsiveness on the part of the townsfolk that the initiation of legal action against female spoken crime took place. Indeed, the occurrence of a cursing situation rarely arises spontaneously. Typically, it is rooted in a lengthy history of underlying issues. Within its social context, cursing primarily revolved around matters concerning property, possessions, livestock, and land. It is worth noting that scolding and cursing were closely intertwined, and both cursing and witchcraft in this region were commonly associated with disputes over property ownership. The fact that female behaviour that was perceived as criminal conceals a distinct socio-economic dimension that has been neglected. Cursing was most common during periods of local economic hardship, and social hardship lay at the root of most cases. From the early sixteenth century there was a consistent chronological pattern in the number of accusations. In the early seventeenth century, a sharp rise in the number of cases appeared from around 1630 to 1640. As disclosed and confirmed in the petitions of the townsfolk, this period was one of pronounced hardship for the communities of the Northwest.

The episodes of cursing that related to Sybill Farclough, Jenet Wilkinson, and Joane Elderson, are typical of both the transgressory conditions and a tightening of the restrictions that were imposed on women's discourse and conduct in the Northwest. However, notwithstanding these regulatory impositions, the most striking feature of the circumstances of cursing and scolding is that the conditions that precipitated legal prosecutions were not instigated by the governing or regulatory bodies—the prosecutions were initiated by the townspeople. However, that is not to say that Justices played no part in the acceleration of cases as they had women arrested without hesitation if they considered that the evidence of the charge brought by the community was sufficient. Highly verbose women became ever more susceptible to accusations and some of their neighbours became more litigious. From 1630 onwards such verbal violence became progressively more closely connected with socio-economic deprivation. Although individuals were particularly concerned about goods, property, and belongings, their petitions disclose a socially disruptive environment that might also be related to a range of divergent issues. These issues consisted of disturbing the peace, unsettling one's neighbours, and violent affray. However, in the period after 1630, petitions and depositions disclose that, of all the different kinds spoken crime, it was cursing that was most connected with loss of property or loss of livelihood. Similarly, there was a progressively intensifying emphasis upon honour, reputation, and social status. Although honour and good reputation had always been important, the records from Cheshire show an obsessive emphasis upon honour and reputation, especially after 1660. The personal properties of good credit, a blameless character, and the pursuit of respectability were issues which were constantly being fought out in the legal arena. The progressive regulation of women's speech and behaviour was a part of this process. There were certainly pockets of crisis and hotspots of gender conflict, but these situations overlay a context of continuous conflict with the influence of the competing ideologies of moral law implemented by the Consistory Courts and exerted by religious control. The potential of female vocal power may well be confirmed by the measures that were taken to silence it. The denunciations and finger-pointing that occurred, and the extent of litigation indicates that women were the focal point of a wider a social battle to maintain their significance in the often turbulent and changing communities of early modern Northwest England.

Notes

1. C. B. Phillips and J. H. Smith, *Lancashire and Cheshire from AD 1540: A Regional History of England* (London and New York, 1994).
2. This figure is derived from E. A. Wrigley and R. S. Schofield, *The Population History of England 1541–1871* (London, 1981).
3. C. B. Phillips and J. H. Smith, op. cit. p. 8.
4. J. Addy, *Sin and Society in the Seventeenth Century* (London and New York, 1989), p. 4.
5. Ibid.
6. The Victoria History of the Counties of England, A History of Cheshire, Volume III (London, 1980).
7. R. C. Richardson, *Puritanism in Northwest England: A Regional Study of the Diocese of Chester to 1642* (Manchester, 1972), p. 1.
8. Ibid. pp. 1–22.

9. R. A. Skelton, *Christopher Saxton's Cheshire, Saxton's Survey of England and Wales* (Amsterdam, 1974).
10. J. Speed, *An Atlas of Tudor England and Wales* (London, 1951), p. 6.
11. J. Thirsk, 'Sources of Information on Population 1500–1760,' *Amateur Historian,* IV (Oxford, 1959), pp. 132, 183, 184. Although not exact, these figures at least provide a working estimate, particularly when they are converted with the average multiplier of 4.75 (being the calculated size of the average family) to arrive at the numbers of individuals probably resident within each household. Deaneries and hundreds had different boundaries. The population figures of the Hearth Tax of 1664 can be compared with the 1563 parochial returns to demonstrate the change in population size and distribution during this period.
12. C. B. Phillips and J. H. Smith, op. cit. p. 8. Presuming the average family was 4.75, the population of Cheshire was approximately 60,339 and Lancashire 82,241. The Hearth Tax returns of 1664 indicate a rise in the population of the region. Cheshire's number of heads of household was 19,825; multiplied by 4.75 the population figure is 94,168; while for Lancashire a head of households' figure of 29,819, multiplied by 4.75 gives a population figure of 141,640.
13. E. A. Wrigley and R. S. Schofield, *The Population History of England 1541–1871* (London, 1981), p. 681. This study shows that in some decades, such as the 1590s, 1620s, 1630s, and 1740s, the incidence of local crises was higher than usual: 'During these decades the national death rate fluctuated violently upwards in one or more years, indicating that the crises in these decades were widespread and that the surges in the national death rates were not simply the product of heavy mortality in a few large parishes.'
14. See also D. Hirst, 'Locating the 1650s in England's Seventeenth Century' History, Volume 81, Number 263, (July 1996), pp. 359–383. Hirst refers to the crisis conditions that were experienced throughout England during the period of the Restoration. He argues that: 'Locally devastating outbreaks of plague at the start of the 1650s were followed by a virulent and almost nationwide fever at the end of the decade.'

15. R. Stewart–Brown (Ed.), *Cheshire Inquisitions Post Mortem*, The Record Society for the Publication of Original Documents Relating to Lancashire and Cheshire, Volume 111 (1938).
16. F. A. Bailey, (Ed.), *Cheshire Quarter Sessions Records for the County Palatine of Chester, 1559–1760,* The Record Society for the Publication of Original Documents Relating to Lancashire and Cheshire, Volume 94 (1938).
17. Ibid. p. 83.
18. Ibid.
19. Ibid.
20. Ibid. p. 137.
21. Ibid. p. 162.
22. Ibid. p. 139.
23. Ibid.
24. Ibid. p. 142. See also, G. P. Higgins, 'The Government of Early Stuart Cheshire,' *Northern History*, Volume 9–11 (Manchester, 1984), p. 32.
25. F. A. Bailey, op. cit. p. 142.
26. Ibid.
27. Ibid. p. 153.
28. Ibid. p. 153.
29. Ibid. p. 152.
30. Ibid. p. 152.
31. Ibid. p. 137.
32. See for example, I. Peck, 'The Great Unknown: The Negotiation and Narration of Death by English War Widows, 1647–60.' *Northern History* 53, No. 2 (2016): 220–235.
33. S. Beale, '"Unpittyed by Any"? Royalist Widows and the Crown, 1660–70.' *Historical Research: The Bulletin of the Institute of Historical Research* 92, No. 258 (2019): 737–753.
34. F. A. Bailey, op. cit. p. 155.
35. Ibid. p. 171.
36. K. O'Brien, 'Companions of Heart and Hearth: Hardship and the Changing Structure of the Family in Early Modern English Townships.' *Journal of Family History* 39, No. 3 (2014): 183–203.
37. CRO Nantwich Poor Rate Assessments, Six Volumes, (D4060/1), P120/4525/219-223, 226–228.
38. R. C. Richardson, op. cit. p. 109.

39. See, for example, K. O'Brien 'Intimate Worlds: Kinship Relations and Emotional Investment Among Nantwich Women 1603–1685,' *Journal of Family History* 41, No. 2 (April 2016): 131–143. This study investigates wills, inventories, and probate records and identifies high numbers of women reinforcing kinship relations, demonstrating commitment, signifying resilience, and arranging emotional investment in female-centred families.
40. Ibid.
41. See, for example, K. O'Brien 'Companions of Heart and Hearth: Hardship and the Changing Structure of the Family in Early Modern English Townships.' *Journal of Family History* 39, No. 3 (July 2014): 183–203. This study investigates wills, inventories, probate records, deeds, poor accounts, and parish records and provides an insight into hardship through a close study of all of the poor in one street in 1664. It finds that poor children worked hard and when apprenticed were also compulsorily separated from the family home and that child mortality was equally high among rich and poor people in early modern Nantwich townships.
42. Ibid.
43. Wyatt, op cit. p. 14.
44. CRO Nantwich Parish Records, 1660–1670.
45. Ibid. p. 25.
46. Ibid. p. 18.
47. Ibid. p. 17.
48. Ibid. p. 18.
49. Ibid. p. 18.
50. K. O'Brien, 'Petitioning, Sexual Impropriety and the Dynamics of Ill Will in Daily Urban Life.' *Urban History* 43, No. 2 (2016): 177–199.
51. Ibid. pp. 4–6.
52. Ibid.
53. P. Crawford, op. cit. p. 14. The figures are derived from E. A. Wrigley, and R. Schofield, op.cit.
54. V. Brodsky-Elliot, 'Single Women in the London Marriage Market, Age Status and Mobility, 1598–1619,' in R. B. Outhwaite (Ed.), *Marriage and Society: Studies in the Social History of Marriage* (London, 1981), pp. 80–100.

55. Quotation taken from *An Ease for Overseers of the Poore* (Cambridge, 1601), pp. 25–26, cited in P. Crawford, op. cit. p. 15.
56. Ibid.
57. Ibid.
58. Ibid.
59. Ibid.
60. P. Crawford, op. cit. p. 18.
61. Ibid. p. 21. Crawford refers to Schofield, who argues that 6–7% of women died in childbirth, and many more, of course, were afraid they would not survive.
62. P. Crawford, op. cit. p. 21. A. Wilson, 'Participant or Patient? Seventeenth-Century Childbirth from the Mother's Point of View,' in R. Porter, (Ed.), *Patients and Practitioners, Lay Perceptions of Medicine in Pre-Industrial Society* (Cambridge, 1985), p. 137.
63. P. Crawford, op. cit. p. 21.
64. See, for example, the letters of Elizabeth Winnington and Katherine Shakerley, CRO DSS1/4/57/11, which contain some details of childbirth. Also consult CRO DDX/384/1 (2), the diary of Sir Thomas Mainwaring, 1648–1659, which refers to the births and subsequent deaths of his children.
65. P. Crawford, op. cit. p. 29.
66. Ibid.
67. CRO EDC5/16/1663 Nantwich. Richard Walthall c. Anne Knutsford for an abusive midwife who lies, steals and swears and CRO EDC5/6/1664. Nantwich, Anne Knutsford c. Barbara Croxton for slander on birth of her child and 'advising her to get rid of it.'
68. CRO EDC5/1668/5.
69. Ibid.
70. Ibid.
71. Ibid.
72. Ibid.
73. Ibid.
74. Ibid.
75. Ibid.
76. CRO EDC/5/1664.
77. Ibid.

78. Ibid.
79. Ibid.
80. CRO EDC5/1663/4/16.
81. Ibid.
82. For information about the scope of Anne Knutsford's practice, see EDC5/1663/54. This archival document provides information about the context in which Knutsford practised in 'the severall townes and parishes of Nantwich'she encompassed in her rounds as midwife.
83. See CRO MF 13 Hearth Tax Records, Nantwich, 1664.
84. See EDC5/1667/2 in which Knutsford's close neighbour, Mr Illedge (he lived nine doors away from her) refers to an argument which occurred 'in the open street in Nantwich in Pepper Street, near Thomas Knutsford's house.'
85. See EDC5/1662/18 in which it is recorded that 'Anne Knutsford is commonly reputed to be the daughter of Raphe Elcocke the younger.' Anne was brought up in a house on Mill Street. Raphe Bostocke of Willaston, of gentle status, 60 years, was a contemporary of her father, Raphe. Widow Margaret Wilkes, of Beam Street, Nantwich was a contemporary of Margery, Anne's mother. She gave evidence to say that she and Anne's mother had lived together in Beam Street, when her husband died. Her brother Samuel was a mercer; in 1662 he was 32 years old.
86. See CRO EDC5/1668.
87. Anne Knutsford gave birth to daughter Jane, on November 5 1662. The three children born between 1671 and 1677, were more likely than not, the children born to her son, Thomas.
88. See J. Addy, (Ed.), *The Diary of Henry Prescott, LL.B.*, Record Society of Lancashire and Cheshire (1987).
89. Ibid. p. 27.
90. Ibid. p. 45.
91. Ibid. p. 13.
92. Ibid. p. 56.
93. CRO EDC5/1662/18/19, Nantwich, EDC5/1663/16 Nantwich, EDC5/1663/54 Nantwich, EDC5/1664/6 Nantwich, EDC5/1664/57, EDC5/1664/68 Nantwich, CRO EDC5/1662/59, EDC5/1667/2 Nantwich, EDC5/1667/62 Nantwich, EDC5/1668/10 Nantwich. Reference was made

within EDC5/1663/4/16 to six separate suits which were settled between neighbours outside the jurisdiction of the Chester Consistory Court.

94. CRO EDC5/1663/54 Prohibition of Practice. This document was fastened to the door of Nantwich Church, at the direction of Richard Walthall, promulgator of the cause, on 5 February 1663.
95. CRO EDC5/1663/4/16 Nantwich.
96. CRO EDC5/1663/4/16 Nantwich, Items.
97. Ibid.
98. Ibid.
99. Ibid.
100. Ibid.
101. Ibid.
102. Ibid.
103. Ibid.
104. Ibid.
105. Ibid. Deposition of Margaret Birkerton.
106. CRO EDC5 1663/4/16, Nantwich. Deposition of Janet Brooket. Brooket asserted the following: 'Anne Knutsford is said to have cursed James Wilson of Namptwich.'
107. Ibid. Deposition of Barbara Croxton.
108. Ibid. Deposition of Jane Wright. Jane Wright snubbed the midwife socially but acknowledged her acquaintance professionally. She stated: 'all though she hath soe often made use of her as a midwife, yet she hath very little acquaintance or familiarity with her at other times.'
109. Ibid. Deposition of Jane Wright.
110. Ibid. Deposition of Margaret Birkerton: 'Anne Knutsford is a woman of a very uncivill and base scandalous language towards people without any cause or provacaccon at all many times and hath abused with her bad tongue both Thomas Proudman and his wife who are very civill persons, and others.'
111. Ibid. Deposition of Margaret Birkerton.
112. Ibid. Deposition of Margaret Birkerton.
113. Ibid. Of her neighbours, Margaret Birkerton had this to say: [the] persons subscribed to the certificate and of what she has heard generally of their good standing they have the report of very civill good people and she believes [they] are soe.
114. Ibid. Deposition of Margaret Birkerton.

115. Ibid. Deposition of Margaret Birkerton.
116. Ibid. Deposition of Thomas Proudman.
117. Ibid. Deposition of Thomas Proudman.
118. Ibid. Deposition of Thomas Proudman.
119. Ibid. Deposition of Thomas Proudman. In his statement, he asserted the following: 'for these reasons .... the neighbours being much offended he believes the contents [of the petition] thereof are true.'
120. Ibid. Deposition of Janet Brooket: 'these differences were ended before Christmas last.'
121. Ibid. Deposition of Janet Brooket.
122. Ibid. Deposition of Janet Brooket.
123. Ibid. Deposition of Richard Jackson.
124. Ibid. Deposition of William Blundell.
125. Ibid. Deposition of William Blundell.
126. Ibid. Deposition of Margaret Wirkstad.
127. Ibid. Deposition of Margaret Wirkstad. 'Anne Knutsford hath a very bad and scandalous tongue and is very apt to slander and abuse her neighbours.'
128. Ibid. Deposition of Margaret Wirkstad.
129. Ibid. Margaret Wirkstad in her statement said the following: [her husband] was 'neare a kin to the party prdcent but how neare she well knoweth not.' Mr Wirkstad was a mariner by trade in 'Namptwich and followed it as long as he lived and since his death her sonne keeps the same ship and this deponent looks to his praise.'
130. Ibid. Deposition of Margaret Wirkstad.
131. Ibid. Deposition of Margaret Wirkstad.
132. Ibid. Deposition of Margaret Wirkstad. Wirkstad stated her affinity with the others in agreeing with the other townsfolk. She asserted she 'believed the contents [of the items to be] true.'
133. For a full account of Anne Knutsfords revelations, see K. O'Brien, op. cit.
134. Ibid. Deposition of Janet Brookett. Several incidents were alleged to have occurred at the home of Mr and Mrs Richard Yorksall, Mr and Mrs Wilson and Mr and Mrs Booth where, it was alleged Anne had been midwife. Similarly, deponents referred to 'poore' people, none of whom provided evidence or signed the petition.
135. Ibid. Deposition of Janet Brookett.

136. Ibid. Deposition of Janet Brookett.
137. Ibid. Deposition of Janet Brookett.
138. Ibid. Deposition of Janet Brookett.
139. Ibid. Deposition of Margaret Jackson.
140. Ibid. Deposition of Margaret Jackson.
141. Ibid. Deposition of Elizabeth Walley.
142. Ibid. Deposition of Elizabeth Brumall: 'she hath heard that the articulate Anne Knutsford hath devulged the secretts of some women in the time of their trauell and particularly of this deponent and such things as were unfitt to be declared, but whether she did soe or noe this deponent can not testifie, but she the said Anne hath denyed that ever she spoke any such words as were charged against her concerning this deponent and wished that she might never enter into the Kingdome of heaven if ever she spoke them.'
143. Ibid.
144. Ibid. Deposition of Edward Blagg.
145. Ibid.
146. Ibid.
147. Ibid.
148. Ibid.
149. Ibid.
150. Ibid.
151. Ibid.
152. Ibid.
153. Ibid.
154. Ibid.
155. Ibid.
156. Ibid.
157. See, for example, EDC51664/68 Anne Knutsford cites Anne Blagg. This cause discloses further antagonism between Anne Knutsford and Anne Blagg. The events recorded in this case took place in July 1663. The conflict began, however, in the early months of 1663.
158. Deposition of Elizabeth Proudman.
159. J. Addy, op. cit. p. 158. Addy suggests that fornication, of course, encouraged bastardy, and that bringing a child into the world was, in a patriarchal society, unacceptable. Furthermore, he argues, tying down the father was an 'unquestionably anti-social act.'

160. See CRO EDC5/13/1675, Nantwich, Andrewes c. Bristowe, Marriage of Richard Walthall to Maria Wilbraham. Richard Walthall paid a bond of five hundred pounds to be married secretly to Maria Wilbraham in the house of Ralph and Margaret Briscoe. See QDR7 MF96/6 where Briscoe has a house listed under non-conformist groups in the Register of Dissenting Meeting Houses, 1689–1853. Andrewes admonishes the 'promoter of the cause.' The meeting house was in Barker Street Nantwich. The entry is dated 15 January 1695 but the meeting house was established before this date.
161. Deposition of Elizabeth Johnson: 'they hold a small garden under Mr Walthall for three lives.'
162. Ibid. Deposition of Elizabeth Cliffe.
163. Ibid. Deposition of Margaret Wirkstad.
164. Ibid. Deposition of Margaret Jeurl.
165. Ibid. Deposition of Elizabeth Church.
166. Ibid. Deposition of Richard Jackson.
167. Ibid. Deposition of Richard Jackson: He testified that Anne is 'too much adicted to lyeing, swearing and cursing and for such a one is comonly taken and reputed in that neighbourhood.'
168. Items against Anne Knutsford: 'for the misdemeanours aforesaid and other reason appearing to the judge….was privately and personally inhibited and publiquely in the congregation soe declared to bee…but have proceeded to exercyze the office of midwife to the wives of John Pratchett, Johnathan Chones and soe are reputed to have done.'
169. Ibid.
170. Ibid. Items against Anne Knutsford, John Wainwright v Anne Knutsford.
171. Ibid. Deposition of Elizabeth Johnson.
172. CRO EDC5/1664/68 Nantwich.
173. CRO EDC5/1668/10 Nantwich.
174. CRO EDC5/1668/10 Nantwich. Responsions of Anne Knutsford and Thomas Knutsford.
175. Ibid. Deposition of Foulke Hart.
176. CRO EDC5/1664/68 Nantwich, Statement of Anne Blagg.
177. CRO EDC5/1664/68 Nantwich, Statement of Anne Blagg.
178. CRO EDC5/1662/59 Nantwich, Anne Knutsford cites Barbara Croxton for Slander.

179. Deposition of Anne Knutsford.
180. CRO EDC5/1664/6 Anne Knutsford cites Barbara Croxton for slander of Knutsford who was midwife to her on the birth of her child and for claiming that Knutsford had advised her to 'get rid of it.'
181. CRO EDC5/1663/54 Suspension revoked.
182. Ibid.
183. Ibid.
184. Ibid. Deposition of Elizabeth Cliffe: 'Made use of Anne Knutsford as a midwife above 14 years agoe.'
185. Ibid. Deposition of Margaret Birkerton: 'Anne is a good midwife and generally accounted soe to be.'
186. Ibid. Deposition of Janet Brookett: 'Anne has had much to do with this family havinge done the office of a midwife to the depot. of sixe children.'
187. Ibid. Deposition of Margaret Robinson: 'About thirteen years ago she had occasion to make use of the articulate Anne Knutsford as a midwife.'
188. Ibid. Deposition of Elizabeth Johnson: 'Anne is a woman very skillfull in her profession and by her endeavours and God's blessing hath laid this deponent in bed of 4 children and she is accounted to be a good midwife.'
189. Ibid. Deposition of Barbara Croxton: 'Anne is an experienced woman in her profession this deponent haveing made use of her in that way and is soe accounted to be.'
190. Ibid. Deposition of Maria Elledge: 'Anne is a skilfull woman in the Art she professeth and is accounted soe to be.'
191. Ibid. Deposition of Elizabeth Walley: ' Of Anne Knutsford she said the following words Anne is a very skilfull midwife, and comonly soe reputed, And (as this depot. hath heard) by Gods blessing hath brought women safe to bed when others could not…she hath many times heard the articulate Anne Knutsford talk merrily but never heard her abuse anyone with her tongue though she hath heard some people say that she hath a bad tongue.'
192. Ibid.
193. Ibid. Deposition of Elizabeth Walley.
194. Ibid. Deposition of Elizabeth Walley.

195. Ibid. Deposition of Elizabeth Brumall: Anne Knutsford haveing taken this deponent sixe children into the world.'
196. Ibid. Deposition of Elizabeth Church.
197. Ibid. Deposition of Margaret Robinson: 'About thirteen years ago she had occasion to make use of the articulate Anne Knutsford as midwife … Anne is a good midwife in this deponents iudgemement and soe accounted to be. And this deponent hath heard she not long since laid a woman in bed when another before her would not do it.'
198. *Ibid. Deposition of Margaret Jackson: 'haveing made use of Anne Knutsford at the birth of seven or eight children as* a midwife … is a very ready handed and powiful woman in her profession.'
199. CRO EDC5/1663/54 Nantwich, Suspension Revoked. The signatories to this document were Frances Fletcher, Grace Bostock, Elizabeth Jackson, Margaret Bostocke, Margaret Mainwaring (her mark), Elizabeth Church, Anne Bowey, Anne Wathmill, Hannah Action, Elizabeth Bromhall, Elizabeth Malley, Elizabeth King, Anne Wenken, Bridgit Seavill, Joane Henshaw, the mark of Jane Beckit, Margaret Parker, Elizabeth Bulton, Robena Milroy, her marke, Anne Masseye, Alice Milton.

CHAPTER 5

Contextualising Customary Knowledge, Mystical Healing, and Cursing

Beyond Medicine: Magical Healing, Love Magic, and Spells in Treating Disease

The use of customary knowledge encompassed a strong and enduring popular belief in the effectiveness of magical healing. In the context of customary knowledge, the inclusion of supernatural forces was integral to the healing process and formed a prominent aspect of the traditions of cunning and magic employed in the practice of medicine. It was a widely shared belief that the involvement of supernatural powers was crucial for the successful recovery of sick individuals. The scope of customary knowledge transcended the bounds of the lay community, as the practice of magical healing was prevalent not only in domestic settings across different regions, but also among astrologers and intellectual individuals at universities who were equally familiar with the healing efficacy of spells. For example, the use of love magic to attract a lover was debated regularly at Oxford University. Debates about love magic took place regularly and they occurred during the years of 1605, 1620, 1637, 1652, and 1669.[1] In addition, spells, prescriptions, and charms of healing were prepared by astrologers. These were prepared mostly for men who wished to have their love returned by women who were the object of their desire.[2] There were numerous love spells, such as those listed in a compendium entitled 'The Preparation of Experiments of Love.' Such spells as these were executed

K. O'Brien, *Cursing, Crisis and Customary Knowledge in Early Modern English Townships*, Palgrave Historical Studies in Witchcraft and Magic,
https://doi.org/10.1007/978-3-031-44045-8_5

by pronouncing special words such as charming words, they were assisted by candles or words that were written on parchment as indicated in the 'charm to make a woman love thee' by speaking 'names over virgin waxe or parchment or any other experiment of love.'[3]

The extent of magical healing is well illustrated in Richard Napier's loose notes of his astrological practice of medicine from 1598 to 1629. Among prescriptions of medicinal astrology there are a broad variety of references to such medical formulas which might deal with any potential supernatural occurrences that might trouble the broader populations.[4] Similarly, the casebook of William Lilly, a practising astrologer in 1648, includes numerous remedies sought by community members to safeguard themselves against witchcraft. These remedies were preserved for use in the various cases where individuals believed they had fallen victim to bewitchment. His casebook documents that he offered counter-spells and prayers as protective measures 'for one bewitched' and for a 'house bewitched.'[5] It provides evidence of the use of incantations and ceremonial expressions to facilitate the conception of a child.[6] During the recitation of the incantation, he proposed the performance of a specific action that involved inscribing Psalm 33, thereby suggesting its potential efficacy in promoting the conception of a child as is indicated below:

> Yf she be yonge and can have no children, wryte this psalme 33. Exultate iusti in domino and these caracters, and perfume them with mastick and laye them to her right arm and she shall conceave.[7] Another to cause conception, wryte these letters in virgin parchment and let the woman beare yt upon her and she shall conceave And yf you will not beleeve yt prove yt on a tree.[8]

Instances of bewitchment were commonly reported within the popular community. Historical records indicate that cunning folk played a crucial role in offering curative remedies, as they were often sought out not only for addressing perceived instances of cursing and enchantments but also for their knowledge and proficiency in popular medicine. Cunning women were highly sought after by the broader populace for their ability to heal individuals suffering from physical and mental ailments in regions throughout England and beyond. Cunning folk played a significant role in Welsh society. They were seen as important figures in the community and resorted to magic for a range of purposes, including healing, protection, and divination and operated within Welsh society.[9]

Cunning women were regularly called upon for assistance during times of crisis. In times of catastrophe, they were called upon to pronounce the healing formulas that would ameliorate disease while nursing back to health the sick children and animals that had fallen prey to illness.[10] Occasionally, cunning women took in those clients who were distressed about their health. Often, they were concerned about regaining ownership of property that they had either lost or were at risk of losing. Such consultation with cunning folk existed throughout England. In Essex, for example, it was quite possible that cunning women were consulted to detect pregnancy.[11] Without question cunning women were consulted about a range of issues associated with childbirth, as well as about forecasting the gender of an unborn child. Such prognostications occurred broadly in the regional Northwest of England as well as in other regions of England.[12] Within a broad synthesis of European women's history and the place of childbirth in early modern society, it is noted that English cunning women performed an invaluable function, particularly within the realm of childbirth:

> At all levels of society, relatives, friends, and neighbours came to help the mother during her labour before the midwife arrived, or (in the case of most villages) the local wise woman who did the job for little or no payment.[13]

Alongside customary knowledge, cunning women were believed to possess extraordinary healing powers and were regarded as capable individuals in their curative practices. The clientele recognised that these women had the ability to tap into supernatural forces that could be harnessed for the purpose of healing and that they held great capabilities within their curative pronouncements. In contrast to the general population, the clergy and Justices of the Quarter Sessions courts held the belief that cunning women might possess a power that was of a diabolic nature, distinguishing them from ordinary individuals. Not all people agreed on this interpretation of medicine. The quotation below gives a first-hand account of a cunning women's skills:

> The spirits which appeare unto them in the Christall, or in the glasse, or water, or any way do speake, and shewe matters unto them [were] holy Angels, or the Soules of excellent men, as of Moses, Samuel, David, and others.[14]

Cunning Women and Interpersonal Relationships

The relationship between cunning women and the broader community varied. They were especially helpful during times of hardship when there was little food security in the Northwest and the health of the townsfolk suffered. During such times of difficulty some cunning folk were asked to find remedies for many of the acute illnesses that afflicted people. They were consulted to assist ailing cattle and, more often, to protect the homes of townsfolk and to free the aggrieved households of what was perceived by the townsfolk to be a supernatural evil influence. The frequency of requests for such protection by the community is indicative of their perceived vulnerability. The townsfolk, recognising their own susceptibilities, turned to cunning women for assistance, highlighting the level of trust placed in their abilities to ward off perceived threats.

In such cases, cunning women, were remunerated with a meal or two, particularly when they were called upon to bestow blessings upon a valuable harvest or sanctify areas where valuable foodstuffs were stored. Distraught townsfolk from Lancashire consulted with cunning folk regularly so that they might express blessings to protect foodstuffs and to make their barns secure.[15] The ritual blessings of the cunning folk offered panic-stricken individuals a level of food security over the annual harvest. In this way the charms of the cunning folk were deemed to have safeguarded the animals that supported their livelihoods in precarious times.

The Cultural Significance of Cursing: An Examination of Popular Beliefs

Amid the varied economic conditions and wider societal context, the belief in magical healing was widely prevalent in the early modern period of Northwest England. As previously mentioned, the sixteenth and seventeenth centuries in England saw the coexistence of various systems of popular belief, such as religion, magical healing, astrology, and bewitchment. Cursing was a fundamental aspect of popular belief during this period. When assessing ideological influences on inhabitants of early modern Northwest England, it is important to acknowledge the indebtedness owed to the earlier investigations into popular cultural beliefs and the transformations that occurred within agrarian society during the latter half of the nineteenth century in Lincolnshire. Central to popular cultural belief in Lincolnshire is the idea that an adherence to popular belief was not only a response to 'the sacred' but was also closely related to the influence of 'supernatural power.' Popular belief was essential to the recurrent problems of human resistance where religious phenomena occurred within a mutable social context, and where churches were forced to compete with each other for dominance of the status quo.[16] An emphasis on 'religions,' which, it has been noted, competed for ideological dominance with the popular belief in supernatural power.[17]In the competition for ideological dominance, orthodox religions emphatically competed with what was considered to be 'lower' expressions of religious phenomena. The process of change that occurred when English society was alienated from its shared past owes much to the transition from oral to literate culture. This is especially true for the battle for control over traditional belief that commenced shortly after the Reformation. The result was that by the twentieth century, popular belief became relegated to the realm of 'superstition.' The persistence of magical practices in the face of modernisation provides a valuable contribution to the study of folklore and popular culture. Cunning was practised throughout Europe and persisted in England into the twentieth century. The decline of magic was not due to a decrease in belief in its efficacy, but rather to changes in the social and economic conditions of rural life. While prosecutions for witchcraft were quite rare, cunning folk could face charges for fraud or similar offences.[18]

A process of transition occurred dramatically during the seventeenth century.[19] Court records express the desperate circumstances of individuals in the communities. During the period from 1630 to 1640 in Northwest England, the increase in litigation produced by the Chester Consistory Court and the Quarter Sessions courts against customary knowledge and cunning practice establishes that the charges of superstitious practice fell upon a wide range of traditional activities and beliefs. Those individuals whose practices could be associated with Catholicism—however innocuous their actual rituals may have been, whether they be 'blessings' or 'casting water' or 'bone-setting,' making prognostications more often became subject to regulation. The legal action taken against cunning folk was time and again originated by a distressed public, who, with no explanation to hand for the disastrous occurrences that befell them, therefore accused cunning people of resorting to the dark side of magic. As with the crimes associated with speech, the simple prayers for healing that were pronounced by cunning women were then depicted as enchantments or even worse, as 'sorcery.' The accusations, however, were rarely inspired by ideology alone. As with cases of cursing, the accusers repeatedly referred to the deaths of children, sickness, the loss of goods, and fear of starvation among the reversals of fortune which consequently provoked their allegations against traditional practices and especially against the cunning folk.

The general public's dissatisfaction with conventional medical treatments paved the way for the enduring reliance on the customary knowledge of cunning folk. Throughout an extended period, these practitioners continued to administer herbal remedies and a diverse array of magical healing practices, remaining relevant well into the nineteenth and twentieth centuries.[20] Consequently, cunning folk played a crucial role in meeting the medical needs of the early modern population through the provision of magical interventions. Serving as healers and adept herbalists, they were frequently summoned to employ their knowledge of magical healing powers to explain inexplicable circumstances. These practitioners enjoyed widespread popularity and were frequently the first point of contact for individuals encountering misfortune. In an examination of folkloric material and newspaper reports of the twentieth century it has been observed that the activities of the cunning folk declined in the twentieth century owing to cultural changes in society unconnected with the medical profession, but which led to a decline in the belief in popular magic.[21] During the seventeenth century in England, personal tragedies were distressingly common, leading to an increased reliance on the services of cunning folk. Their practices were sought more frequently as a means of coping with the frequent occurrences of personal misfortune. While the formal work of the apothecary was closed to women, customary medicine was practised widely, and it offered a way of life to women. It was illegal for women to give advice or to provide more complex remedies, domestic medicine was practised by many women in the domestic setting. The practice of popular healing within domestic settings was also adopted by select women from the broader community. Such individuals were highly respected and renowned for their mastery of traditional healing techniques that had been passed down over time. In this regard, cunning women not only took a chance in extending their knowledge beyond the home, but they also risked their reputation. In some more desperate cases or when a community turned against them, they even risked their lives. The reason why customary knowledge was so fraught with complication lay in the potential failure of customary popular therapies. Cunning folk faced the risk of community backlash if their treatments failed, with hostile reactions often being rapid and brutal. Nonetheless, despite the potential dangers, these practitioners persisted in their work across the region, administering their customary healing practices. Some women and, on occasion, some men achieved considerable renown within the local community. The reputation of more accomplished practitioners extended far beyond the community and their therapeutic treatments were sought near and far, and, in some cases, distressed members of the public might travel many miles merely to consult with them. Cunning women themselves often travelled on horseback to attend to patients. One instance records the details of a woman who travelled for three days at a time to assist a sick family.[22] The finer points of the practices of cunning women like these, are recorded in legal actions and disclosed in petitions. The petitions that were presented by the townsfolk give information about the circumstances in which the practices of the cunning folk were the subject of suspicion. The narratives that surfaced in the petitions that were brought by the townsfolk, and that initiated the prosecutions of the cunning folk are examined more closely below.

Sudden Waves of Illness: 'Your Petitioners Humbly Prayeth'

During the most arduous phases of severe affliction, the local inhabitants found themselves increasingly burdened with despair. In their pleas for aid, they elucidated numerous details pertaining to the nature of their maladies, thereby weaving a comprehensive narrative of their hardships. Through these petitions, an overwhelming sense of dread and trepidation is clearly conveyed, encapsulating profound fear. Some petitions relate the circumstances in which the services of cunning folk were essential, while others relate to the happenings that occurred around magic and the issue of curses. Such petitions are repeatedly associated with cunning women and with practice of customary medicine and the treatments, diagnosis, and cure. The cases that were brought before the Quarter Sessions courts establish that the petitions of disgruntled townsfolk serve to communicate the predicaments they encountered where the community could turn against cunning folk in times of acute hardship. In simple terms, people were afraid. They directed their anguish toward cunning folk who they then held accountable for the sickness that befell them and their families. Often, cunning folk were consulted to find a remedy for sick children, as it was children that were most vulnerable during waves of illness. When they were powerless to find a cure, they were then singled out for issuing curses and were held responsible for causing the deaths of children by supernatural means. In most Quarter Sessions court cases, cunning women turn out to be incriminated as the most likely instigation of the waves of illness that swept through the community.[23]

One such situation occurred in 1629, when members of the community of 'Little Boulton,' which was suffering a wave of disease, turned against a cunning woman of some renown, whose reputation was widely known across the communities. Mother Nuttall was called upon to assist a sick family. When the children of the family died, the townsfolk soon after denounced Mother Nuttall to the court for practising by diabolical means. According to Jane Chisnall, the trouble arose from an ongoing dispute between Richard Nuttall, the cunning women's son, and William Chisnall, Jane Chisnall's brother. William was also a well-known Lancashire wise man whose activities were recorded in Quarter Sessions in 1629. Nuttall's blessing ritual was described as 'casting water' which was a known method that might bring about a cure for the sickness that had befallen a family. When he tried to assist by these means, his methods then became the subject of suspicion. Jane provided the court with the following evidence of the pain caused by illness:

> Her brother called the mother of Richard Nutall a witch whore (as her brother told her) and Richard said unto him thou had best to take heede what thou sayes for my mother will take courses with thee, where upon the day after the sd William fell lame (by reason of the extreme payne he was in) as though they had cast water upon him. William said alsoe hee must have Nuttals mother sent for because he knewe she had done him harme, the mother of William made answere she should not be sent for, and she saw her sonne for foure or five dayes continued the same, and some tymes withall despaired of his speech [he could not speak].[24]

Nuttall's mother, who was a known cunning woman, was sent for to see if she might be able to help. At first, reluctant to get caught up in such a dangerous situation, she refused. Due to her exhaustion from extensive work, she expressed her inability to personally attend to the patient. Instead, she expressed her desire to assist in some manner and reached an agreement to send her son William Nuttall as a substitute. She informed the court that her son, who was frequently relied upon to assist the community, had previously ridden for three consecutive days to attend to someone else and was equally fatigued as a result. Her depositions disclose that instead, she would offer a spoken healing wish and indicated that 'she would pray for him.' However, under pressure from the community, she gave in and agreed to attend to William Chisnall. During her visit she offered a diagnosis and pronounced that he would recover in a little over a week. Shortly after Mother Nuttall's departure, William swiftly recovered. However, the illness must have been contagious. Shortly after her visit, Chisnall's mother became ill and died. Several other members of the family were stricken, including Jane Chisnall, who herself was struck down by the illness. It was at this point that the distressed Chisnall family felt that Mother Nuttall and William Nuttall were responsible for causing their problems by employing magical resolutions. They subsequently accused them of cursing, sorcery, and bewitchment as is indicated in the witness deposition below:

> William being instructed of his mother not to give Nuttall's mother any foule wordes said hee knewe not what she had done but he prayed her to doe him some good and she said she would pray for him and said he would mend and soe went her way after which he suddenly mended. Immediately after this examinates [the person being examined under oath] mother fell sore sicke and she her selfe lame, was extremely troubled with some sorcery, and she was taken after the same manner and the mother of this examinate within six weekes after, dyed, and this examinate thinks and is verily persuaded that she, Nuttals mother did bewitch them and that she released her self her brother and sister. Her mother in the time of her sickness told her she was not affrayed of Nuttall's mother, but she thought she was a witch.[25]

The Chisnall family, along with numerous other households in the vicinity, experienced the rapid spread of a contagious illness accompanied by fever. As the affliction affected the Chisnall family, their perception of Mother Nuttall and her son underwent a significant shift. At a critical juncture, when the family reached a breaking point, they denounced the cunning woman who had previously endeavoured to assist them. Although the account is clear enough about the reproof of the community, the sources do not offer distinct outcome about the fate that befell Mother Nuttall and her son, William.

'Blesser' and 'Cunning Woman' Mary Shaw

In a similar situation to that of the Nuttall cunning folk, in the same year, a renowned and so called 'Blesser' and popular 'Cunning woman' Mary Shaw gave an account of her activities when she was examined by George Ireland, Justice of the Peace, at Southworth. Her words provide further clarification about the role of cunning women who worked to restore the health of their patients. Through her narrative, the author conveys valuable insights into the multifaceted nature of the assistance provided by cunning women to community members afflicted by illness. According to Mary Shaw's proposition, cunning women exhibited generosity in sharing their extensive customary knowledge and frequently demonstrated good will by freely applying their skills to aid those in need. Shaw reports that a significant number of cunning individuals declined to accept any form of payment when assisting families during challenging circumstances. Similarly, Anne Urmeston, the daughter of William Urmeston of Crofte, a tailor, confirmed that she, too, was familiar with the efficacy of Mary Shaw's efforts. She even swore before the court that Mary Shawe, wife of Henry Shawe of Crofte, a tailor, was a renowned healer. She disclosed the details of one such occasion during which time she had returned from 'milking Edward Dowson's kyne' in August 1630. She made known that one time she had encountered Mary Shawe who then suggested that Anne 'might give God thankes for her amendment' having prepared a remedy that cured Nicholas Hadfield's farm animals. However, Anne said that she was unaware that day of any healing that Mary had done. Mary's testimony shed light on the fundamental aspects and the extent of Mary Shawe's reputation regarding her profound knowledge of customary practices and her healing abilities:

> Mary Shawe tould this examinante that shee hadd beene at Nicholas Hadfeilds and that shee hadd done good, and never did any Hurt, and that shee could do some litle thinges, but never tooke any money, but what they would give her of good will and did att the same tyme Confesse that shee Came into Hadfeilds howse and that there was a pigge fell downe very sicke. And thereuppon she went into a Chamber there and was very sicke and then Nicholas Hadfeild caused a possett to bee made for her, but tell she was amended shee could not eate yt, but after shee came out of the Chamber shee said that under God and her the pigg was amended.[26]

The deponents' narratives confirm that in conditions of sudden adversity, livestock was extremely valuable. Thus, the curative powers the cunning folk possessed became yet more highly valued. Such was the situation with 'Blesser' Mary Shawe who, it was claimed, had restored the health of numerous livestock, both of pigs and the cows that belonged to Nicholas Hadfield. Other neighbours, such as John Key and Robert Gaskell, testified to having consulted with her and spoke of the extent of her curative powers. They confirmed that she did not curse and did not accept financial reward, and that Mary Shaw was especially conversant with the customary remedies that she applied to cure sick animals, as is confirmed in the statement below:

> John Key, sonne of Henry Key of Crofte, Lynen Webster, saith that Ann Urmeston tould this examinate that Mary Shawe said that under God and herself shee hadd amended a pigg of Nicholas Hadfeilds Robert Gaskell of Crofte, aforesaid husbandman, sworne and examined saith that Mary Shawe was with this examinate and other his neighbours, to helpe upp a Cow of Nicholas Hadfeilds, but did not see her blowe in the cowes mouth, nor use any Charme to his knowledge, but further saith that shee ys generallie suspected to be a Blesser.[27]

Petitions and 'Strange and Sudden Diseases'

Multiple testimonies from the townspeople make mention of abrupt episodes of illness. Throughout the decade from 1630 to 1640, the scourge of illness, that was most likely to have been measles, spread very quickly to other neighbourhoods.[28] It was during such precarious times as these that a cunning man, known as Thomas Hope of Aspull, was contacted to assist the children of individuals who were stricken with illness. At the same time, horses and livestock also became ill. In 1638, Thomas Hope was called upon to explain the extent of his practice as legal proceedings had been taken against him. In his response he gave an account of the extent of the healing activities that he carried out. He was examined at Standish by William Leigh, Justice of the Peace, of Lancaster. Hope's account brings to light the high regard the community had for the cunning folk. It offers some details of the ways in which the healing practices of the Lancashire cunning folk were relied upon by those in the community who suffered ill health. Hope explained that he had healing powers and professed in his deposition how it was that he came to be invested with healing powers. He explained that when he was ten years old he went, with John Hale of Frodsham, to Rome where he stayed for seven weeks. During his time there he claimed to have washed in water which left marks on his arms. These marks, he claimed, had conferred on him a most remarkable capacity for curing sickness. He stated that this gift brought about in him a predisposition for restoring health and that he felt that it was his responsibility for treating illness in both humans and animals. In his deposition he explained the nature of his ability and gave an account of his work and how he had been able to alleviate suffering in both animals and humans:

> ...when he was but ten yeres of age he went with one John Hale of Frodsome to Rome where he continued about seven weakes, and after came into Frodsham and he saith that att his being in Rome he was washed in a Chamber with water by vertue of which water he hath helped horses, beasts and some children, and cured their maladies.[29]

Hope's predicaments arose through the deterioration of a professional relationship with his patients, Margerie and William Mullineux. The decline of the relationship occurred after the cunning man Hope was summoned to attend to sick children. Margerie and William Mullineux then insisted that Hope was responsible for the deaths of their children who had died after a long period of illness. Margerie Mullineux subsequently denounced the cunning man, telling the court that Hope claimed to heal 'by the name of Jesus' and that Thomas Hope said that in Jesus' name that he would pray for them:

> Margerie the wife of William Mullineux of Westhoughton sworne and examined saith that about two years since her son being dead, Thomas Hope of Aspull came unto her and told her that a prayer was sayd for him. And another tyme another of her sonnes dyed about two yeares being sicke she sent unto Thomas Hope for helpe who ansered that if she then had not taken him upp he had dyed, and she demaunding by what meanes he did that and other thinges, he said by the name of Jesus, And Margerie Mullineux further saith that she demanding of Hope who had done them that hurt had answered he could not tell, But shee should knowe 'itt' by some signe after he went awaye, whereupon one Sibyll Hyton then came into the house to borrowe a cart-rope then Hope said when she was gone that she could let noe other but come come in, and warned this examinate

> she should not lett Sibyll Hyton have Any thinge from her But that she shuld first put salt into itt.[30]

Margerie deposed that Hope also threatened her and stated that if she blew the whistle on him that he would withhold a cure:

> And told her that if shee did complayne of them or descrye them he could never cure Any more diseases for he further told her there was halfe a dozen witches thereabout whereof Agnes Hurst was chiefe of the fold And named noe more saveing a man and his wife who had noe children, and were as badd as Agnes Hurst, but who they were by name he declared not.[31]

It was later in May 1638, that Margerie Mullineux took out legal proceedings against Thomas Hope. In this case William Leigh heard evidence from physician, Christopher Leigh of Rumworth, who claimed that Margerie, who he described as being 'over-raught', was a patient of his. Nevertheless, he also implied that Hope had invoked supernatural forces and insisted that Hope was responsible for her misfortune:

> On Saturday last, he comming unto the house of William Mullineux in West Haughton and heareing that Thomas Hope had been there and suspectinge that some practice had been done upon Margrett Mullineux then his patient, sent to Hope to learne what he had practized and done unto Margrett Mullineux; who told him she was over raught and that he knewe who did itt as well as he himeself that did itt. And promised she should have noe further hurt untill this matter were tryed.[32]

The details presented in Thomas Hope's legal depositions substantiate the perilous nature of practising medicine during that time. The cunning individuals undoubtedly took risks in communities that were driven to desperation by illness, material losses, and the heart-breaking deaths of their loved ones. As with similar cases, Hope's problems began when he failed in his attempts to cure sick children. At this point his healing methods became the focus for grief-stricken and desperate parents, who, with no other explanation for their misfortune, then sought to blame Hope and wreak revenge on the cunning man who had failed to heal their sick children. Thomas Hope was soon desperate himself, for he knew that had he been found guilty by a Quarter Sessions Justice, and that he would certainly be imprisoned. At that point he then denounced other cunning folk who, he claimed, resorted to cursing and employed 'charms and inchauntements.' His efforts to direct attention away from himself, and on to Agnes Hurst, however, paid off, because Agnes Hurst was later herself denounced for speaking ill and her case is discussed further below.

Clearly, the cunning folk were easy targets. Thomas Hope's circumstances have much in common with those of Sybill Farclough. The name 'Sybill Farclough' was inseparable from illness, decayed crops, and bad luck. Moreover, she was claimed to have been a proficient curser. Between the years of 1634 and 1638 she was accused of cursing many people numerous times. Her behaviour was described as 'lewd,' and she was often accused of 'bewitchment' or 'magick.'[33] When children became ill she too found herself charged with their deaths. The petitions of local inhabitants reveal 'strange and sudden diseases' and the turn of events was attributed to Farclough's 'cursing,' 'violent and wicked speeches,' 'magick,' and 'wicked and malicious tongue.' That the circumstances of hardship and vulnerability occurred over a four-year period is suggestive of an acute ongoing crisis in the Orrell community. The grief caused by loss and sickness that formed the driving force behind petitions is well documented in the Lancashire Quarter Sessions records. It is echoed many times in the evidence of the Chester Consistory Court records as well as in the Quarter Sessions of Cheshire. Such evidence is indicative of the circumstances of sporadic crisis in certain isolated towns and villages throughout Northwest England between 1630 and 1640.[34]

Sybill Farclough's case is important because it lays bare three important and common themes. First, it demonstrates the ways in which the frequent deaths of children were often associated with charges of cursing and sorcery. Second, it indicates that Sybill's power was owing to the deep underlying fear of a powerful cursing woman, and that fatal cursing power was commonly assigned to cunning women who were trying to lend a hand during times of hardship. Third, Sybill's case elucidates the details of the close connection that existed between the remedy and failed attempts to nurse back to health, after which soon followed the accusations of negligence and suspicious malpractice in these areas.

The case of Agnes Hurst is one that reveals that there were also specific networks of suspicion at grassroots level which were specifically directed at the activities of women. For example, on 23 July 1638, at Manchester General Sessions of the Peace, Roger Gregory of Westhaughton brought a petition before the court to force the appearance of 'material witnesses' who had declined to comment, to disclose all they knew in relation to a charge against Agnes and Margaret Hurst, who had been accused of pronouncing curses:

> Agnes Hurst and Margaret Hurst were indicted for witchcraft charms and inchauntements, and your petitioner there obeyed an order from this Court for your witnesses who were Considered to bee materiall to goe before some justices of peace to give informacion against them and for her sheweth that there are some persons whom this Informacion conciders to be very materiall who deny and refuse to goe before any Justice of peace to give any information against them. Your petitioners humbly prayeth that your good worships would bee pleased to grant your warrants directed to the Constables of the severall townes where your sessions dwell, to charge and command the persons concerned to be materiall witnesses to repaire before your Justices of peace to give informations against Agnes Hurst and Margaret Hurst to you and they may be bound over to your Generall Sessions of Assizes goal delivery and your petitioner as in duty bound will ever pray.[35]

The Hurst sisters were the casualties of a network of suspicion. As with Thomas Hope‘s case, the Mullineux sought to shift the blame for the children‘s deaths to practitioners of ‘charms and inchauntements.’ Thomas Hope, through his determination to save his own neck, clearly exposed several members of the community to the suspicion of sorcery. What such incidents reveal are the ways in which accusations came about and the social dynamic which drove such accusations. In this particular case, like many others, the presence of illness and the premature deaths of children is strikingly apparent.

There were other cases involving the pronouncement of prayers which were brought before the court. For example, at Chadderton in 1634, a cunning man known as Henry Baggillie asserted that he knew a charm that was useful for curing both humans and cattle. The charm, he said, was inherited from his father, who, according to Baggilie, had learned it from a travelling Dutch man. The charm which Henry related to the court, was a simple prayer and had very little to do with sorcery, as the following deposition will demonstrate:

> About twentie years since, this examinant's father was taught by A Dutcheman certaine Englishe wordes and praiers to repeate, whereby to blesse or helpe anie sicke person or cattell in there extremetie.[36] Tell thee

> thou for Spoken Toothe and Tongue: Hearte and Hearteraithe: Three things thee boote moste: the father sonne, and holighoste, with the Lordes praier and thee Beleeve three tymes over.[37]

According to the evidence of Henry Bagillie, there was much need of the healing charm, during the years of 1632 and 1633. During this year so many people became ill that his services were called upon regularly to help both people and animals:

> all which wordes and the manner of speakinge them: hee learned of his father and hath made use of dyverse times though more frequently for these two yeares last paste, when people have come to him to blesse there friendes or cattell. And further he confesseth that alwaies when hee came to the partie ill affected, if the same needed his blessinge, then he pronounced the wordes and praiers in utteringe [sic] the of the wordes and duringe all the tyme of his blesinge, hee for all suche tyme hath alwaies beene suddenlie taken with sickness or lamenesse and that alwaies in the same manner that the man or beaste that hee blessed was troubled withall.[38]

This cunning man did not profit from his healing methods, and he would not accept a payment for these healing services. However, he did disclose that he might sometimes enjoy a meal with the family:

> that what hee hath blessed hath recovered and he hath only receaved Meale, or Cheese or Comodities of the like nature, but never did take silver or anie other rewarde but such as before hearein is Acknowledged.[39]

Despite Bagillie being an obvious blesser and healer, and his words merely an assertion of healing, Edmund Assheton, the Justice found him guilty. His note that read 'guilty' at the bottom of the manuscript page and the conclusion of Justice Edmund Assheton almost certainly condemned Henry Bagillie to a dubious future.'[40]

Starving and Homeless: 'Your Petitioner Cripell Almost Starved for Want of a Habitation'

The Justices of the Quarter Sessions Courts were not always so ruthless when dealing with people who were suffering hardship. They occasionally showed mercy. In some situations, they might offer support and sympathy to the petitioners who were in extreme poverty. This is the case with the petition of John Rosthorne who explained in his petition that he was homeless and close to starvation. In such cases of utter desperation, the justices might respond sympathetically to a petition that requested compassion. In 1663, John Roshorne, who was a labourer of Little Bolton in Lancashire, told his story of how he became embroiled in a disagreement with his landlady's brother. His petition, reproduced below, gives a clear account of the severe hardship that he endured:

> your petitioner being a very poore Lame Cripell who formerly followed the ocupation of Miller but for the space of fourteene years last past hath not beene able to work at a mill, your petitioner hath lived in Littel Boulton for the space of five years last past and upwards att the house of William Stone and coming upon atime in my landlords house my landlady William Stone's wife tould mee of a nighbours wife and Thomas Warde wiffe which had gotten a women to spit her some grout to quicken in a barril which a littell before had been left under a spout and when the barrill was emptied she tould mee there was two or three water toads in itt. Goeing to one Adame Stones house his daughter Dorothy tould mee the same story and throughe the story I had heard of my landlady, she said she thought I was a witch and she having a brother fallinge sicke shortly after Mr Hon Seefeild of Boulton tould mee hee heard on 21th July 1663 Adam Stone say that hee suspected mee to be a witch and that he threatened to further a warrant for mee and Mr Seefeild wished him to take heed what hee did and said for hee had known mee this twenty or thirty years and neither knew nor heard nothinge to mee where upon these reports my Landlord William Stone July 7th 1663 did give mee warning to provide a plea for my selfe on the 15th September and hee tould mee that if Mr Seefeild would wittness what he said to mee I might have a warrant against them.[41]

John Rosthorne's petition provides valuable insights into the rapid escalation of community finger-pointing and the momentum it gained within the community. In times of the sudden onset of illness, individuals such as Rosthorne were forced to respond with equal rapidity if they were to thwart the legal actions that were taken against them by their resentful neighbours. The petition conveys Rosthorne's indignation and the potential damage to his reputation as well as the maltreatment he suffered at the hands of his neighbours when he admonished them 'as if I had been some theefe.'[42] When people were afraid of what they believed he might be capable of doing to them and refused to accommodate him, he was forced to live on the streets. When he applied to the Justices for poor relief, his plea was recorded as follows: 'may it please your good worships to grant your petitioner relief who is allmost starved for want of a habitation.'[43] In this case, the Justice was merciful and poor relief was granted. A note at the bottom of the page read: 'Done. Provided relief and cleared of charge.'[44]

The Justices of the Quarter Sessions were not so generous to women that they suspected of cursing. Neither the petition of 80-year-old Ann Baker of Warrington, nor the signatures of 13 people in support of her petition, would move Justice William Weast to show compassion for Ann Baker who was an inmate, at Warrington in 1658. Ann Baker, who was also known as a cunning woman, was not as fortunate as John Rosthorne. She was imprisoned without delay. However, not all members of the community agreed that she was a threat to them and the signatures which appear on the petition are indicative of the concern that many members of the community felt at the imprisonment of such an elderly woman. The petitioners communicated a great deal of empathy for the elderly woman and sympathised with her sorry situation. The petitioners may also have been inmates themselves or prison wardens at the jail from where Anne Baker made her plea. Their words are telling of their concern and the petition read as follows:

> Your petitioner beinge within the Comon Gayle at Lancaster upon the suspition of sorcerie or witchcraft and nothing prouved againste her, and remaineth here still for not paying her feese wich shee can not produce, nor pay haveing no frends to Looke upon her, but hath sould all her clothes her hatt and aprine and all that shee hath and now lieth sore sicke in bed, and is not able to stir or to helpe her selfe any way.[45] May it therefore please your good worship to take into your grave Consideration the poore and Miserable Condition of your afflicted petitioner and release her from prison and shee as in duetie bound, will ever prey wee whose names are heare subscribed are daylie witnesses of her miserable condition being a woeman of fourscore years of age or thereabouts.[46]

The petition, however, was presented in vain. William Weast's blunt reaction, was recorded in the single order. 'Nothing.'[47] Despite the concern of the community, Ann Baker received no poor relief. She most likely died of starvation in prison.

The petitions of the popular community confirm that their accusations sometimes continued beyond the extent of periodic crises. However, it was above all, during periods of acute waves of illness that cunning women were most at risk. If they failed in their attempts to nurse the sick back to health, they were condemned by their patients for invoking supernatural forces, when they were then reported and subsequently imprisoned. This occurred in 1657, when, in a similar situation to that of Anne Baker, a widow Margery Greene of Ince in Macclesfield, petitioned that she and her children were starving because she was held responsible for the adversities that were experienced by the Ince community. A note from Justice Butterworth that read 'Nothing,' at the bottom of the petition is a clear indication that no mercy was forthcoming for either Margerie Green or for her children. She may have starved in prison.[48] Her children, perhaps, may have met with a similar fate. Her petition recited the details of her dire situation and is informative about the lack of compassion for cunning women such as Margery Green:

> Your poore petitioner fyndeth her selfe sore wronged and disgreaced by Thomas Bradshaw of Ince, Mr Ralphe Browne, Mrs Elizabeth Goodlaw and her sonne Christopher, Elizabeth Jolly of Ince spinster, Katherine Ford of Wigan widow, and by Jane the wife of Edward Marsh of Wigan who have all accused slandered and said and reported your petitioner to be a witch insomuch that your petitioner and her childen are lykely to be famished by reason that noe one (through these reports) will give them any releife but push them from their doores.[49]

At Lancashire Quarter Sessions in October 1661, an unnamed female reported a cunning woman to the magistrates. She was distraught because the cunning woman had failed in her attempt to cure an ailing colt. The petitioner wrote that she was afraid of the cunning woman and was vociferous in her pursuit of her saying that she was anxious for the Justices to issue a warrant for the cunning woman's arrest. Her words testify to the fact that she had on previous occasions been 'bound.' Having herself been accused previously, this petition was prompted by her desire to protect herself from further accusation. The petition discloses how the petitioner was clearly frightened to speak. Her petition confirms that the dispute concerned the death of a young horse and that when she had failed to cure the colt, she then became a suspect of speaking ill and the cause of evil supernatural intervention. The petition discloses that threats of violence were made. Although her fate is not known, her petition set out below tells her story:

> Nouble gentle men I desire you to consider of this women what kind of acourse of life shee hath lived in the first of her time shee lived with her husband as man and wife and was not so and after they were maried shee went away with another man besides her husband and shee goes in the name of a witch for which a child which the mother of the child was tought to get blud of them to cure the child, and shee did go and the child recovered well and shee was taken one morning killing of a nebours Coult and the other daye the Coult dyed, and they threaten me that they will make me to breake my bones or they will make my bones Clater in my skin and they say that they will hange me at the sessions or they will be hanged themselves and if shee meete me far from any house shee will say nothing to mee but if shee be neare any house shee will cry out for helpe and as for my part I never spoake word to her since I was bound and as for his part hee hath bin arraigned and since stole close of a hedge and I can bringe witness of this all if you plese to grant mee a warrant for them.[50]

An indication that people were suffering hard times is also demonstrated in the alleged thieving of a neighbour's livestock. One such alleged theft transpired in 1641 when a Recognisance Bond was issued by John Butterworth, Justice of the Peace. The bond required that Alice Schofield, a known cunning woman of Castleton, present herself before the Justices of Manchester Great Sessions to hear the charges of supernatural 'devilish' practices that had been made against her. During this time, she was accused of attempting to find stolen cattle, sheep, and a hen at the request of her neighbours, James Newbold and John Seildon, and by prognosticating the birth of a child. She was required to answer charges of using the 'sieve and shears,' a practice which was ill favoured by the court. The cunning woman of Castleton had been presented to the court on other occasions, and John Chadwick, Labourer, of Belfield, brought several 'Bills of Indictment' against her.[51] If the charge was proved against her at Manchester Quarter Sessions, she would have been imprisoned. The bond stated the following details:

> the Courte shall injoyne her commanding the devillish practising of a sieve and a pair of sheeres to know whoe had stoulen the sheepe, the goods and Chattel of James Newbold of Castleton aforesayd, and a hen from John Seildon of Belfield in the parish of Rochdale, and to know whether Jane Broasly at Cydeon nowe with Child, and Mary the daughter of the aforesayd John Feilden were with Child.[52]

The Quarter Sessions petitions of the Northwest show that there was a consistent chronological pattern of accusation throughout the sixteenth and seventeenth centuries with an increase in the number of cases during the decade from 1630 to 1640. In the Chester Consistory Court and the Quarter Sessions courts, the period of 1630 to 1640 shows an increase in petitions and litigation driven by acute instability. This critical period of socio-legal unrest was again repeated in the decade from 1660 and 1670.[53] The records disclose that townsfolk were being set upon by sudden illness. The subsequent emotional turmoil that followed is presented in each of the petitions of the townsfolk. The petitions reveal that the status of those who tried to help and failed was almost as precarious as those who were requesting assistance. While the situation of precarity varied from place to place, the community swiftly changed from indigence to one of malevolence, in seeking legal retribution against the cunning folk when they proved to be unsuccessful in their attempts to bring sick children back to health. During the legal hearing, there were urgent attempts to shift attention away from themselves. In such circumstances as these the cunning person was made vulnerable. Some cunning folk, in desperation and in fear of their lives, disclosed the names of other known practitioners of the healing arts who were then similarly accused of cursing or sorcery.[54]

Overall, the petitions that were presented to the Quarter Sessions and subject matter of the depositions of the Church courts of the Northwest disclose that English state and society were quick off the mark when it came to bringing legal opinion to bear on a range of traditional healing activities. However, as disclosed above, it was during acute downturns exacerbated by the constant worry that was brought on by cycles of illness that the townsfolk took legal action. Some instances were simply matters of slander or defamation, but some incidents that involved imprecation led to prolonged legal actions and held serious outcomes for healers as well as those who were involved with them. Paradoxically, it was in such difficult times as the casualties of cycles of illness that the skills of the cunning folk were in greatest demand by those members of the community. These were indeed dangerous times. Those who offered their assistance to those who were stricken were required to proceed with caution. Narratives of petitions point out that the main source of trepidation in the community was caused by infant deaths. During times of acute misfortune, the individuals who were once their patients, turned against them. This was especially the case when a young member of the family died. Those who failed to restore the sick back to health were at the mercy of a bereft community that was driven to extremes by grief and one which sought a way to make sense of their suffering by petitioning for redress of grievance, or worse, through a legal course of action, one which would often result in a poor outcome for the cunning folk.

Everyday Remedies for Household Healing

Although the use of popular traditional medicine practised by cunning women faced scrutiny, it is important to recognise that customary healing methods were widely embraced by the broader community. Scholars have proposed the notion that domestic medicine played a significant role in the healing practices of the community. Many gentlewomen in the early modern period were expected to have knowledge of customary methods of healing. They set aside kitchen gardens for such purposes and often provided medical assistance to the people that they employed on their estates. In addition, they recorded numerous medicinal recipes and noted the more popular conventions of domestic medicine. There is significant attention to detail regarding the knowledge of magical healing. The practices of supernatural healing can often be found documented in the diaries, letters, and handbooks of affluent members of the community, kept within their private homes. Women's customary knowledge was extremely important to the informal practice of medicine in early modern England. Indeed, one historian claims that 'the preparation of medical remedies was one of the skills expected of a housewife.'[55] So important was her work in the application of medicinal skills, that it has been suggested that 'apothecaries did the same job as the housewife but on a more extensive basis.'[56]

The private papers and letters of wealthier families of the Northwest display customary knowledge that reveals that although the cunning folk may have practised in poorer communities of the Northwest, they alone were not responsible for community healing. Women were informally involved as apothecaries, herbalists, and writers of medical recipes. It is not simply that women took over from their apothecary husbands. There was a familiarity with the traditions of medicine beyond the involvement in a business enterprise and this existed in some of the wealthiest households, just as it did in some of the poorest. Although the letters and diaries of wealthy men and women recorded medicinal remedies, they also often documented the frustrations, hopes, and fears of the mothers and fathers who were concerned about their families. The diaries of Sir Thomas Mainwaring, who was a Justice of the Peace in Nantwich, Cheshire between the years of 1648 and 1659, expressed great concern about his wife and new-born because of a 'child born before its time.'[57] Similarly, the letters of Katherine Shakerley of Hulme tell of the anxiety she felt about the well-being of her family. Shakerley referred to the doctors she had dealings with. Her words recount the fears she held concerning the welfare of her children, especially during the time of the plague. In one letter, she brings up the subject of the plague, which fell upon the Northwest in 1665. In her letters she alludes to it colloquially as 'the sicness.'[58]

The letters and private papers of several men and women are also full of remedies that were used for the kinds of illnesses that aggrieved people in Lancashire and Cheshire over three hundred years ago. Their household papers register a variety of important remedies for salves, burns and swellings, gallstones, piles, earache, and countless other minor injuries. As was the practice among the cunning folk, animals were as important as people and they were revered within the household. So, in addition to the remedies for common complaints, there are numerous remedies which were used to assist animals and diseased horses. Documented alongside the more minor ailments are medications for several serious diseases such as the plague and the smallpox. The appearance of such serious diseases as smallpox appearing alongside more minor ones is perhaps an indication that life-threatening diseases were treated on a regular basis and just as often as minor complaints.

An endorsement of the harmonious relationship that existed between the apothecary and the gentlewoman is noted in the letters of prominent families of Lancashire and Cheshire. Lady Katherine Shakerley of Hulme, for example, when writing to her friend Elizabeth Winnington in 1662, cited the accomplishments of the Chester apothecary Dr. Pennington most favourably. A grateful Shakerley congratulated him on his skill as a healer, as this extract from her letter will confirm: 'Dr Pennington came to see my sonn and gave him these things which I thank God he has found a great deal of good by.'[59] Similarly, Elizabeth Winnington, or ('Betty' as she was known to Shakerley), also told of her close association with a local apothecary when she wrote: 'I am very well after my fisicke.'[60] So often was Elizabeth Winnington in contact with Chester apothecary, Mr Heath, that she advised her friend to send her letters there. She wrote: 'you may conveniently every Saturday get a letter unto mee if you cause it to be left at Mr Heath's shopp, the apothecary neare to the Easte gate in Chester.'[61] Judging by their reports, women such as Lady Katherine Shakerley and Elizabeth Winnington were well versed in the art of domestic treatment and its application in the domestic sphere.

Lady Jane Stanley belonged to a prominent Lancashire family, and she prepared and applied domestic medicine by her own hand. Lady Jane Stanley was especially knowledgeable about the treatment of stomach complaints. She was above all proficient in the preparation of remedies to counteract the symptoms of nausea. The same remedy, she suggested, could also be used for treating gallstones. In a one-page manuscript was noted 'Lady Jane Stanley's receipt for Bilious Complaints [and] relief for Gall Stones.'[62] She proposed a remedy to relieve the symptoms and suggested a combination of 'aloes and mastic' which remedy is even now used for digestive issues. Her directions for the preparation of the remedy appeared as follows:

> Powder these ingredients separately, mix them well with a sufficient quantity of syrup of wormwood. Put three grains into one pill. Great care must be taken that the Aloes are properly prepared with a strong tincture of liquorice. Take one two or three pills. As they operate every day at dinner or supper that they may digest with the food, they must not on any account be taken fasting. Continue the use of these pills for three months and take them afterwards as you find it necessary. It has been known to make one perfect by taking it twelve months in cases of the Gallstones.[63]

In a slightly later period in a letter dated 1670 are the details of a herbal remedy that was sent through the mail by a loving mother to her son who was suffering the miseries of earache. Her letter contained directions to make an oil to cure an ear infection, and an herbal solution to soothe the pain was included. As recorded on the manuscript, the remedy provided directions for the application of the remedy, and was a decoction of some of the following herbs:

> Origannum, cummon, wormwood, pennyroyal, mother of thyme, sage, mint, centaurie, common mallow and marsh mallow, of each a small handfull, of chamomel, Rosemarie flowers of each a pinch (as much as you can take up between your two fingers and your thumb) of cinnamon and cloves, of sack, a quarter of an ounce.[64]

The directions for preparing the medication involved boiling a mixture of wine and water. The wine and water were then bottled as per the following instructions: 'boyle these in a pint and a half of spring water and as much good white wine, until half a pint be unfinished, when it is colde, strayne it and keep it in a bottle.'[65] It was then regularly applied to the affected part and an oil placed into the ear. An order to keep the ear warm with wool was recorded thereon as follows:

> Morning and night make hot six or seven spoonsfull of this liquore and dipping a spoone into it apply it to your eare and when it grows colde squeeze out your liquor, and warming it again, apply it after the same manner three or four times. When you have thus washed your ears droppe into them two or three drops of the oyle which I have sent you making it prettie hot, and then put into your ears a little black wool.[66]

Therapies such as the ones mentioned above were shared among friends and neighbours, often recommended with the intention of aiding with various ailments and complaints. For example, in a loose manuscript, prepared by an unknown author, in 1640, is provided a 'A Receipt for Piles.'[67] In another undated manuscript, probably late seventeenth or early eighteenth century, there are recorded the details of how to prepare a medicine known as 'Johnson's Salve' (Johnson presumably being the person who prepared it). This cure was described as 'an excellent salve, or ointment for white swellings, biles, [boils] gatherings, burns, scalds, sprains, sore throats or to heal after a blister.'[68] The manuscript conveys that this ointment was sent to one known as Mr Finney of Oversleyford. It was an all-purpose salve, used for a range of skin complaints. The fusion of herbs including honey, beeswax, and oil was recorded for this remedy and is set out below:

> Have ready 12 ounces of honey in a jar, in which you intend to keep the Ointment, which must stand near the Fire till quite warm, then cut into small pieces 4 ounces of Bees Wax, and 6 ounces of Dyachylon cum Gum, put into an Iron Pan with half a pint of Sweet Oil, let them simmer over a very slow Fire till dissolved, but not to boil, stirring all the time. Mix these very slowly with the Honey stirring them very well, whilst another person stirs the Ingredients in the Pan as pur'd out, that the Gums may not settle, let the Ointment be continued to be stirred till quite cold.

As with the solution for earache, the remedy recommended a guide to follow for its application. The instructions convey the extent of the knowledge that Johnson had as he demonstrated a most thorough understanding of how to deal with burns, scalds, infections, and abscesses. Johnson's strategy for dealing with inflamed or infected areas was to apply a 'plaister' with the following instructions for its application:

> [It] Must be renewed every 24 hours, and covered with a soft flannel—if applied soon to any swelling, it will reduce, it but if matter is formed will bring it forward, break it and heal it, if the skin is not very thick, should that be the case, apply a white-bread poultice, with honey instead of oil, when the swelling appears ready to break, this will be found to answer without lancing apply lint with salve to keep the holes open as long as possible, put a large plaister over.[69]

As for burns and scalds, Johnson suggested applying 'some sweet oil on the plaister, with a feather, which may be often repeated.'[70] For sprains he suggested the following: 'rub first with warm oil before the fire, then put on the plaister and repeat the running two or three times a day.' For swellings: 'If [there is] any proud flesh upon old sores, burn alum upon a heater till done boiling, powder it fine, and with a little wet lint, apply the alum to the sore under the plaister.'[71] As established by an assortment of letters and papers from Cheshire the use of herbal medicine certainly continued in this area throughout the eighteenth century. Thomas Finney of Cheshire, 'a known druggist and a gentleman remarkable for his honour and integrity,' put together a list of drugs required by an apothecary.[72] On his list, which was dated 1761, there appeared 'myrrh, aloe, camphor, opium and angelica,' along with an order for 'half a hundred weight of the best English gentian root,' which he described as 'old sound and good.'[73] The cost of his order, sent to John Pickard, apothecary, was £14 1*s.* 2*d.*

Household remedies such as those above played an important part in everyday healing. The women of most prominent families displayed knowledge and skill in this area. Some, of course, were more knowledgeable than others. One woman who was particularly well-versed in the art of healing was Madam Eliza Cholmondeley who held a formidable collection of healing remedies several of which possessed ritual magic. A selection of the most popular remedies appears in more detail below.

Remedy, Ritual, and Herbal Medicine: Eliza Cholmondeley's Insight into Traditional Healing Practices

Customary remedies, rituals, and herbal cures were circulated regularly among gentlewomen. Elizabeth Cholmondeley or 'Eliza,' as she was more familiarly known, came from Hodnet. She possessed a formidable repository of customary healing knowledge. Eliza was the daughter of Baronet Henry Vernon and was married to Robert Cholmondeley at Hodnet on the 6 April 1675. Robert, of Vale Royal Cheshire, was the eldest son of Thomas Cholmondeley, who was Sheriff of Cheshire from 1660 to 1661 and member of Parliament for the county in 1669. Robert died at the young age of 28 and was buried in the Cholmondeley vault in the Church at Minshull in December 1679.[74] In Eliza Cholmondeley's 'Receipt Book,' there are thirty formulas to cure both serious of diseases and less life-threatening illnesses. In one remedy she gives a demonstration of how to deal with the ravages of plague in her remedy of how 'To make a plague water.'[75] In another remedy, she discloses how she had formulated a treatment 'against the smallpox.'[76] On occasion, she drew on the knowledge of other women, but on the whole, Eliza Cholmondeley chiefly aided others with her own personal cures. She had a good understanding of the dangers of childbirth, through a prescription to ease a difficult birth, which she described as 'a drinck to cause easie labour.' In addition, she was familiar with herbal formulas with which to bring a pregnancy to full term through 'a powder against miscarriage.'[77] Within Eliza's assortment of medications were popular cures that were given to her by relatives or friends. One such remedy for stomach ache known as 'Mrs Whiteleys way to make the Spirit of Oranges,' was given to her by a neighbour. An alternative cure for the same ailment was passed on to her by her cousin. This remedy she named 'My Cousin Crewe's Water for the Colick.' Her friend Lady Bridgeman gave her a prescription for a health-promoting drink which was recorded in her book as 'My Ladie Bridgeman's Water.'[78]

Eliza Cholmondeley carefully noted the details of the important remedies for the illnesses that afflicted those around her. Unlike the healing methods of Bald and Macer, her knowledge was not presented in any formal way. It was recorded in an unpretentious fashion and was probably intended first and foremost for private use, but, on occasion, the medicines, such as the one below for the treatment of kidney stones were also circulated among friends. For example, the remedy, 'Madam

Beestons Water for the Stone,' is indicative of the presence of the spoken charm ritual. The following herbal remedy, for kidney stones, is vaguely charm-like. Observe how it refers to a proposed most efficacious time for taking the potion only 'at the full, and at the change of the moon.' It was also considered to be more effective if it was taken 'with the milk of a *red* cow.'[79] The remedy, which used a few well-selected herbs, was created as follows:

> Take saxifrage, peligree of the wall, wild thyme and parsley of each handful. Then good radish roots sliced. Steep these all night in a gallon of milk of a red cow. The next day distill it on an ordinary still, when you take off this water take six spoonfuls of it and as much white rhenish wine, slice a little nutmeg into it and sweeten it with sugar and make it blood warm. Drink it evening and morning three days together at the full, and at the change of moon, take it last at night and first in the morning, use some moderate exercise after it in the morning but not at night.[80]

Eliza's book features a remedy which was perhaps the most important of all her remedies. This cure is entitled 'Herbes for the Cordiall Water.'[81] Eliza's Cordiall Water, despite its name, should not be mistaken for a fruit drink or contemporary cordial water. It was a medicinal treatment comprising around thirty beneficial herbs. This concoction was highly regarded for its health-promoting properties. Additionally, it was consumed as a preventive measure against the plague and smallpox and proved particularly effective in managing cases of fever. Eliza believed that the Cordiall Water was particularly effective in alleviating convulsions. It was administered to young children as a preventive measure against the highly fatal plague and smallpox, both of which posed significant threats during the early modern era.

According to the Shakerley letters, smallpox and plague were rife, especially in the year 1665. In her remedy to prevent smallpox were 30 herbs which were combined in the 'Cordiall water potion.' This remedy as it appeared in the manuscript, is presented below:

> Sage, celandine, rue, rosemary mugwort, pympernell, drogone, scabiousa, seordine, arens, lavender, ergnundie, balme, bettony flowers and leaves, century flowers and hops, angelica sweet, marjorum, wermwood, marigold, mynte, rosemary flowers, cowslip flowers. Of each of these one handful, also the roses of elepistines, licorich, zedner and angelica of each, half and ounce.[82]

Eliza proposed that the following directions be taken for the preparation of the herbs which were to be prepared according to the following instructions:

> Wipe the herbes with a dry cloth, clean them and add a small slice of the roots. Mingle them, steep them in four quarters of best whyte wyne and one quarter of such and putting it in a great pot. Then, in each glass, season, and keep them close covered. One night stirring them twice one day then distill them in an ordinary still but not in limlocke paste but keep your still close that no air come forth but with paste and of the dough mingled with old boyled almeric and so the whyte of the egg lest it run. With it fire the keeping quart, of the first water itself and three pints of the second and much of the last and meekest. The water is to be taken warm with a little sugar and take a spoon full the stronger in the masker of it. At a time you may give two spoon fulls to a little child. It is very good to serve it against the infection smallpox or plage and it is very good in convulsions.[83]

In addition to formulating her own medicinal solutions, Eliza demonstrated a steadfast commitment to implementing the principles she advocated. Her resolute belief in the therapeutic potential of each of her remedies was evident. For example, in the preparation of an all-purpose balm, which is like the remedy for Johnson's salve above, she recorded instructions of how to prepare a treatment which was known in 1677 as 'Lucutellus Balsome.'[84] Eliza praised the efficacy of the balsam and found many uses for it which she recorded under the heading of 'The Virtues of the Balsome.' The 'virtues' of the treatment were many and diverse. Lucutellus Balsome was said to have cured 'wounds, burnings, scaldings, fissures and headaches by anointing the temples.' According to Eliza, it cured people of 'stitches, wind colick,' by 'taking it with a quantity of an nutmeg and sack or red wine.' It was said to have cured 'an ulcer within' and soothed the 'biting of a mad dogge or beaste.' In addition, it was considered to be an effective preventative against 'the plague, by anointing the nostrils and lips.' It was a corrective against parasites and skin eruptions, and it was also said to have been 'good against worms and cankers.' The balsam was effective in preventing excessive bleeding from a wound, for, according to Eliza's Receipt Book, 'it will stench the blood of any.'[85]

The combination of herbs for this medication were 'venus of turpentine, oil of olives, yellow wax, natural balsom, oil of Saint John's Wort, oil of red sandis powdered, and six spoonfuls of sack.' Eliza's instructions for the preparation of Lucutellus Balsome appear below:

> Cut the wax and only melt lest it catch the fire and put the turpentine to it—being washed three times in damask rose water. Having mingled the solid oil with the sack, put it through it and put them all on the fire and stir them till they boil. If it boil much it will run over. Suffer it to cool for a night or two until the water and wine be sunk all to the bottom, then make holes in the stuff so that the water may run out of it which being done put over the fire again, put then to it the balsom and St. John's oil, and when it is melted, put in the Sandis, and stir it well so that all may incorporate together. When it begins to boil almost a quarter of an hour, take it off and stir it for two hours, till it begin to grow thick and cold then keep it for your use in a galley pot.[86]

Among the many illnesses that affected early modern townsfolk the 'Droppsie' and 'Jaundus' were two common illnesses in Cheshire in 1677. For relief of the symptoms of these maladies Eliza prepared a therapeutic drink that was produced from the ashes of 'Green Broom.' She also produced a further healing strategy which involved placing elder leaves to the legs. This procedure was known to cure the illness with or without the help of the ashes of broom. Eliza's directions for the formulation of the remedy for the Droppsie or the Jaundus is reproduced below:

> *A Recipe for the Droppsie or the Jaundus*[87]
>
> Take green broom and burn it to ashes, then take a good big spoonful thereof and put it to a pint of rennish wine overnight and let it steep therein until the next morning, then shake it well together, and drink the moyetie in the morning and the rest at the four of the clock, in the afternoon let this continue for a fortnight or three weeks or longer as you find the effects of it., otherwise apply to the shin bones from the knee to the instep elder leaves with fasting spittle, take out the hard vein which runs along the leaf lest it should hurt, and place the leaves athwart to the bones, stalk, rind or bottom of the leaf must be placed inward to the leg, the other outward all along the shin bone as aforesaid, if the patient's stomache can not bear the taste of the ashes he may have the use of the wine alone, but it hath a much better effect with the ashes, this recipe was given by Madam Mariana Selwell and cured the old lady Mulgrave of her distemper.

Eliza Cholmondeley's and Jane Stanley's written works on herbal medicine attest to their proficiency in customary domestic healing practices. Eliza Cholmondeley's Receipt Book is a prime example of how women during the seventeenth century employed their knowledge of herbal remedies to safeguard their families against fatal illnesses like smallpox and the plague. Among their most successful cure is the remedy to deal with convulsions brought on by fever in children. In the domestic sphere there was a close association between women and the local apothecary. However, all the remedies that appear in women's letters and diaries support the views of those historians of medicine who argue that the housewife carried out the work of the apothecary—only on a wider basis. As is established in the extracts above, this was certainly the case in the Stanley and Cholmondeley homes.

Women were expected to exhibit fortitude and ingenuity in times of hardship. Women possessing knowledge of traditional healing practices were often approached by distressed individuals seeking assistance during family illnesses. Such curative work typically involved reciting uncomplicated prayers or performing rituals. However, if the remedies failed, the women would face condemnation from the community. Resilient and resourceful, women's curative work often involved speaking simple prayers or rituals. But should they fail to cure they were denounced by the community. By the time news of their curative activities had reached the lawsuit stage their actions were misinterpreted as sorcery. when, particularly during times of social stress, the community denounced the cunning folk to the Justices, who dealt with them very harshly and often imprisoned them. During such hard times, resourceful women gathered wild herbs and edible plants such as common arens, along with healing herbs such as century, and sought to stave off hunger with the 'common wood pea.' Eliza Cholmondeley's Receipt Book includes remedies to deal with the smallpox and the plague that so blighted the inhabitants of seventeenth-century Cheshire. Stanley's Receipt Book, private papers of apothecaries, the letters and diaries of women, and the details of the broader community each demonstrate that spoken ritual played a part in the customary healing traditions of early modern Northwest England. The deposition of women like Jane Chisnall, for example, communicates how Mother Nuttall and her son, William, were summoned to the homes of sick people. Cunning women such as Mary Shaw granted a free service in support of the troubled townsfolk and she rarely accepted payment but, in difficult times herself, she rather wished for something to eat instead of payment. In times of great sickness, townsfolk were troubled by the scourge of illness which affected their families and there was the ever-present threat of child mortality, which was high during this period. The depositions indicate that there was food insecurity, money shortages, and uneasiness about property ownership and these circumstances combined to create an unstable environment for the townsfolk.

Unveiling Women's Emotional Struggles through Letters, Petitions, and Testimonies

Although women's letters and writings often focused on healing, they also frequently revealed accounts of suffering, sorrow, and susceptibility, including instances of domestic violence within the family. The collective petitions, letters and depositions of women of early modern Northwest England bring together the intimate details about the nature and the extent of the violence that was experienced by women in the townships. Domestic violence sometimes underscored the context of cases of cursing. Petitions, depositions, and personal letters from women offer a vivid portrayal of the conflicts they encountered in their everyday existence. These writings frequently include descriptions of brutality within their intimate and marital relationships. These exposés are frequent in the narratives that are presented in the 'causes.' Petitions similarly draw attention to the dynamics of ill will that drove the townsfolk to assemble to condemn what the court subsequently recognised as transgressors of a moral code. Women's narratives in their legal depositions communicate the particulars of grief, hardship, and vulnerability of these women who would survive dangerous violence. They are equally clear in conveying the conditions that women had to deal with during periods of crisis. The experiences of such women were also drawn against the vagaries of an unpredictable means of support and made worse by the sporadic periods of severe economic downturn that made their lives even more difficult.

It has been noted that the structure of the control of violence in the individual and in the state is linked, and that the superiority attained by violent means to control the behaviour of others has not yet been sufficiently explored.[88] The claims that medieval English society was excessively violent have received some support from researchers on the subject of violence that occurred during the early modern period who argue that 'violence was never far from people's lives because through discipline and punishment it was central to any attempt to exercise power.'[89] The use of shaming rituals and whipping for moral discipline confirm that the state used violence in order to repress and, in the early modern period, Church courts took on the role of a moral gate-keeper.[90] The debate about the levels of violence in early modern society is ongoing with the so-called 'pessimists' identifying a society as one that is 'unloving' and 'uncaring.'[91] The so-called 'optimists' claim that early modern English society was largely humanised and that it was not overtly violent.[92] Women's narratives certainly confirm not only that violence was widespread but also that it occurred often. These themes of debate require further research within the context of the social and economic conditions that were often the driving force behind such aggression.

The human emotional response to the adversity that was the driver behind the socio-economic statistics of early modern Northwest England is noticeably expressed in a female narrative of hardship. Female narrative confirms that interpersonal relationships were shaped by the secular and Church courts in early modern communities and, as explored above, these records incorporate detailed data about the language that offended communities, and which drew the resentment of ruling authorities. There was a steady increase in court business with three distinct high points in the distribution of prosecutions during the three decades: 1610 to 1620, 1630 to 1640, and 1660 to 1670.[93]

Desperation was a central theme repeated in the petitions of women who were concerned to remain in employment, or to define paternity, to protect property, to thwart violence, or to maintain equilibrium against 'disturbers of the peace.' Petitions that were made to the Justices of the Peace for poor relief were often a positive means of alleviating hardship in the short term as these petitions were often successful in achieving relief from poverty.[94] Such narrative casts light on the connection between the violence directed at women and material hardship and the outpouring of grief that occurred during such periods of difficulty.[95] Within the general patterns of shifts and changes that took place in the financial system and social structure of the Northwest regions of England, and the several local 'spasmodic' and intense social and economic downturns, the evidence of the human impact of such socio-economic hardship is laid bare in the words of disturbed petitioners. Some of these accounts are investigated further below.

'Throtled into Kindness': The Dark Realities of Interpersonal and Domestic Violence in Early Modern Society

To fully understand the prevalence of domestic violence in early modern communities, it is imperative to examine the interpersonal violence that gave rise to legal action. Legal documentary evidence provides information about the more intimate details of the circumstances of women who resort to legal means to find a way out of violent circumstances. While some women sought legal intervention to end domestic violence, their personal letters reveal that they often turned to friends and neighbours for support in times of desperation.

A Cheshire woman's harrowing account of domestic violence was conveyed in a letter that detailed the extreme brutality she endured at the hands of her husband, as evidenced by the following lines:

> It is not the fashion in Chesher for wifes to be either thretned or Throtled into cindness. I wish for this 7 yeres I had no grete cas to have wepte and Groned under the mightey borden of your oncindneses to me.[96]

The letter was written by Mrs. Elizabeth Dobson who expressed these thoughts on her experiences of domestic violence in a letter dated 1682 which she wrote to Lady Shakerley, who was the Chatelaine of Chester Castle, in Cheshire. She and Lady Shakerley were lifelong friends. In the letter, Mrs Dobson distinctly states that her husband, Edward Dobson, who was a lawyer at Gray's Inn, London, unambiguously married her so that he could better his own financial position. In addition to resisting her husband's abuse, she also employed legal means to prevent him from coercing her into relinquishing her property. This highlights the recurrent issue of women's property ownership, as evidenced by the consistent theme of women's petitions and letters, which reveal the persistent challenges women faced in retaining ownership of their property. Mrs Dobson's letters state that she used the law to resist all her husband's attempts to coerce her into settling her properties in his favour. Women like Mrs Dobson were frequently in danger of losing their personal property and sought legal recourse by bringing their cases before the courts, a situation common to many women in their community. The Chester Consistory Court in Northwest England provided such a course of action to women who were threatened, beaten, or suffered some other kind of physical abuse. The petitions of the Cheshire and Lancashire Quarter

Sessions courts presented by women indicate that they were in a precarious position. In addition, some were subject to violent behaviour, usually, although not always, at the hands of a male.

There is some evidence to suggest that violence against women was not an inherent or accepted aspect of domestic life. Although women were sometimes the victims of domestic violence and assault in marriage, the community, the Church court and the secular courts recognised that violent behaviour was morally wrongful that was and ruled strictly against violent offenders. The petitions and depositions of those caught up in violent dispute often convey intimate knowledge of the distribution of community power. Petitions are especially informative about the relationships between families, as well as recording issues that arose through difficult interpersonal relations with their neighbours. Overwhelmingly the petitions, letters and depositions identify the community as a primary locus of conflict, especially when the inhabitants found themselves to be in precarious financial circumstances.

Though women were subject to regulation and governance from above and presented a high profile for verbal transgression, their petitions, letters, and depositions indicate that they turned to the court for justice in matters of violent misconduct. Women frequently violated the law. They were denounced for participating in crimes such as stealing and receiving stolen goods. Studies of the Church court records of Wiltshire suggest that women were more likely to be presented to court as they were 'predisposed' to verbal violence and tended to avoid physical violence.[97] Evidence from the Church courts, Quarter Sessions and Assize courts discloses that female participation in violent crime was high. Women were frequently involved in violent crimes such as assault.[98] Research into the extent of patriarchal control indicates that discord within the household was a regular event in early modern England. The 'war of words' approach surveying the incidence of spoken violence in early modern England, concurs with the view of a violent society. Evidence from legal bodies similarly illustrates that women pursued lawsuits in Church courts and secular courts, against relatives, neighbours, against each other, and, in some instances, they brought legal action against their marital partners. Women were often put to the test in legal battles, some of which went on for years, sometimes a decade or more, in a maze of suit and countersuit.[99]

As set out above, on 5 February 1663, many Nantwich townsfolk organised a petition against midwife, Anne Knutsford. In total 19 members of the community signed the petition, after which 30 people more appeared in court to give evidence and a further 93 people were indirectly involved in the case. Although the petition was directed at the midwife primarily for the charge of cursing, numerous additional charges of verbal infringement were alleged to have offended the good will of the community. Those called, were required by the court to give evidence about 'Items,' or a list of charges, which were read out in the court. However, in cases of domestic violence women took successful legal action against offenders for violent affray. This legal action took account of violence at the hands of their husbands. Such conflict as this was indicated in the records and reported on. It was not remarkable for a woman to bring a husband to court for domestic violence. The records of the Chester Consistory Court reveal that, besides achieving success in court against violent behaviour, some women who were assaulted by their husbands, charged, fought, and occasionally won, legal battles against their husbands for assault. According to the petitions and depositions that were presented to the court, women might also occasionally have resorted to physical violence to resolve outstanding disagreements.[100] It is the wide variety of these cases that contain the emotional and more intimate details of the circumstances of those women who were involved in domestic violence and who resorted to the court for legal redress.[101]

Some women expressed their dissatisfaction with violence in their domestic situation and sought to bring about change by resorting to the law. They retaliated to threatening behaviour by taking legal action, and by bringing violent behaviour to the attention of the court. The depositions of witnesses indicate that neighbours were offended by violent actions against women and in some cases of extreme domestic violence the neighbours offered women their support and provided a refuge for them to stay and, sometimes, they also appeared as witnesses to offer more formal support. In domestic situations involving physical violence, the lawsuits discussed here illustrate that women were not the passive victims of domestic brutality. In one incident of rough treatment in Cheshire in 1630, the injured woman brought her case to court and won. Subsequently she received financial compensation when the court ordered her husband to pay for causing her injuries. In another similar case, in the same year, a woman took her husband to court for attempted murder and sexual assault. Her case was also considered sympathetically by the court. For example, challenging the conflict that occurred in the home was Anne Houghe of Runcorn, who gave evidence to the court against her husband, Thomas Houghe for domestic violence. Anne Hough reported that she encountered persistent acts of physical abuse at the hands of Thomas Houghe who was her husband. Her depositions confirm that Thomas Houghe was financially well off, and that he owned what the court described as 'copyhold' land and earning 20 shillings a year from running a ferry boat. The court found that Houghe, who had a reputation as a renowned drinker, was guilty of inhumane and violent behavioor. The charge against him was recorded as follows:

> Thomas Houghe hath given himselfe to immoderate and excessive drinkinge and hath bine often distempered with drinke and then as well in his drunkenness or att other times hath often inhumanely beaten Anne his wiefe.[102]

The court recorded that in December 1630, Anne Houghe narrowly escaped Thomas Houghe's rage and was so afraid of being killed that she was forced to run from her home. She recalled how she was given refuge and was offered somewhere to stay by her neighbours who then took her into their home:

> by reason of his crueltie Thomas Houghe hath forced her at nighte to rune naked and without clothes forth of her bed and to shelter and hide her selfe from him in a neighbours house.

In their depositions, the neighbours convey the circumstances of how Thomas Houghe then followed Anne, and violently forced his way into their home where he searched for her. He was armed with a weapon. They deposed that they were afraid that if he had caught up with her, he might well have killed her. The court took a dim view of Houghe's cruelty and violent assaults on Anne with a pair of fire tongs. It scandalised them to find out that he also put their young child in danger and that he had attacked Anne even as she tried to shield their child from his blows:

> Thomas Houghe did strike and beate the said Anne his wiefe with a paire of Iron fire tongues in such fierce cruell and inhumane manner that by reason of his force and longe continued beatinge up, the most pte of her armes, sides, backe, thighes and legges were and are bruised and made blacke and blewe, and her childe then being in her arme she could not save herselfe but rather submitted herselfe to his violence than to endanger the liefe of her childe.[103]

In evaluating the fine he would receive for his violent conduct, the court required detailed knowledge of Houghe's income. Thomas Houghe was forced to pay compensation to his wife for her injuries. There is no sum mentioned in the record. There were other parallel situations to that of Anne Houghe that were dealt with by the court. In similar circumstances, Mary Bennett, who also gained the support of the court, deposed against her husband and gave evidence to the court which indicated that a charge of violent assault be made against her husband. In this case, however, there is no evidence to suggest what Bennett's punishment was. He was, however, found guilty.[104]

The background to the disharmony that provoked townsfolk to elicit legal action against their neighbours was widespread. Numerous women were incriminated for their violent behaviour and some were accused of murder. For example, in November 1616, 31-year-old Elizabeth Corkerton of Wybunburie was accused of murdering Bridget Wood. The records, however, make no explicit reference to Corkerton's fate.[105] However, a closely documented sequence of violent events involving a different female offender transpired in Tarvin, near Chester, in 1607, when Elizabeth Brynne terrorised the local community. She was also accused of soliciting, of prostitution, of behaving in a drunk and disorderly way, of immoral behaviour and lastly, was charged with attempted murder. Often at odds with other inhabitants in the town, she was reputed to have 'carried a knyffe under her apparel.' An unlucky individual entered into a heated exchange of words with her. He gave evidence to the court as follows: 'She [Brynne] was buying a mantle in Margery Massies entrye and because he gave her some crosse wordes she wente home and fetched a knyffe under her apparell and would have stabbed him.'[106]

Brynne was also the proprietor of an alehouse. The records show that she was widely known to be both a prostitute and a customer of gigolos. Amongst other violations she was accused of harlotry, pimping, and of exhorting women to prostitution. A deponent claimed as much in the following statement: 'Anne Horkenhull (being then her house mayde) was to occupy a man and she shulde give her 20 shillings …and she would have the other… also she keepeth herself to her house a younger man with money.'[107]

The court heard that Brynne was not averse to ale and was often discovered in the alehouse drunk. Previously she had been bound over to keep the peace for drunkenness when she approached the husband of Elizabeth Browne making indecent suggestions. As deponent, Elizabeth Brown, claimed: 'She had beene bounde for drinking and was drunke when she went to Ralph Browne and would have been nought with him. Elizabeth Browne wyeff of Ralph Brown did affirm this the last day of August 1607.'[108]

Elizabeth Brynne had threatened several individuals in Tarvin. According to the records she obtained a great deal of satisfaction from doing so. It was claimed by one deponent that she 'fought with John Tibson and broke his heade and was merrie for the sinne.' In a petition brought by the community, 14 distinct charges were made against her. While wielding a knife, she fought with a neighbour, John Woodwarde, and was almost successful in achieving his decapitation, as the following deponent states: 'she fought with John Woodwarde and would have had his head.'[109] She also had no qualms about attacking and stealing at knife-point. The same deponent also claimed she was a thief: 'In the falling out with John Tibson she carried a knyffe under her apparel and meetinge him at the Crosse in Tarvinne would have robbed him.'[110]

Seemingly, those who drank in Brynne's alehouse did so at their own risk. According to the Quarter Sessions records she almost killed one customer as one deponent testified: 'she would have killed James Hignette in her owne house.'[111] Brynne jealously guarded her property, goods, and livestock. According to reports she did not hesitate to defend them by violent means: 'Hynrie Sympson chaced her swyne out of the church yarde, she sayde if she had him out of the town, she would kill him.' According to the reports, it was commonplace for her to carry arms, but the accounts about her behaviour with offensive weapons do not correspond. Some deponents said she *bore* weapons for assault, for example: 'she carried a dagger or longe knyffe to have stopped Thomas Sympson.' Some said, however, she *threatened* to use weapons with force, as follows: 'seeinge Simpson come into the towne said that *if she had* a knyffe she would thrust it into his guttes.'[112] While the Chester Consistory Court recorded in detail the misdemeanours of Elizabeth Brynne, it did not establish how she responded to the charges, or what her punishment was. However, the most serious charge against her was that of attempted murder. If found guilty of these offences she would have received a fine, a public whipping, or incarceration.[113]

Societal Changes and Their Impact on Women's Roles and Interpersonal Relationships

The speech and activities of women were influenced by a range of changes in society. The changeable economy influenced modes of governance and such societal changes significantly not only affected gender relations but interpersonal community relationships. Changes in the economy, in religion and, as discussed more especially, by the radical religious ideas of Calvin. There were restraints placed on the female sphere of existence and an ideological battle for control stemmed from such restrictions There was a transformation in the Northwest region in the later seventeenth century, which in general terms was a period that saw a disparate distribution of economic growth.[114] There was acute change in society that boosted the economy, and which brought with it a 200% population growth. By the later seventeenth century, the national population that withstood economic hardship ranged from 35 to 50%.[115] The reasons for this change in the region occurred through an intensification of commerce through trade routes. It is also through this new progress in business that the word of Calvin was disseminated and which, at the same time, drove the proliferation of the dogma of Puritanism that so influenced the lives of women and their interactions.

Protestantism was influential in the transformation that took place in the townships of Northwest England. The growth and spread of Puritanism in the diocese were widespread and and this was conspicuous in the ongoing struggle for religious non-conformist domination of the female sphere. The radical doctrines of Calvinism were carried through trade connections with London.[116] Protestant preachers were employed to convert Catholics to the reformed Church. In southeast Lancashire and northeast Cheshire, a Calvinist clergy refused to conform to the prescribed liturgy and became established there. There are several opposing views regarding the effectiveness of non-conformist preaching ministers. Some historians argue that, owing to organisational and financial problems in the diocese, the effectiveness of preaching ministers in a large unruly diocese is open to question.[117] However, an alternative argument proposes that radical preaching was well received.[118] Without a doubt, the favourable reception given to Calvinism promoted radical thinking and according to expert opinion, the growth and spread of Puritanism in the diocese went unchecked.[119] Pastoral and woodland areas, such as those of Cheshire, provided the most conducive environment for Puritanism to flourish. Puritanism was based on the Godly household in which women were expected to be subservient and was strongest in the eastern, pastoral areas of Lancashire and Cheshire. All three of these elements, the pastoral background, family solidarity, and Puritanism were connected.[120] Puritanism was especially strong in Cheshire.[121] In the period 1630 to 1640 the stronghold of Puritanism in the archdeaconry of Chester was in the east. It has been noted that it was:

> a pastoral area with growing trade and industry. The local evidence suggested a distinct similarity between the distribution of Puritanism and that of market towns—a finding which lends weight to the frequently made generalisation that Puritanism took firmest root in the most thriving and economically developed parts of the country.[122]

It is well known that there was a compatibility of Puritan dogma with the capitalist objectives of the emerging middle class, where the religious discourse stressed the inherent inferiority of women, with the role of middle-class women within the domestic sphere. The Puritan 'push,' as it is known, came about through the growth of market towns which began to prosper in early-seventeenth-century England. It also had a good reception from large prosperous towns, such as Manchester.[123] The parochial character of Puritan belief has been noted and is described as being 'local in organisation, local in structure, and above all local in its impact.'[124] Of all towns, Manchester had the closest and most regular ties with London and in consequence it also had the largest Puritan contingent of all towns in the Northwest.[125] As the state of affairs with Manchester demonstrates, London's impact on the nation was important from both the economic and social point of view.[126]

Canon law meant that the act of damaging another's reputation was illegal in early modern England.[127] The opportunity to control female language arose through the indoctrination of Puritanism. The numbers of Puritan ministers increased principally between the years of 1620 and 1642. Their sermons were designed to have emotional appeal 'to stir up the people's affections with pithy matter and a warm delivery.'[128] The power of the ministers increased as they occupied more influential positions within secular law. For example, Christopher Hudson's lecture opposing Sabbath-breaking and the sin of drunkenness at Lancashire assizes in Preston, in 1631, was well received, and this incident further exemplifies the influence that Puritan ministers exerted upon the community through the justice system.[129] Between 1646 and 1658 the magistrates were very active in their prosecution of social space such as the ale houses that had long been enjoyed by the popular community. In addition, Puritans associated the rituals of Catholicism with popular superstitious belief and condemned them both. The popular healing traditions of the cunning women were often interpreted by them as sorcery and described by them as witchcraft. Sunday sports, ale-churches, and dancing were frowned upon while attitudes hardened towards single mothers who, owing to their economically unsupported status were labelled as 'bastard-bearers.' Lancashire was more vulnerable to such radical thought because ministers, who believed Catholicism was rife, felt that the moral welfare of Lancashire was more at risk. Even though the Cheshire authorities were somewhat more moderate in dealing with matters concerning magic, 11 persons were hanged for the customary practices of cunning which was interpreted as witchcraft between the years of 1580 and 1709.[130] Hangings took place with greater regularity in Lancashire. At Lancaster Assizes fifteen women and five men were brought to trial on one occasion in 1612. Eight women and two men were hanged, while the oldest woman died in prison.[131] In some areas, women made up the majority in the Puritan contingency. Some, like Elizabeth Symons of Nantwich, refused to go to church. In 1611 she was charged at the Chester Consistory Court, not with recusancy but with 'wilful forwardness.'[132] Such unmitigated opposition to strict religious control indicates that women, despite the obvious pressures to conform to a required standard of speech and conduct continued as best they could to be assertive in maintaining their rights and privileges.

Conclusion

The desire to shape female speech and behaviour according to a prescribed prototype ensured the continuous regulation of women's language and activities, ultimately leading to male-dominated governance. There were strict measures imposed on women whose conduct failed to meet the prescribed standards. The legal machinery was systematic in its castigation of women who asserted themselves out loud. A lawfully endorsed, brutal punishment of women embodied by an inherently aggressive social order turned on women in times of adversity. Cursing, scolding, and chiding were systematically punished, and women were publicly shamed and 'proclaimed' at the cross in the marketplace. Guilt by association with known cursers meant that accused women were further marginalised. When cursing involved the death of a person, women were found guilty and executed.

When closely examined, it is clear that individuals lodging complaints against women for cursing commonly intended to undermine women's agency and control over their possessions. Such challenges resulted in sequestration of female property. Outspoken women or women of ardent sexual comportment were frequently punished. Cicilia Collinge, who was accused of demonstrating 'lewde and naughte' conduct, was severely criticised and was made more vulnerable, while the male consort with whom she had an affair did not encounter an accusation. An initial charge like this one often concluded with an accusation of cursing. When Sybill Lingard appeared before the Chester Consistory Court accused of having an 'abusive tongue' she later became accused of cursing.[133] Her depositions convey that she was rendered desperate with grief when her child died.[134]When first her husband became ill and then later her child died, she was charged with placing a curse on her own family and was subsequently held responsible for causing their deaths.[135]

A discernible pattern of interconnected allegations gradually unfolded over the course of several decades, culminating in a final accusation of cursing. This historical configuration of the three main stages of accusation ranges broadly from an allegation of 'thief', then of 'prostitute', and then of 'curser.' Over time ill will simmered below the surface to emerge years later in a charge critical of a woman as a 'curser.' This was so with the long-running Elderson curse, when, as the proprietor of a popular alehouse, she occupied a space that officials judged undesirable for a woman of 'good character.' When, in 1636, she was accused of running a brothel, the charge progressed to one of receiving stolen goods. Further imputations were directed at her over the years to the extent that she was rendered vulnerable to the gravest charge of cursing. The background to the curse divulges significant insights into the premeditated seizure of her property, as initiated by the complainant Elizabeth Baxter who asserted ownership of Elderson's house. Plagued by sorrow and driven by the need to secure her own shelter, Baxter attributed the demise of her sons to the curse. However, Elderson refuted these allegations, challenging the legitimacy of Baxter's claim. Such crisis conditions impelled the strong female presence in courts, where petitions expressed an overwhelming concern about uncertain economic conditions. In the parishes of the Northwest, there were catastrophic levels of mortality. Such elevated levels of mortality indicate disease or famine or perhaps both. Several periods of intensified social crisis provided the push for the escalation of charges against garrulous women. During the period from 1541 to 1700, women were represented in more than 90% of cases of crimes of speech in the Chester Consistory Court. The court records of Northwest England suggest that incidents of women's verbal wrongdoing, especially cursing, increased most perniciously during challenging times. Three distinct periods saw significant social unrest which occurred in the decades 1610 to 1620, 1630 to 1640, and 1660 to 1670. Within the general patterns of shifts and changes that took place in the economy and social structure of the Northwest, in the decades 1610 to 1620, 1630 to 1640, and 1660 to 1670, there were also several local 'spasmodic' social and economic downturns. Evidence of the human impact of economic decline is recorded in the depositions of the distressed petitioners and the heartbreak they expressed in the depositions reveals the range of the emotional responses that lay behind socio-economic statistics.[136] Seeking to rationalise unfathomable misfortune, individuals filing petitions vividly express the profound emotions they underwent during times of financial adversity. Through their narratives, they elucidate the explicit reasons behind their recourse to magical traditions, as they grappled with the ravages of destitution, rampant afflictions, and the heart-wrenching bereavement of their dear ones.

As divulged by the curse of Anne Knutsford, many tradesfolk, gentlemen, and gentlewomen, were hard-pressed to protect their credit and good name yet they were forced to do so to remain economically active.[137] Knutsford's curse shed light on the refusal to provide financial commitment in support of a child. Women's sexual adventures raised issues of bastardy, prostitution, and concubines. In revealing such information, Knutsford's curse did much to discredit the townsfolk. Her curse disclosed the details of improper affairs which resulted in bastardy, where gentlewoman Dorothy Hussey 'kissed out her rent' with Captain Walthall for 'fifty shillings a year.'[138]Knutsford's curse uncovers the pronounced disagreement among the townsfolk regarding the economic hardships they faced. Women who were caught up in the matter were concubines who were 'paid' by Walthall or 'paid' him in sexual services for the rent on their properties. One gentlewoman, Mrs Cliffe, it was said, received 'forty pounds a year' from Sir Philip Egerton, and Samuel Hussey's wife, received 'fifty shillings a year' from Captain Richard Walthall. According to law, the children born from such relationships were referred to as bastards as they were born as the result of fornication outside of wedlock, and in the common law court, fornication was punished very severely.

Townsfolk's testimonies give accounts of social adversity, conflict, and economic hardship inflicted upon communities during the Civil War. Women accused of engaging in verbal offences faced public whippings or imprisonment, while other townspeople were incarcerated for minor thefts involving just a few shillings. These examples illustrate the severity of the punishments imposed for various transgressions during this tumultuous period. The records from the Cheshire Inquisitions Post Mortem,[139] Cheshire Quarter Sessions.[140] and Chester Consistory Court examined above, each confirm profound community distress. Townsfolk who were employed by local gentry refused to work, neighbours were at loggerheads with each other, and Churchwardens repeatedly found themselves the targets of hatred which escalated into violent acts. Neighbours fought each other over trivial matters, some clashed in church, pushing each other out of pews, anxious to maintain their status in a church hierarchy that reflected the social order of the town. Nurses who were forced to look after plague victims and then cheated of their pay had their objections heard by the Justices of the Peace at Quarter Sessions. Starving, 'maymed soldiers' of the 'Scotch' invasion appealed for justice, as did the many widows of soldiers who died in the wars.

The deeds of false practitioners of cunning are well documented.[141] However, during precarious conditions, the application of genuine customary knowledge was crucial to the well-being of the community. While it was common for women in difficult conditions to look after their own health, they turned to cunning women who were more conversant with the ways and means of long-established treatments. In times of danger, some people perceived customary knowledge erratically, especially during intervals of cyclical illness. Women struggled to stay alive. They were hell-bent on ensuring the survival of their children. At every turn, they sought to overcome the ravages of food insecurity and disease. During the seventeenth century, in the towns and villages that were scattered throughout the Northwest that were already affected by hunger, many people came to be at the mercy of waves of disease. Entire families fell victim to illness, with some experiencing devastating losses. In townships such as Ormskirk, Little Boulton, Chadderton, Ashton-in-Makerfield, Orrell, and Ellell, the inhabitants suffered more acutely. As a cunning man, Henry Baggillie of Chadderton, in 1634 explained, his healing 'wordes were made use of dyverse times, though more frequently for these two yeares last past.'[142] In the same way, the community of Little Boulton, in 1629, during a wave of disease, turned against cunning man William Nuttall when children were struck down, became 'lame' and died.[143] Their testimonies give voice to the experiences of people who were made desperate by hunger and in fear for their lives. They reveal that when all else failed, they turned to magic, customary knowledge, and magical practitioners with the hope of stimulating preternatural powers so that they might harness the power of magic to safeguard the well-being of their families.

The radical doctrines of Calvin were carried through trading connections from London and the 'Godly' household grew to be strong in the eastern pastoral areas of Lancashire and Cheshire. Despite the reaction against Puritanism in the wake of the Restoration, by 1660, its ideology dominated the Quarter Sessions Courts of the Northwest. At the same time as an ideological battle was being fought out in legal, social, spatial and linguistic domains, there were periods of economic contraction and scarcity in the region. In a situation of ongoing gender conflict, those women who were in the vanguard of the struggle to defend themselves from encroaching ideological control consistently resisted and challenged the moral values that were imposed on them. Throughout the decade from 1630 to 1640 in Lancashire, customary magical expression, issuing curses, and composing charms in the Northwest came to be perceived by the Justices of the Peace as sorcery. However, a striking feature of this decade is that accusations of bewitchment were often instigated by the neighbours of the accused. Women became more susceptible to accusations. In response to the prosecutions initiated by the townspeople, the Justices responded quickly and mercilessly. From 1630 onward, spoken violations were unambiguously related to poor socio-economic conditions. Women's depositions over and over again expressed their concerns about the threat to their property and belongings.

The curse cast by Sybill Farclough exemplifies a recurring pattern observed in cases of curses involving the tragic demise of children. Sybill's tumultuous relationships with both relatives and neighbours culminated in her being accused of inflicting a curse that led to the untimely death of a child. Spanning four years, Sybill's cursing episodes unfolded chronologically. This prevalent fear of women who engaged in cursing practices was deeply ingrained within the societal fabric, often accompanied by an intimate association between cursing and witchcraft, particularly in certain regions. Sybill's cousin, Margery Ireland, brought several proceedings against her and deposed that Sybill was well known to possess almighty supernatural powers. An acute crisis existed in Orrell, where death, 'sudden diseases,' and anxiety about property ownership were expressed by Sybill's neighbours, who were in deep distress. Jenet Wilkinson of Ellel, Lancashire, was implicated in a cursing case that began in the year 1629, but which comprised an extended history of more than ten years.[144]The circumstances behind Jenet's curse were somewhat different from Sybill Farclough's curse. This instance of cursing was, in origin, a dispute about property ownership. Several key people that were involved were landowners. Jenet's cursing case originated in the year 1629 and developed to a timeline of more than ten years. In a dispute about property ownership, the key people that were involved in the matter were described as landowners. Complainants expressed concern about Jenet's magical abilities and bore witness to the power of Jenet's curse. Others believed that they were 'forsworne' and then appealed for a counter-bewitchment, and subsequently went to see a cunning woman to search out a cure for the curse. However, in fear for her life, nothing would induce the cunning woman to assist. She refused to offer a counter-spell for fear of the end result.[145]

In the ongoing gender struggle that followed the imposed regulation of female language and conduct, scores of women resisted the unrelenting attempts to control their movements. Some were forced to defend against attacks on their status and property.[146] In their depositions, women expressed their opposition to societal and legal constraints and social control. At the same time, women of professional standing, such as midwife, Anne Knutsford, were required to conform to the imposed standards. She spoke too freely about sexual impropriety so inflaming the fragile relationships that existed in an extremely volatile community. Simultaneously, amid an environment of ceaseless conflict, women found themselves facing mounting pressure as they were progressively stripped of their esteemed status and autonomy, being relegated to a state of dependence on men. Notably, in Lancashire, the local Justices of the Peace exhibited an unwavering determination to prosecute women who failed to adhere to the prescribed standards of morality, displaying a remarkable intensity in their efforts.

The result of the ideological battle for control is put plainly into words in women's petitions. When precarious conditions prevailed, gender relations worsened. It was at difficult times that the community moved to blame their fellow citizens for their misfortune. When the customary treatment they expected would cure them came to nothing, they held cunning women accountable. Women's petitions voice anguish and convey the precise details of when people turned against each other. Intimate and emotional, petitions are full of expressions of sorrow, grief and fear. Hostility was directed at individual women who were singled out and held responsible for creating the hard times the community faced. Elderly Ann Baker was fearful that she would die of starvation in prison.[147] Margery Greene of Ince in Macclesfield, who was held responsible for the adversities that afflicted the Ince community, petitioned that she and her children were starving.[148] One recalls how neighbours threatened a cunning woman with a beating and wanted to have her hanged at the 'sessions.'[149] John Rosthorne petitioned that he was homeless and close to starvation. He was lucky and released from prison.[150] The dread of starvation was a frequent motif of the petitions of the townsfolk. Some lost hope. In this environment of deficiency, women's struggles multiplied as they faced further personal tragedies through the loss of farm animals or goods, or experienced infertility, affliction, family breakdown, infidelity, abandonment in pregnancy, homelessness, and hunger.

The petitions of the distressed townsfolk further confirm that women were undoubtedly influenced by a series of socio-economic ups and downs in society. The ravages of hunger, waves of disease, and substantive losses were many. Towns and villages such as Ormskirk, Little Boulton, Chadderton, Ashton-in-Makerfield, Orrell, and Ellell were critically affected at different times. When a wave of disease struck Little Boulton in 1629, the community turned against Mother Nuttall and her son William Nuttall when children were struck down, became 'lame' and died. Women's testimonies spell out how women were made desperate by hunger and in fear of their lives. Some, such as Sybill Lingard, were abandoned during pregnancy. Issuing curses, reverting to customary magical lore, and speaking charms were perceived by the Justices in the Northwest as sorcery. Sybill Farclough, Jenet Wilkinson, and Joane Elderson were particularly vulnerable to accusations, and the contextual backdrop of cursing incidents reveals the profound hardships experienced during the decade spanning from 1630 to 1640. In response to accusations, which originated from the townspeople, the Justices of the Peace acted swiftly and frequently employed harsh measures. However, the most noteworthy aspect of female speech transgressions during the period from 1630 to

1640 is that the majority of accusations were instigated by fellow citizens and sometimes even family members of the accused individuals issued complaints.

Nevertheless, the power engendered by ritual cursing proved to be a worthwhile substitute for female high political engagement. Women repeatedly proclaimed their discontent in opposition to the social conditions and legal measures were taken to silence them. Despite the pressures on women to comply with patriarchal standards of conduct, they continued to give voice to their discontent. In numerous English regions, comprising Devon, London, Somerset, Wiltshire, and Cheshire, women challenged the ideological constraints that were placed on them. Some went through the legal system for their own ends while others sought a positive outcome through petitioning for fair dealing. They elevated their right of speech in an effort to be heard in private in the home and in the public domain, whether they were vocal in the mercer's shop or grocer's shop, on the streets, in the ale house, in the court, or, when under pressure from social and economic constraints, through asserting their dissatisfaction and gaining further momentum by invoking the magical potential expressed in the formal curse. Issuing a curse enabled women to gain some control in a much-conflicted community. Through cursing they were able to perform their protests publicly at the same time as they were able to gain power over their enemies. However, the shift that cursing women achieved was not incremental, nor was it progressive. Often, the traction it gained was short lived. Though temporary in nature, a magical imprecation was an effective means of exerting power over those who believed themselves to be at the mercy of a curse. It allowed cursing women to shift the balance towards the outcome they desired. Their encounters changed their calamitous circumstances for the better, while in some cases, although in the short term, they reconfigured their contexts sufficiently for them to survive a major disaster. This temporary halt to misfortune sometimes allowed women some breathing space, enabling them to rise above the difficult circumstances that life presented them with. Despite the consequences of possible prosecution and the transgression of legal standards, the curse presented women with an alternative medium of communication when experiencing violent oppression. For desperate women, dispossessed, forced out of their homes, threatened with imprisonment, corporal punishment, fines, abandonment, ostracism or worse, during such times of crisis the ritual of cursing presented a potent force. When they experienced an unusual bout of bad luck or experienced the deaths of their children, were stricken with sickness, or fear of starvation or loss of goods, the practice of cursing provided a unique platform on which they expressed grief and anger and served to draw public attention to injustice. By relying on a deeply ingrained faith in the supernatural and the immense power of God, the ritual curse remained a potent verbal weapon. Through the curse, women could evoke a terrifying ordeal, more frightening than any demonic force. Within an ongoing state of conflict, women found solace in the deployment of ritualistic curses as a potent weapon of verbal aggression. Cursing served as a last resort for women enduring dire circumstances, as they fought to preserve their own lives. While curses offered a momentary respite from misfortune and a formidable means of altering the course of events in their favour, they also exposed women to legal repercussions that posed a genuine threat to their very existence. Despite the prevailing male-dominated governance, women subverted the imposed limitations to achieve a deep-seated political influence and personal agency by engaging in the practice of cursing. They harnessed the power of speech to interrupt patriarchal dominance and asserted a unique class of social authority by calling forth the power of the curse.

Notes

1. See, for example, A. Clark, (Ed.), *Register of the University of Oxford*, (1571–1622), vol. 1, Oxford Historical Society (1887).
2. Bodleian Library, Oxford, Ms.e. Mus, 173, 'An Experiment for love,' 'To make a woman love thee.'
3. Ibid.
4. See, for instance, Bodleian Library, Oxford, Ashmolean Manuscripts, No. 181, p. 135.
5. See, also, Bodleian Library, Oxford, Ashmolean Manuscripts, Casebook of William Lilly, Numbers, 184, 178, 185, 420, 210, 427, 547 (contains a whole file on witchcraft), 749, 1488. Remedies against it are contained in 1417 V.16, 1442 V1 27, 1447, 1X. Cases of people who thought to themselves to be bewitched are found in 182, 1076, 153, and 1447, 1X, 14, 1488, 11,35, 1730 artt. 35, 82 contains 'a prayer for one bewitched,' and 178,31, prayer for 'a house bewitched.'
6. Bodleian Library, Oxford, Ms e. Mus., 243, folio 13.

7. Ibid.
8. Ibid.
9. O. Davies, 'Cunning-Folk in England and Wales During the Eighteenth and Nineteenth Centuries.' *Rural History* 8, No. 1 (1997): 91–107.
10. See for example, K. O'Brien, 'Petitioning, Sexual Impropriety and the Dynamics of Ill Will in Daily Urban Life'43, No. 2 (May 2016): 177–199.
11. For an early study that examines cases in regional seventeenth-century Essex investigating archival sources from Church court records and witchcraft concerning an economic context, see A. Macfarlane, *Witchcraft in Tudor and Stuart England: A Regional and Comparative Study* (London, 1970), p. 121. For belief in popular magic deriving from folkloric tradition and newspaper sources, see also, O. Davies, 'Cunning-Folk in the Medical Market-Place during the Nineteenth Century.' *Medical History* 43, No. 1 (1999): 55–73.
12. See, for example, Lancashire Record Office, (hereafter LRO) QSB1/255/38 where cunning woman, Alice Schofield, in 1641, was consulted to diagnose the gender of the unborn child of Jane Broasly using the 'devilish' practice of 'sieve and shears.'
13. O. Hufton, The Prospect Before Her: A History of Women in Western Europe, Volume One, 1500–1800 (London, 1995), p. 182.
14. A. Macfarlane, *Witchcraft in Tudor and Stuart England* (London 1970), p. 126.
15. See, for example LRO DDX/471/1, Charms to cure a horse, and LRO DDX/611/4/8, Charms to be spoken over a house and a barn.
16. J. Obelkevich, *Religion and Rural Society in South Lindsey*, 1825–1875 (Oxford, 1976).
17. Ibid.
18. O. Davies, 'Cunning Folk and Witchcraft in Twentieth-Century England,' *Folklore* 129, No. 2 (2018): 119–132.
19. Thomas, Religion and the Decline of Magic.
20. For the practice of cunning in the nineteenth century see O. Davies, 'Cunning-Folk in the Medical Market–Place during the Nineteenth Century.' *Medical History* 43, No. 1 (1999): 55–73.
21. Ibid. p. 55.

22. See, for example, LRO QSB1/139/85 1630, the case of Lancashire cunning man William Nuttall, (whose mother, was also a cunning woman), who travelled by horseback for three days.
23. See also, J. Obelkevich, *Religion and Rural Society in South Linsey, 1825–1875* (Oxford, 1976). Obelkevich emphasises the role of the wise man. He claims that women who could cure animals were the exception rather than the norm. However, the wise folk of the Northwest were not public figures, but they were well known in the community. For some European comparisons, see also D. Gentilcore, 'Was there a "Popular Medicine" in early modern Europe, *Folklore* 115, No. 2 (August 2004): 151–166. Gentilcore proposes that based on Italian evidence it is impossible to draw absolute distinctions between schooled medical professionals, ecclesiastical healers, and illiterate 'wise-women,' as there were important differences in the guiding mentality behind each approach.
24. LRO QSB1/139/85 1630, Lancashire wiseman, William Nuttall, charged with witchcraft.
25. Ibid. Deposition of Jane Chisnall.
26. LRO QSB1/78/49, 1630, Examination of Mary Shawe of Crofte, Blesser.
27. Ibid. 'Sworne' examination of Robert Gaskell.
28. For adversity caused through the epidemics of measles in the Northwest, see Karen O'Brien, 'Companions of Heart and Hearth: Hardship and the Changing Structure of the Family in Early Modern English Townships,' *Journal of Family History* 39, No. 3: 196.
29. LRO QSB1/202/89, 1638, Examination of Thomas Hope of Aspull, Blacksmith and cunning man.
30. Ibid. Sworne deposition of Margerie Mullineux.
31. Ibid.
32. Ibid. Sworne examination of Christopher Leigh of Rumworth, Physician.
33. LRO QSP/1634–1638. Sybill Farclough.
34. C. B. Phillips and J. H. Smith, op cit. p. 11. See also Wrigley and Schofield, op. cit. p. 651, C. D. Rogers, *The Lancashire Population Crisis of 1623* (Manchester, 1975), and A. Appleby, op. cit. p. 147. These studies support the view that there were a number

of spasmodic local crises in the Northwest, especially during the 1590s, 1620s, and 1630s.

35. LRO QSP/324/20, 1638.
36. LRO QSB1/139/81, 1634, Examination of cunning man, Henry Bagillie.
37. Ibid.
38. Ibid.
39. Ibid.
40. LRO QSB1/139/81, 1634. Examination of cunning man Henry Bagillie and the note of Edmund Ashheton. His activities were interpreted by Ashheton as 'witchcrafte.' Bagillie may have hanged.
41. LRO QSP/268/6, 1663. The petition of labourer John Roshorne of Little Bolton.
42. Ibid.
43. Ibid.
44. Ibid. Note of the Justices of Lancashire Quarter Sessions Court.
45. LRO QSP165/12 The Petition of Ann Baker of Warrington.
46. LRO QSP165/12 The names subscribed are T. Barrow, Hariot, John Coulthroft, Bennit, Thomas Parkinson, George Chorlton, Janice Whitworth, John Renshall, William Sharlock, George Almred, Richard Mather.
47. Ibid. The note of William Weast, Justice, at Warrington.
48. LRO QSP151/21. Note of Justice Butterworth.
49. LRO QSP151/21, 1657. The petition of Margerie Greene of Ince.
50. LRO QSB9P0/214/8, 1661. Petition of unnamed woman accusing another of failing to cure a colt. Probably a recognisance bond was issued against her.
51. Ibid.
52. LRO QSB1/255/38, 1641. Recognisance bond of Alice Schofield, cunning woman.
53. K. O'Brien, 'Companions of Heart and Hearth: Hardship and the Changing Structure of the Family in Early Modern English Townships.' *Journal of Family History* 39, No. 3 (2014): 183–203.
54. Ibid.
55. L. Conrad, M. Neve, V. Nutton, R. Porter, A. Wear, *Members of the Academic Unit, The Wellcome Institute for the History*

of Medicine, London, The Western Medical Tradition, 800 BC to AD 1800 (Cambridge, 1995), p. 298. For further information regarding the involvement of women as apothecaries, midwives and healers, See also, J. Bennett, *Women's Work in a Changing World 1300–1600: Ale, Beer and Brewsters in England* (Oxford: Oxford University Press, 1996), B. Ehrenreich, and D. English, *Witches, Midwives and Healers: A History of Women Healers* (London, 1974), L. Pollock, *With Faith and Physic: The Life of a Tudor Gentlewoman, Lady Grace Mildmay 1552–1620* (London, 1993), V. Nutton, *Ancient Medicine* (New York 2004), C. Webster, *Paracelsus: Medicine, Magic, and Mission at the End of Time* (Yale University Press, 2008).

56. Ibid.
57. CRO DDX 384/1 1648–1659.
58. CRO DSS1/4/47–64.
59. CRO DSS1/4/40 1–84, 1662.
60. CRO DSS 1/4/50 1–84, 1663.
61. CRO DSS 1/4/50 1–84, 1663.
62. CRO DAR/6/60.
63. CRO DAR/6/60.
64. CRO DSS/1/1/37.
65. CRO DSS/1/1/37.
66. CRO DSS/1/1/37.
67. CRO DSS/1/4/51.
68. CRO DFF/162/122.
69. CRO DFF/162/122.
70. CRO DFF/162/122.
71. CRO DFF/162/122.
72. CRO DFF/26/2–3. List of Medicines.
73. Ibid.
74. CRO D/4367/1AQ2BES Eliza Cholmondeley, 1677, Receipt book. The above information is written at the beginning of the book and is recorded as being 'collected from the pedigree of the Cholmondeley family as set out in Ormerod's Cheshire.'
75. Ibid. p. 13.
76. Ibid. p. 27.
77. Ibid. p. 30.
78. CRO D4367/1AQ2BES Eliza Cholmondeley, 1677, Receipt book.

79. Ibid.
80. Ibid.
81. Ibid.
82. Ibid.
83. Ibid.
84. Ibid.
85. Ibid.
86. Ibid.
87. Ibid.
88. J. Goudsblom and S. Mennell, (Eds.), *The Norbert Elias Reader: A Biographical Selection* (Oxford, 1998).
89. S. Amussen, 'Punishment, Discipline and Power: The Social Meanings of Violence in Early Modern England,' *Journal of British Studies* 34, No. 1 (January 1995): pp. 1–34 and S. Amussen, *An Ordered Society: Gender and Class in Early Modern England* (Oxford, 1988).
90. Wardens listened carefully to the hearsay that was circulating in the community.
91. Those who believe that early modern society was excessively violent include J. A. Sharpe in 'The History of Violence in England, Some Observations,' in *Past and Present* No. 108 (London, 1988), pp. 206–215, and L. Stone, 'Some Interpersonal violence in English Society 1300–1980' *Past and Present*, No. 10, (London, 1988), pp. 22–33.
92. A. Macfarlane and S. Harrison, *The Justice and Mare's Ale, Law and Disorder in Seventeenth-century England* (New York, 1981), and K. Wrightson, *English Society, Poverty and Piety in an English Village, Terling 1541–1871* (London, 1986).
93. The circumstances of the dynamics of ill will are further explored in K. O'Brien, 'Petitions, Sexual Impropriet and the Dynamics of Ill Will.' No court matters were heard during the interregnum between 1650 and 1660. When the Consistory Court resumed business in 1660, there was a rise with 841 causes being heard between 1660 and 1670. The highest annual increase within the second peak decade of 1660 to 1670, took place in 1663, when the court heard 126 causes in a single year.
94. See, for example, a series of petitions that includes transcriptions of petitions (written requests) that were submitted to the Quarter Sessions in S. Howard (Ed.) *Petitions to the Cheshire Quarter*

Sessions, 1573–1798, *British History Online* http://www.british-history.ac.uk/petitions/cheshire [accessed 12 February 2020].

95. For petitions concerning the peasantry and structures and consistency of rural social relationships, see R. Houston, *Social Relations and Economic Life on Landed Estates, 1600–1850* (Routledge, 2014). See, also J. Healey, *The First Century of Welfare—Poverty and Poor Relief in Lancashire, 1620–1730* (Boydell and Brewer, 2014) which offers a regional study of poverty and its relief in the seventeenth century by drawing on thousands of individual petitions for poor relief presented by paupers themselves to magistrates, exploring the social and economic world of England's poorest people. For the later period and popularisation of petitioning, for repeal of the Contagious Diseases Acts, see also, Richard Huzzey and Henry Miller, 'Petitions, Parliament and Political Culture: Petitioning the House of Commons, 1780–1918,' *Past & Present*, 13 April 2020. See also the ways in which First Nations challenged British colonial authority in from the earliest days of colonisation through the act of petitioning. In an analysis of First Nations petitions, my publication entitled *Petitioning for Land* follows colonialism and investigates First Nations rights and the range of legal encounters that initiated the many petitions of First Nations of modern British colonies. K. O'Brien, *Petitioning for Land: The Petitions of First Peoples of Modern British Colonies* (Bloomsbury 2019).
96. CRO Shakerley of Hulme and Somerford Correspondence and Papers, DSS1/4/57/11. The correspondence dated c.1662 to 1672 addresses domestic and personal matters, family, health, doctors, servants, deeds of settlement, legal disputes, land taxes, the great plague of 1665, and the fire of London. Also petitions and documents from the Lancashire Record Office are referred to as LRO.
97. M. Ingram, *Church Courts, Sex and Marriage in England, 1570–1640* (Cambridge, 1988) and M. Ingram 'Scolding Women Cucked and Washed,' in J. Kermode and G. Walker, (Eds.), *Women, Crime and the Courts in Early Modern England* (London, 1994).
98. Ibid.
99. See, for example, the causes relating to midwife, Anne Knutsford, from Nantwich, CRO EDC5/1662/18/19, EDC5/1663/16,

EDC5/1663/54, EDC5/1664/6, EDC5/1664/57, EDC5/1664/68, EDC5/1667/2, EDC5/1667/62, EDC5/1668/10. The conflict between those involved in these cases went on for more than ten years.

100. See, for example, CRO DDX96/5, 'The Misdemeanours of Elizabeth Brynne of Tarvin.'
101. The following records are useful in documenting violence. CRO Ecclesiastical Records, Chester Consistory Court: Caveat books 1619–1791: (EDC4), Citations books, 1693–1944: requiring appearance at court (EDC3, EDD1), Court books 1502–1976, matrimonial, testamentary and tithe cases (EDC1), Court Papers 1525–1860 (EDC5), Deposition books 1529–74: evidence of witnesses (EDC2), Penances and excommunications 1606–1786 (EDC6, EDX). Chester City Record Office: Extracts of Fines (QSPE), Rolls of Offences, Gaol and House of Corrections, 1575 (QAG). Lancashire Record Office: Quarter Sessions Bonds and Petitions (QSB and QSP). Liverpool Record Office: Minute Books from 1550, The Moore deed and letters 1300–1800, The Norris deeds and papers. The records of Lancashire and Cheshire Quarter Sessions, the Liverpool Town Books, the various Manorial Courts of Cheshire, and other subsidiary regulating bodies of the Northwest contain details of domestic violence. Since the Church courts operated in 450 places in England during the early modern period there is no shortage of comparative material.
102. CRO EDC5/1630/45. These details were heard by Thomas Stafford in 1630.
103. CRO EDC5/1630/45.
104. CRO EDC5/73/1638.
105. CRO EDC5/1616/30 Winwick.
106. Ibid.
107. Ibid.
108. Ibid.
109. Ibid.
110. Ibid.
111. Ibid.
112. Ibid.
113. CRO DDX/96/5 /1610 List of Misdemeanours of Elizabeth Bruyne (sic) of Tarvin.

114. A. Shepard and J. Spicksley, 'Worth, Age and Social Status in Early Modern England' *Economic History Review*, 64 (2011): 516.
115. A. Shepard, 'Poverty, Labour and The Language of Social Description in Early Modern England,' *Past and Present*, 201, (2008): 55.
116. C. B. Phillips and J. H. Smith, op. cit., p. 60.
117. Ibid.
118. R. C. Richardson, *Puritanism in Northwest England* (Manchester, 1972).
119. Ibid. p. 94.
120. Ibid.
121. For details of the religious distribution of Nantwich, see CRO D4059/9, and see also details of James Hall 's notebook, who wrote about Nantwich in the seventeenth century in his draft manuscript of 7 Miles Around Nantwich. See also CRO EDC5 1693/21 Chester, Holy Trinity, which records the details of a book written by Alderman Wilcock in 1693 in defence of the Church of England. He attacks Presbyterians and dissenters.
122. R. C. Richardson, Puritanism in Northwest England, p. 114.
123. Ibid.
124. Ibid. p. 183.
125. Ibid. p. 77.
126. C. Hill, *Society and Puritanism in Pre-Revolutionary England* (1964) and W. K. Jordan, *Philanthropy in England*, 1480–1660 (London, 1959) and *The Social Institutions of Lancashire, 1480–1660* Chetham Society, third series, II, (Manchester, 1962), and P. Collinson, 'The Godly: Aspects of Popular Protestantism in Elizabethan England,' *Past and Present Conference Papers* (1966), as cited by Richardson, op. cit. pp. 181–183.
127. R. M. Helholz, *Roman Canon Law in Reformation England* (Cambridge, 1990), p. 6.
128. R. C. Richardson, op. cit. 42.
129. R. C. Richardson, op. cit. 52.
130. C. B. Phillips and J. H. Smith, op. cit., p. 61.
131. A. White (Ed.), *A History of Lancaster 1193–1993*, (Staffordshire, 1993), p. 64.
132. R. C. Richardson, op. cit., p. 108.
133. CRO EDC5/1630/50.
134. Ibid.

135. Ibid.
136. K. O'Brien, 'Petitioning, Sexual Impropriety and the Dynamics of Ill Will in Daily Urban Life' p. 53.
137. C. Muldrew, 'Debt, Credit, and Poverty in Early Modern England,' in R. Brubaker, R.M. Lawless and C.J. Tabb (eds.), A Debtor World: Interdisciplinary Perspectives on Debt (Oxford, 2012), 9–32.
138. Ibid.
139. R. Stewart-Brown (Ed.), *Cheshire Inquisitions Post Mortem*, The Record Society for the Publication of Original Documents Relating to Lancashire and Cheshire, Volume 111 (1938).
140. F. A. Bailey, (Ed.*), Cheshire Quarter Sessions Records for the County Palatine of Chester, 1559–1760*, The Record Society for the Publication of Original Documents Relating to Lancashire and Cheshire, Volume 94 (1938).
141. O. Davies, *Popular Magic: Cunning Folk in English History*. (London, England; Hambledon Continuum, 2007).
142. LRO QSB1/139/81, 1634. Examination of cunning man, Henry Bagillie.
143. QSB1/139/85 1630. Lancashire Wiseman, William Nuttall.
144. LRO QSB1/64/21–23, 1629.
145. LRO QSB1/64/21–23, 1629.
146. See also, K. O'Brien, O'Brien, 'Petitioning, Sexual Impropriety, and the Dynamics of Ill Will in Daily Urban Life' p. 2.
147. LRO QSP165/12 The Petition of Ann Baker of Warrington.
148. LRO QSP151/21.
149. LRO QSB9P0/214/8, 1661. Petition of unnamed woman accusing another of failing to cure a colt.
150. LRO QSP/268/6, 1663. The petition of Labourer John Roshorne of Little Bolton.

Bibliography

Manuscript Sources

1. Bodleian Library, Oxford

Ashmolean Manuscripts Ms.e. Mus.

Ashmolean Manuscripts, Casebook of William Lilly, Numbers, 184, 178, 185, 420, 210, 427, 547, 749, 1488.

Ashmolean Manuscripts, 547, Gifford, G., 'A Dialogue Concerning Witches and Witchcrafte.'

2. Cheshire Record Office

(a) Ecclesiastical Records, Chester Consistory Court

Caveat books 1619–1791 (EDC4)

Citations books, 1693–1944: requiring appearance at court (EDC3, EDD1)

Court books 1502–1976, matrimonial, testamentary and tithe cases (EDC1)

Court Papers 1525–1860 (EDC5)

Deposition books 1529–1574: evidence of witnesses (EDC2)

Penances and excommunications 1606–1786 (EDC6, EDX)

(b) Visitation

Clergy call books c.1532–1562, 1671–1908, details of clergy, schoolmasters, surgeons and midwives.

(c) Wills and Probate Records

Diocesan series (disputed wills) 1487–1800 (WC)

Infra series 1600–1641, 1660–1697, 1729–1857 (WI)

Supra series 1545–1650, 1660–1858 (WS)

Wills in the bishop's registers 1492–1829 (EDA2)

K. O'Brien, *Cursing, Crisis and Customary Knowledge in Early Modern English Townships*, Palgrave Historical Studies in Witchcraft and Magic, https://doi.org/10.1007/978-3-031-44045-8

(d) Private Deposits: Estate and family
Cholmondeley of Cholmondeley
Nantwich Manor and Hundred Court records 1547–1840
Crewe of Crewe
Nantwich rentals 1664–1667 (DCR)
Delves-Broughton of Doddington
Deeds to Wybunbury and townships (DDB)
Shakerley of Hulme and Somerford
Shakerley of Hulme and Somerford Correspondence and Papers. Letters of Katherine Shakerley and Elizabeth Winnington (DSS1/4/48–64)
Stanley of Alderley
Family correspondence and papers 1650–1884 (DSA)
Wilbraham of Nantwich
Deeds 1260–1889 and poor accounts 1668–1674 (DWN)
Wilbraham Almshouses (DCH)
Cowper
Papers and correspondence
(e) Antiquarian Collections
Countess of Warwick Fee, Nantwich 23 October 1632, in D4059/30 James Hall's notebook.
James Hall, *Nantwich,* 1899.
James Hall's notebook and his draft of *7 Miles Around Nantwich* D4059/9.
Notebooks of James Hall, historian of Nantwich (D4059)
Documents Oswald Cockayne, Leechdoms, Wortcunning and Starcraft of early England; being a collection of documents, for the most part never before printed, illustrating the. country before the Norman conquest Volume 1
(f) Microfilms and Lists
Hearth Tax, Nantwich 1664 (MF13)
Nantwich Parish Records 1539–1923, (P 120, MF 80)
Nantwich Chapel Houses 1689–1853, (QDR7 MF96/6)
(g) Civil Parish and Township
Audlem: overseers of the poor 1635–1836
Baddiley: overseers of the poor c.1684–1843
Wybunbury: overseers of the poor 1652–1831
(i) Manorial court
Nantwich Manor List, fines, (DCH)
Salt Bonds (DCH)
The Manor court rolls of Audley Fee, Nantwich, 1578–1653, the Countess of Warwick Fee, Nantwich. The court rolls of Nantwich.
(j) Miscellaneous
Almanac of Moore, Frances, 1751, owned by Samuel Hurlbutt, March 1751 (DDX)

Almanack 1775, The Gentleman's Diary (DDX 352/20)
Arrangement of pews. A copy of the uniformity of the church of Nantwich, 1633 (P120/4525/253)
Bastardy Bonds, DCH/M/32/11.
Bastardy bonds of Robert Cholmondely (DCH/M/32/11)
Cowper Collection, The Buglawton Rent (DCC/36)
Eliza Cholmondeley's Receipt Book (D4367/1AQ2BES)
Lady Jane Stanley's receipts (DAR/6/60)
Letter of James I (DCR)
'Macer's Herbal' D/4398/1
Nantwich Poor Rate Assessments, Six Volumes, (D4060/1) 5), P120/4525/219–223, 226–228.
Prescriptions (DCH), (DAR), (DFF)
Stanleys of Alderley (1620–1760) (DDX/361)
The Earl of Cholmondeley's Eastral Rowls from October 1711 to 14th May, 1712. (DCH/M/37/73)

(k) Monumental Inscriptions

Monumental inscriptions (D5104)

3. Chester City Record Office

Extracts of Fines (QSPE)
Rolls of Offences, Gaol, and House of Corrections, 1575 (QAG)

4. Lancashire Record Office

Charms and Spells (DDX)
Quarter Sessions Bonds and Petitions (QSB and QSP)

5. Liverpool Record Office

Minute Books from 1550
The Moore deed and letters 1300–1800
The Norris deeds and papers
William Curtis, *Flora Londensis,*1777–1787, plates and descriptions of plants that grow wild in the environs of London. Illustrations engraved by William Kilburn. Sansom and Sowerby from drawings by Kilburn, Sowerby, Pts. 1–5, roy. Fo. Londong (1777–1799) pl. 434, hand coloured.

6. Oxfordshire Record Office

Archdeacon's papers, Oxon from 1616 to 1679.
Oxford Church Court deposition books.
Oxfordshire Diocesan Papers from 1542 to 1694.

Contemporary Printed Books

Potts, T., *The Wonderful Discovery of Witches in the County of Lancaster*, (1613)

Books and Articles

Addy, J., *Sin and Society in the Seventeenth Century* (London and New York, 1989).

Addy, J., (Ed.), *The Diary of Henry Prescott, LL.B., Deputy Registrar of Chester Diocese*, Record Society of Lancashire and Cheshire (1987).

Aldridge, N., *Demographic Shifts in the Urban Network of Cheshire, 1560–1660*, Les Petites Villes en Europe Occidentale (Lille, 1987).

Amussen S., 'Punishment, Discipline and Power: The Social Meanings of Violence in Early Modern England', *Journal of British Studies* 34, no. 1 (January, 1995).

Amussen, S., 'Women's voices in Seventeenth-Century England' *Journal of British Studies,* 35, no. 1 (January 1996): 114–118, review of P. Mack, *Visionary Women: Ecstatic Prophecy in Seventeenth-Century England* (Ithaca, 1993).

Amussen, S. D., *An Ordered Society: Gender and Class in Early Modern England* (Oxford, 1988).

Amussen S. D. and Underdown, D., *Gender, Culture and Politics in England, 1560–1640 Turning the World Upside Down* (London: Bloomsbury Academic, an imprint of Bloomsbury Publishing Plc, 2017).

Ankerloo, B., and Henningsen, G., (Eds.), *Early Modern European Witchcraft* (Oxford, 1990).

Appleby, A., *Famine in Tudor and Stuart England* (Liverpool, 1978).

Arkell, T., 'Multiplying Factors for Estimating Population Totals from the Hearth Tax,' *Local Population Studies* XXVIII (Spring, 1982).

Bailey, F. A., (Ed.), *Cheshire Quarter Sessions Records, With Other Records of the Justices of the Peace for the Country Palatine of Chester, 1559–1760*, The Record Society for the Publication of Original Documents Relating to Lancashire and Cheshire, Volume 94 (1938).

Bailey, F. A., (Ed.), *Prescot Quarter Sessions Records, 1447–1600,* The Record Society of Lancashire and Cheshire, Volume 89 (1937).

Bailey, F. G., *Gifts and Poison: The Politics of Reputation* (Oxford, 1971).

Bakhtin, M., *Rabelais and His World,* translated by Helene Iswolsky (Bloomington, 1984).

Barry, J., *Witchcraft and Demonology in South-West England, 1640–1789.* 1st ed. (London: Palgrave Macmillan UK, 2012). https://doi.org/10.1057/9780230361386.

Beier, L. M., *Sufferers and Healers in Early England: Studies in Social and Intellectual History* (London, 1987).

Bennett, J., *Women's Work in a Changing World 1300–1600: Ale, Beer and Brewsters in England,* (Oxford: Oxford University Press, 1996).

Bennett, J., *History Matters: Patriarchy and the Challenge of Feminism* (Philadelphia: University of Pennsylvania Press, 2006).

Bennet, J. M., *Women in the Medieval Countryside: Gender and Household in Brigstock Before the Plague* (New York, 1987)

Bever, E., 'Popular Witch Beliefs and Magical Practices.' in Levack, B. P., *The Oxford Handbook of Witchcraft in Early Modern Europe and Colonial America* (Oxford: Oxford University Press, 2013).

Bogiato, J., Green, A., and Lobban, M., *Law, Lawyers and Litigants in Early Modern England*, Essays in Memory of Christopher W. Brooks (Cambridge, 2019).

Blackwood, B. G., 'The Lancashire Gentry and the Great Rebellion 1640–1660', *Chetham Society*, 3rd Series, XXV (1978).

Blackwood, R., 'The Lancashire Cavaliers and Their Tenants', *The Historic Society of Lancashire and Cheshire*, LXV11 (1966).

Borsay, P., *The English Urban Renaissance: Culture and Society in the Provincial Town 1660–1770* (Oxford, 1989).

Bossy, J., *The English Catholic Community 1570–1850* (London, 1975).

Brazier, M. and Fox, S., 'The Regulation of Midwives in England, c.1500–1902.' *Medical Law International* 20, no. 4 (December 2020): 308–338.

Briggs, R., 'Women as Victims? Witches, Judges and the Community in Early Modern France', *French History*, 5 (1991).

Brodsky-Elliot, V., 'Single Women in the London Marriage Market, Age Status and Mobility, 1598–1619', in R. B. Outhwaite (Ed.), *Marriage and Studies in the Social History of Marriage* (London, 1981).

Butler, J., *Bodies That Matter: On the Discursive Limits of Sex* (London: Routledge, 2014).

Callow, J., *The Last Witches of England: A Tragedy of Sorcery and Superstition* (London: Bloomsbury Academic, 2022).

Chamberlain, M., *Old Wives Tales, Their History, Remedies and Spells* (London, 1981).

Chapman, C. R., *Ecclesiastical Courts, Their Officials and Their Records* (Dursley, 1992).

Cixous, H., and Clement, C., *The Newly Born Woman* (Manchester, 1986).

Clark, A., (Ed.), *Register of the University of Oxford*, (1571–1622), Volume 1, Oxford Historical Society (1887).

Clark, A., 'Whores and Gossips: Sexual Reputation in London 1770–1825', in A. Angerman, G. Binnema, A. Keunan, V. Poels and J. Zirkzee, (Eds.), *Current Issues in Women's History* (London, 1989).

Clark, A., *Working Life of Women in the Seventeenth Century*, 3rd edition (London and New York, 1992).

Clark, P., and Slack, P., (Eds.), *Crisis and Order in English Towns, 1500–1700: Essays in Urban History* (London, 1972).

Clarke, P., and Slack, P., (Eds.), *English Towns in Transition* (London, 1976).

Chamberlain, M., *Old Wives Tales: Their History, Remedies and Spells* (London, 1981).
Cohn, N., *Europe's Inner Demons* (London, 1975).
Collinson, P., 'The Godly: Aspects of Popular Protestantism in Elizabethan England', *Past and Present Conference Papers* (1966).
Conrad, L., Neve, M., Nutton, V., Porter, R., Wear, A., Members of the Academic Unit, The Wellcome Institute for the History of Medicine, London, *The Western Medical Tradition, 800 BC to AD 1800* (Cambridge, 1995).
Crawford, P., 'The Construction and Experience of Maternity,' in Valerie Fildes, (Ed.), *Women as Mothers in Pre-Industrial England, Essays in Memory of Dorothy McLaren* (London and New York, 1995).
Crawford, P., 'Rethinking the Familiar: Domestic Relations, Property and Law in Early Modern England', *Journal of British Studies* 35, no. 3 (July 1996)
Crawford, P., *Women and Religion in England, 1500–1720* (London, 1993).
Cressy, D., 'Purification, Thanksgiving and the Churching of Women in Post Reformation England', *Past and Present*, Numbers 138–141 (March, 1996).
Culpeper, N., *The Complete Herbal* (London, 1953).
Cust, R., 'Honour and Politics in Early Stuart England: The Case of Beaumont versus Hasting', *Past and Present*, Number 14 (November 1995).
Davidson, H. E., *The Lost Beliefs of Northern Europe* (London, 1993).
Davies, O., *Cunning-Folk: Popular Magic in English History* (London, 2003).
Davies, O., 'Cunning-Folk in the Medical Market-Place during the Nineteenth Century.' *Medical History* 43, no. 1 (1999): 55–73.
Davies, O., 'Cunning-Folk in England and Wales During the Eighteenth and Nineteenth Centuries', *Rural History* 8, no. 1 (1997): 91–107.
Davies, O., *Popular Magic: Cunning Folk in English History* (London, England: Hambledon Continuum, 2007).
Davies, O., 'Magic in Common and Legal Perspectives,' in David J. Collins (Ed.), *The Cambridge History of Magic and Witchcraft in the West: From Antiquity to the Present* (Cambridge: Cambridge University Press, 2015), pp. 521–46.
Davies, O., 'Cunning-Folk in the Twentieth Century.' in *Popular Magic* (United Kingdom: Bloomsbury Publishing Plc, 2007).
de Blécourt, W., 'Witch Doctors, Soothsayers and Priests. On Cunning Folk in European Historiography and Tradition,' *Social History* 19, no. 3 (October 1994): 285–303.
de Blécourt, W., and Davies, O., *Witchcraft Continued Popular Magic in Modern Europe* (London: Manchester University Press, 2004).
de Blecourt, W., Hutton, R., and. La Fontaine, J. S., *Witchcraft and Magic in Europe the Twentieth Century* (London: Athlone Press, 1999), p. 191.
Dolan, F. E., *Dangerous Familiars: The Representation of Domestic Crime in England, 1550–1700* (Ithaca and London, 1994).

Dolan F. E., *Marriage and Violence: The Early Modern Legacy* (Pennsylvania: University of Pennsylvania Press, 2009).
Donoghue, E., *Passions Between Women, British Lesbian Culture 1668–1801* (London, 1993).
Dore, R. N., *The Letter Books of Sir William Brereton, Volume One, January–May 1945*, The Record Society of Lancashire and Cheshire, Vol. CXXIII (Cheshire, 1984).
Earwaker, J. P., (Ed.), *The History of the Church and Parish of St. Mary on the Hill, Chester* (London, 1898).
Eccles, A., *Obstetrics and Gynaecology in Tudor and Stuart England* (London, 1982).
Ehrenreich, B., and English, D., *Witches, Midwives and Healers: A History of Women Healers* (London, 1974).
Erickson, A. L., 'Common Law Versus Common Practice: the Use of Marriage Settlements in Early Modern England', *Economic History Review*, 2nd series, 43 (1990).
Erickson, A. L., *Women and Property in Early Modern England* (London and New York, 1993).
Evendon, D., *The Midwives of Seventeenth-Century London* (Cambridge, 2000).
Favret-Saada, J., *Deadly Words: Witchcraft in the Bocage* (Cambridge, Cambridgeshire: Cambridge University Press, 1980).
Fildes, V., (Ed.), *Women as Mothers in Pre-Industrial England, Essays in Memory of Dorothy McLaren* (London and New York, 1990).
Fletcher, A., *Gender, Sex and Subordination in England, 1500–1800* (1995).
Forbes, T. R., 'Midwifery and Witchcraft', *Journal of the History of Medicine and Allied Sciences* 17 (1962).
Gaskill, M., *The Ruin of All Witches, Life and Death in the New World* (London, 2021).
Gelis, J., *History of Childbirth: Fertility, Pregnancy and Birth in Early Modern Europe* translation by R. Morris (Cambridge, 1991).
Gentilcore, D., 'Was there a "Popular Medicine" in early modern Europe?', *Folklore* 115, no. 2 (August 2004): 151–166.
Ginzburg, C., *The Night Battles: Witchcraft and Agrarian Cults in the Sixteenth and Seventeenth Centuries* (Baltimore, 1983).
Goodare, J., Martin, L., and Miller, J., *Witchcraft and Belief in Early Modern Scotland.* Edited by J. Goodare, L. Martin, and J. Miller. 1st ed. 2008 (London: Palgrave Macmillan UK, 2007).
Gough, Richard, and David. Hey. The History of Myddle. Harmondsworth, Middlesex ; Pengui, 1981.
Gowing L., *Common Bodies: Women, Touch, and Power in Seventeenth-Century England* (Haven: Yale University Press, 2003).

Gowing, L., 'Secret Births and Infanticide in Seventeenth-Century England', *Past and Present* (August, 1997).
Gowing, L., *Women, Sex and Honour: The London Church Courts, 1572–1640* (London, 1995).
Gowing, L., *Domestic Dangers, Women, Words and Sex in Early Modern England* (Oxford, 1996).
Griffths, P., Fox. A., and Hindle, S., (Eds.), *The Experience of Authority in Early Modern England* (New York, 1996).
Grosz, E., *Volatile Bodies: Towards A Corporeal Feminism* (Australia, 1994).
Haigh, C., *English Reformations: Religion, Politics and Society Under the Tudors* (Oxford, 1993).
Hall, J., *A History of the Town and Parish of Nantwich* (Manchester, 1883).
Hall, J., *Nantwich* (Manchester, 1899).
Hammington, M., *Hail Mary? The Struggle for Ultimate Womanhood in Catholicism* (London, 1995).
Harland J., and Wilkinson, T., *Lancashire Folk Lore* (1867).
Harland J., and Wilkinson, T., *Customs, Lancashire Legends, Traditions* (1883).
Harris, T., (Ed.), *Popular Culture in England c.1500–1850* (London, 1995).
Healey, J., *The First Century of Welfare—Poverty and Poor Relief in Lancashire, 1620–1730* (2014).
Herrup, C. B., *The Common Peace: Participation and the Criminal Law in Seventeenth Century England* (Cambridge, 1987).
Hester, M., *Lewd Women and Wicked Witches—A Study of the Dynamics of Male Domination* (London and New York, 1992).
Higgins, G. P., 'The Government of Early Stuart Cheshire,' *Northern History* XII (Manchester, 1976).
Hill, C., *Society and Puritanism in Pre-Revolutionary England* (London, 1964).
Hill, C., *The Century of Revolution 1603–1714* (London, 1974).
Hindle, S., 'The Shaming of Margaret Knowsley: Gossip, Gender and the Experience of Authority in Early Modern England', *Continuity and Change* 9 (1994).
Hindle, S., *English Society in Crisis 1560–1640* (Manchester, 1998).
Horwitz, H., and Polden P., 'Continuity or Change in the Court of Chancery in the Seventeenth and Eighteenth Centuries' *Journal of British Studies* 35, no. 1 (January 1996).
Horwitz, H., 'Record-Keepers in the Court of Chancery and their Record of Accomplishment in the Seventeenth and Eighteenth Centuries,' in *Historical Research*, The Bulletin of the Institute of Historical Research, Volume 70, Number 171 (February 1997).
Houlbroke, R. A., *Church Courts and the People During the English Reformation, 1520–1570* (Oxford, 1979).

Houston, R., *Social Relations and Economic Life on Landed Estates, 1600–1850* (Routledge, 2014)

Howard, S., *Petitions to the Cheshire Quarter Sessions, 1573–1798*, *British History Online* http://www.british-history.ac.uk/petitions/cheshire [accessed 12 February 2020].

Hufton, O., *The Prospect Before Her: A History of Women in Western Europe, Volume One, 1500–1800* (London, 1995).

Hughes, G., *Swearing: A Social History of Foul Language, Oaths and Profanity in English* (Oxford, 1991).

Huzzey, R., and Miller, H., 'Petitions, Parliament and Political Culture: Petitioning the House of Commons, 1780–1918,' *Past & Present*, 13 April 2020.

Ingram, M., *Church Courts, Sex and Marriage in England, 1570–1640* (Cambridge, 1988).

Ingram, M., 'Scolding Women Cucked and Washed,' in J. Kermode and G. Walker, (Eds.), *Women, Crime and the Courts in Early Modern England* (London, 1994).

Jordan, W. K., *Philanthropy in England, 1480–1660* (London, 1959).

Jordan, W. K., *The Social Institutions of Lancashire, 1480–1660* (Manchester, 1962).

Karras, R. M., *Common Women; Prostitution and Sexuality in Medieval England* (New York and Oxford, 1996)

Kamensky, J., *Governing the Tongue: The Politics of Speech in Early New England* (New York and Oxford: Oxford University Press, 1997).

Kermode, J., and Walker, G., (Eds.), *Women, Crime and the Courts in Early Modern England* (London, 1994).

Kounine, L. and Ostling, M., (Eds.), *Emotions in the History of Witchcraft*. 1st ed. 2016 (London: Palgrave Macmillan UK, 2016).

Ladurie, E. L. R., *Jasmine's Witch* (Aldershot, 1983).

Lawton, R., 'Population Trends in Lancashire and Cheshire from 1801' *The Historic Society of Lancashire and Cheshire* CX1V (1962).

Levack, B., *The Witchhunt in Early Modern Europe* (London, 1987).

Levack, B. P. (Ed.), *The Oxford Handbook of Witchcraft in Early Modern Europe and Colonial America* (Oxford: Oxford University Press, 2013).

Lindberg, C., *The European Reformations* (Oxford, 1996).

Loades, D., *Revolution in Religion: The English Reformation 1530–1570* (Cardiff, 1992).

MacCulloch, D., *The Later Reformation in England, 1547–1603* (New York, 1990).

MacDonald, M., *Mystical Bedlam: Madness, Anxiety and Healing in Seventeenth-Century England* (Cambridge, 1981).

Macfarlane A., and Harrison, S., *The Justice and Mare's Ale, Law and Disorder in Seventeenth-Century England* (New York, 1981)

Macfarlane, A., *Witchcraft in Tudor and Stuart England: A Regional and Comparative Study* (London, 1970).

Mack, P., *Visionary Women: Ecstatic Prophecy in Seventeenth-Century England* (Ithaca, 1993).

McClintock, A., *Imperial Leather: Race, Gender and Sexuality in the Colonial Contest* (Routledge, 1995)

Marland, H., (Ed.), *The Art of Midwifery: Early Modern Midwives in Europe*, The Wellcome Series in the History of Medicine (London and New York, 1993).

Mendelson, S. and Crawford, P., *Women in Early Modern England, 1550–1720* (Oxford, 1998).

Mendez, A., *Hell is Empty: Demonology, Witch Hunts, and Reformation in Early Modern England in Sixteenth and Seventeenth Centuries* (Valencia: University of Valencia Press, 2020).

Mendez, A., 'Feeling with Demons. Demonology, Puritans and Emotional Discipline in New England (c.1660–1700)', *Histories of Emotion* (2022): 1–16.

Millar, C. R., 'Diabolical Men: Reintegrating Male Witches into English Witchcraft.' *The Seventeenth Century* 36, no. 5 (2021): 693–713.

Millar, C. R., *Witchcraft, the Devil, and Emotions in Early Modern England* (Taylor and Francis, 2017).

Midelfort, H. C. E., *Witch-Hunting in South-Western Germany, 1562–1684* (Stanford, 1972).

Milhous, J., and Hume, R. D., 'Eighteenth Century Equity Lawsuits in the Court of Exchequer as a Source for Historical Research,' in *Historical Research* (The Bulletin of the Institute of Historical Research), Volume 70, Number 172 (June 1997).

Moffatt, C. R., *Magic and Witchcraft in Early Modern Scotland* (London: Palgrave Macmillan, 2018).

Monter, E. W., *Witchcraft in France and Switzerland; the Borderlands During the Reformation* (Ithaca, 1976).

Moreton-Robinson, A., *Talkin' Up to the White Woman: Aboriginal Women and Feminism* (St Lucia: University of Queensland Press, 2000), pp. 179–186.

Muldrew, C., *The Economy of Obligation: The Culture of Credit and Social Relations in Early modern England* (New York, 1998).

Nutton, V., Ancient Medicine. 2nd ed. Milton Park, Abingdon, Oxon: Routledge, 2013, C. Webster, *Paracelsus: Medicine, Magic, and Mission at the End of Time* (Yale University Press, 2008).

O'Brien, K., The Larrakia Petitions for a Treaty and Land Rights. *UK Parliaments Petition Committee*, October 2019.

O'Brien, K., *White Magic and the Cunning Folk: Charms and Blessings in Northwest England* (Liverpool: The Bluecoat Press, 2001).

O'Brien, K., 'Petitioning, Sexual Impropriety and the Dynamics of Ill Will in Daily Urban Life.' *Urban History* 43, no. 2 (2016): 177–199.

O'Brien, K., "Companions of Heart and Hearth: Hardship and the Changing Structure of the Family in Early Modern English Townships." *Journal of Family History* 39, no. 3 (2014): 183–203.

O'Brien, K., 'Intimate Worlds: Kinship Relations and Emotional Investment Among Nantwich Women 1603–1685.' *Journal of Family History* 41, no. 2 (2016): 131–143.

O'Day, R., *The Debate on the English Reformation* (London, 1986).

O'Day, R., review of A. Fletcher, *Gender, Sex and Subordination in England, 1500–1800 (1995) The English Historical Review*, April 1997, CX11, no. 446: 419.

Obelkevich, J., *Religion and Rural Society in South Linsey, 1825–1875* (Oxford, 1976).

Ogilby, J., *Britannia: Volume the First, or, an Illustration of the Kingdom of England and Dominion of Wales, By a Geographical and Historical Description of the Principal Roads thereof: By John Ogilby Esq., His Majesty's Cosmographer*, Theatrum Orbis Terravum, series of Atlases in Facsimile, 5th Series, Vol. II (Chicago, 1979).

Pelling, M., 'Medical Practice in the Early Modern Period: Trade or Profession?' *The Society for the Social History of Medicine Bulletin* XXXII (1983).

Phillips, C. B. and Smith, J. H., *Lancashire and Cheshire from AD 1540, A Regional History of England* (London and New York, 1994).

Piccope, G. J., (Ed.), *Lancashire and Cheshire Wills and Inventories from the Ecclesiastical Court at Chester*, Chetham Society, Old series, LI and LV (1860 and 1861).

Peck, I., *Recollection in the Republics: Memories of the British Civil Wars in England, 1649–1659*. 1st ed. (Oxford: Oxford University Press, 2021).

Peck, I., 'The Great Unknown: The Negotiation and Narration of Death by English War Widows, 1647–60.' *Northern History* 53, no. 2 (2016): 220–235.

Pócs, É., 'Curse, Maleficium, Divination: Witchcraft on the Borderline of Religion and Magic,' in Willem de Blécourt, Ronald Hutton, and J. S. La Fontaine (Eds.) *Witchcraft and Magic in Europe the Twentieth Century* (London: Athlone Press, 1999), pp. 174–176.

Pollock, L., *With Faith and Physic: The Life of a Tudor Gentlewoman, Lady Grace Mildmay 1552–1620* (London, 1993).

Porter, R., (Ed.), *Patients and Practitioners: Lay Perceptions of Medicine in Pre-Industrial Society* (New York, 1985).

Porter, R., 'The Pharmacology of Sacred Plants, Herbs and Roots,' in C. A. Faraore and D. Obbink (Eds.), *Magika Hiera: Ancient Greek Magic and Religion* (Oxford, 1991).

Purkiss, D., *The Witch in History: Early Modern and Twentieth-century Representations* (London and New York, 1996)

Richardson, R. C., *Puritanism in Northwest England* (Manchester, 1972).

Rogers, C. D., *The Lancashire Population Crisis of 1623* (Manchester, 1975).

Rollison, D., *The Local Origins of Modern Society: Gloucestershire, 1500–1800* (London and New York, 1992).

Roper, L., *Oedipus and the Devil, Witchcraft, Sexuality and Religion in Early Modern Europe* (London and New York, 1994).

Rowlands, A., *Witchcraft and Masculinities in Early Modern Europe*. Edited by A. Rowlands. 1st ed. 2009 (London: Palgrave Macmillan UK, 2009).

Rublack, U., 'Pregnancy, Childbirth and the Female Body in Early Modern Germany,' *Past and Present,* Number 150 (February 1996).

Rushton, P., 'Women, Witchcraft and Slander in Early Modern England: Cases from the Church Courts of Durham, 1560–1675', *Northern History* Volume XV11–XV111 (Manchester, 1986).

Sawyer, R. C., 'Strangely Handled in All Her Lyms': Witchcraft and Healing in Jacobean England', *Journal of Social History*, 22 (1989).

Sainsbury, J. 'Barry, Jonathan. Witchcraft and Demonology in South-West England, 1640–1789.' *CHOICE: Current Reviews for Academic Libraries.* American Library Association Choice, 2012.

Scarre, G., *Witchcraft and Magic in Sixteenth- and Seventeenth-century Europe* (London, 1987).

Sharpe, J., *Defamation and Sexual Slander in Early Modern England: The Church Courts at York* (York, 1980).

Sharpe, J., *Crime in Seventeenth-Century England: A County Study* (Cambridge, 1983).

Sharpe, J., 'The History of Violence in England, Some Observations', *Past and Present*, no. 108 (1988).

Sharpe, J., *The American Historical Review* 118, no. 5 (2013): 1600–1601. Available at: http://www.jstor.org/stable/23784716.

Sharpe, J., *Instruments of Darkness: Witchcraft in England 1550–1750* (London, 1996).

Shepard, A., 'Worthless Witnesses? Marginal Voices and Women's Legal Agency in Early Modern England,' *Journal of British Studies,* 58 (October 2019): 717–734.

Shepard, A. 'Poverty, Labour and The Language of Social Description in Early Modern England', *Past and Present*, 201, (2008), 55.

Shepard A. and Spicksley., J. 'Worth, Age and Social Status in Early Modern England' *Economic History Review* 64 (2011): 516.

Shoemaker, R. B., *Prosecution and Punishment: Petty Crime and the Law in London and Rural Middlesex, c.1660–1725* (Cambridge, 1991).

Shoemaker, R. B., *Gender in English Society 1650–1850: The Emergence of Separate Spheres?* (London, 1998)

Simpson, J., 'Witches and Witchbusters.' *Folklore* 107 (1996): 5–18

Skelton, R. A., *Christopher Saxton's Cheshire, Saxton's Survey of England and Wales* (Amsterdam, 1974).

Speed, J., *An Atlas of Tudor England and Wales 1627 Forty Plates from John Speed's Pocket Atlas of 1627*, introduced and described by E. G.R. Taylor (London, 1951).

Stallybrass P., and White, A., *The Politics and Poetics of Transgression* (London, 1986).

Stavreva, K., *Words Like Daggers: Female Speech in Early Modern England* (Nebraska, 2015)

Stewart-Brown, R., (Ed.), *The Cheshire Inquisitions Post Mortem*, The Record Society for the Publication of Original Documents relating to Lancashire and Cheshire, Volume 111 (1938).

Stone, L., 'Some Interpersonal Violence in English Society 1300–1980', *Past and Present*, no. 10 (1988).

Stretton, T., *Women Waging Law in Elizabethan England* (Cambridge: New York, 1998)

Sylvester D., *A History of Cheshire* (London, 1980).

The Victoria History of the Counties of England, The Victoria County History of Chester, Volume I (Oxford, 1987).

The Victoria History of the Counties of England, A History of Cheshire, Volume II (Oxford, 1979).

The Victoria History of the Counties of England, A History of Cheshire, Volume III (Oxford, 1980).

The Victoria History of the County of Chester, Volume I (Oxford, 1987).

Thirsk, J., (Ed.), 'The Market Town, The Marketing of Agricultural Produce,' in *The Agrarian History of England and Wales Volume V, 1500–1640* (Cambridge, 1987).

Thirsk, J., (Ed.), 'Sources of Information on Population 1500–1760, *Amateur Historian*, IV (Oxford, 1959).

Thirsk, J., *The Agrarian History of England and Wales Volume IV, 1500–1640* (Cambridge, 1967).

Thomas, K., *Religion and the Decline of Magic, Studies in Popular Beliefs in Sixteenth- and Seventeenth-Century England* (London, 1971).

Twemlow, J. A. (Ed.), *Liverpool Town Books, Proceedings of Assemblies, Common Councils, Portmoot Courts, 1550–1862,* Volume II, 1571–1603 (Liverpool, 1935).

Underdown, D., 'The Taming of the Scold: the Enforcement of Patriarchal Authority in Early Modern England,' in A. Fletcher and J. Stevenson, (Eds.), *Order and Disorder in Early Modern England* (Cambridge, 1985).

Underdown, D., *Revel, Riot and Rebellion: Popular Politics and Culture in England 1603–1660* (Oxford, 1985).

Walker, G., 'Women, Theft and the World of Stolen Goods,' in J. Kermode and G. Walker, (Eds.), *Women, Crime and the Courts in Early Modern England* (London, 1994).

Walker, G., *Crime Gender and Social Order in Early Modern England* (London, 2003)

Walker, G., 'Framing Premodern Desires Between Sexuality, Sin and Crime: an introduction,' in Lidman, S. et al. (Eds.), *Framing Premodern Desires. Sexual Ideas, Attitudes and Practises in Europe* (Amsterdam: University of Amsterdam Press, 2018).

Warner J. and Lunny, A. 'Marital Violence in a Martial Town: Husbands and Wives in Early Modern Portsmouth, 1653–1781,' *Journal of Family History* 28 (2003): 261.

Waters, T., 'Irish Cursing and the Art of Magic, 1750–2018.' *Past & Present* 247, no. 1 (2020): 113–149.

Wear, A., (Ed.), *Health and Healing in Early Modern England: Studies in Social and Intellectual History* (Aldershot, 1998).

White, A., (Ed.), *A History of Lancaster 1193–1993* (Staffordshire, 1993).

Wilson, A., *The Making of Man-Midwifery: Childbirth in England, 1660–1770* (New York, 1987)

Wilson, A., 'Participant or Patient? Seventeenth Century Childbirth from the Mother's Point of View,' in Porter, R. (Ed.), *Patients and Practitioners: Lay Perceptions of Medicine in Pre-Industrial Society* (Cambridge, 1985).

Wrightson, K., *English Society, Poverty and Piety in an English Village, Terling 1525–1600* (London, 1986).

Wrigley, E. A., and Schofield, R. S., *The Population History of England 1541–1871* (London, 1981).

Wrigley, E. A., *People, Cities and Wealth: A Simple Model of London's Importance in Changing English Society and Economy, 1650–1750* (Oxford, 1987).

Wyatt, G. M., 'Nantwich and Wybunbury, 1680–1819: A Demographic Study of Two Cheshire Parishes', *The Historic Society of Lancashire and Cheshire*, Volume 139 (Liverpool, 1990).

Walker, T. D., 'Doctors, Folk Medicine and the Inquisition: The Repression of Magical Healing in Portugal during the Enlightenment', *The Medieval and Early Modern Iberian World* 23 (2005): xvi–433.

Wilby, E., *Cunning-Folk and Familiar Spirits: Shamanistic Visionary Traditions in Early Modern British Witchcraft and Magic* (Brighton, 2005).

Young, F., *Magic as a Political Crime in Medieval and Early Modern England: A History of Sorcery and Treason*. International Library of Historical Studies (London and New York: I.B. Tauris, 2018).

Dissertations

Thompson, J. A., *'Her Good Name and Credit': The Reputation of Women in Seventeenth-Century Devon*, PhD thesis (Cincinnati, 1987).

Index

K. O'Brien, *Cursing, Crisis and Customary Knowledge in Early Modern English Townships*, Palgrave Historical Studies in Witchcraft and Magic,
https://doi.org/10.1007/978-3-031-44045-8

GPSR Compliance

The European Union's (EU) General Product Safety Regulation (GPSR) is a set of rules that requires consumer products to be safe and our obligations to ensure this.

If you have any concerns about our products, you can contact us on ProductSafety@springernature.com

In case Publisher is established outside the EU, the EU authorized representative is:

Springer Nature Customer Service Center GmbH
Europaplatz 3
69115 Heidelberg, Germany

The manufacturer's authorised representative in the EU is Springer Nature Customer Service Centre GmbH, Europaplatz 3, 69115 Heidelberg, Germany. If you have any concerns regarding our products, please contact ProductSafety@springernature.com

Printed and bound by CPI Group (UK) Ltd, Croydon, CR0 4YY
28/09/2026
02224072-0009